Reunion Revisited

1930s ECUMENISM EXPOSED

Mark Vickers

GRACEWING

First published in England in 2017
by
Gracewing
2 Southern Avenue
Leominster
Herefordshire HR6 0QF
United Kingdom
www.gracewing.co.uk

All rights reserved.
No part of this publication may be reproduced, stored in a retrieval system, or transmitted in any form or by any means, electronic, mechanical, photocopying, recording or otherwise, without the written permission of the publisher.

The right of Mark Vickers to be identified as the author of this work has been asserted in accordance with the Copyright, Designs and Patents Act 1988.

© 2017 Mark Vickers

ISBN 978 085244 916 5

Cover design by Bernardita Peña Hurtado

Typeset by Word and Page, Chester, UK

CONTENTS

List of Illustrations	vi
Abbreviations	vii
Foreword	ix
Preface	xiii
'The Ultra-Catholic'	xix
1. 'A serious misunderstanding'	1
2. Catholic Reunion	19
3. 'The best men in the Church'	61
4. 'Our Anglican friends'	85
5. The Thackeray Hotel	129
6. Cadogan Gardens	173
7. St Ermin's Hotel	187
8. 'The Next Step'	205
9. A Different Direction	239
10. *Ut unum sint*	253
Appendix. The Oxford Movement: A Centenary Manifesto	265
Sources and Bibliography	271
Index	279

ILLUSTRATIONS

The Chairman
Sir James Marchant   3
(© National Portrait Gallery, London)

The Catholics
Cuthbert Butler   68
(Downside Abbey Trustees)

Alban Goodier   73
(English Province of the Society of Jesus)

Martin D'Arcy   77
(© National Portrait Gallery, London)

Bede Jarrett   79
(Dominican Council, English Province of the Order of Preachers)

The Anglicans
Dr Scott   91
(Nigel Lambert)

Spencer Jones   98
(Anne Gurini)

Henry Fynes-Clinton   105
(Rector and Churchwardens, St Magnus-the-Martyr, London)

Robert Corbould   110
(Rector and Churchwardens, All Saints, Carshalton)

Leslie Simmonds   117
(Vicar and Churchwardens, St Mary with St Alban, Teddington)

William Monahan   120
(Principal and Governors of Pusey House: Monahan Papers)

ABBREVIATIONS

AAW	Archives of the Archbishop of Westminster
ABSI	Archives of the British Province of the Society of Jesus
APUC	Association for Promoting the Union of Christendom
BCA	Beda College Archives
BIY	Borthwick Institute, York
CPCU	Council for Promoting Catholic Unity
CU	Confraternity of Unity
CUO	Church Unity Octave
CUOC	Church Unity Octave Council
DAA	Downside Abbey Archives
GARC	Graymoor Archives and Records Center
LPL	Lambeth Palace Library
MAA	Malines Archdiocesan Archives
OUL	Oxford University Library
OUSR	Oxford University Society for Reunion
PHA	Pusey House Archives
SCM	Student Christian Movement
SCR	Society for Catholic Reunion

For Richard Murray
who is ultimately responsible for this book
— and much else

FOREWORD

In the early months of 1914 a young Oxford clergyman wrote a satire in the style of Swift on the new enthusiasm for Christian unity. Ronald Knox's *Reunion All Round* was a 'Plea for the Inclusion within the Church of England of all Mahometans, Jews, Buddhists, Brahmins, Papists, and Atheists, submitted to the consideration of the British Public'. Knox, son of an Establishment bishop, reduced to absurdity the cheerful willingness of certain Anglicans to ditch doctrines for the sake of religious reconciliation. He does not restrict his modest proposal to the boundaries of Christianity. Mohammed should be seen as 'a good, sound Protestant', whose 'quarrel with the debased Church of his time was mainly about its heathenish Mariolatry, and the unduly strict views it held about marriage'. Knox-Swift suggests that the hierarchy should be alternately Christian and Muslim, with Pashas serving under Archbishops and Mullahs functioning as Rural Deans. In the all-inclusive Church of England of the future, the Pope would be given the status of a retired missionary bishop, and the Cardinals of the Roman Church dispersed among the common rooms of Oxford and Cambridge, 'where they could exercise to the full their talent for intrigue without having any serious effect, for good or ill, upon the destinies of the nation'. Even atheists would be drawn into the fellowship, for 'we, who are conscious of the supreme being as existent, and those others who are conscious of Him as non-existent, are each of us looking at only one half of the truth'.

Knox's pamphlet is good fun, but it has a serious purpose: it was a warning against the dangers of indifferentism and doctrinal relativism in the discussions of the denominations. It was precisely this tendency in the 'Pan-Christian' movement that Pope Pius XI condemned in his encyclical *Mortalium Animos* of 1928:

> Shall we suffer, what would indeed be iniquitous, the truth, and a truth divinely revealed, to be made a subject for

compromise? [. . .] If our Redeemer plainly said that His Gospel was to continue not only during the times of the Apostles, but also till future ages, is it possible that the object of faith should in the process of time become so obscure and uncertain that it would be necessary today to tolerate opinions which are even incompatible one with another?

At the very time in which the Pope's encyclical was promulgated, a group of Anglican clergymen were engaged in a dialogue with senior Catholic theologians quite different in its principles and methods from the ecumenism of their contemporaries, even those engaged in the better known Malines conversations. These were the so-called 'Anglo-Papalists', clerics of the Established Church, who professed their adherence to the entire teaching of the Catholic Church on faith and morals. They were the foes of Modernism in all its forms, and shared Pope Pius's zeal in opposing any compromise of 'truth divinely revealed'. It is the story of their quest for reunion and its final failure that Fr Mark Vickers tells in this ground-breaking book.

In his comic poem, 'The Ultra-Catholic', Eric Mascall, the greatest, perhaps the only Anglican Thomist, pokes gentle fun at the Anglo-Papalist contradiction of accepting the authority of the Pope, while remaining out of communion with him:

> The Holy Father I extol in fervid perorations,
> The Cardinals in Curia, the Sacred Congregations;
> And, though I've not submitted yet, as all my friends expected,
> I should have gone last Tuesday week, had not my wife objected.

The 'Ultra-Catholic' Papalists, reciting their Latin breviaries in empty churches buried deep in the countryside, seem like classic English eccentrics out of the pages of Wodehouse, endearing and amusing, but of no intellectual weight and interest. However, as Fr Vickers shows from his painstaking work in the archives, this judgement is not just. Many of the Anglo-Papalists were learned men, with a deep and extensive knowledge of the Tradition, especially of the Church Fathers, and served their parishes as devoted pastors. They had good humour, but nothing of the frivolity and effeteness of mainstream Anglo-Catholicism, which they abhorred.

One of Fr Vickers's most significant achievements in this book is to show that the Anglo-Papalist critique of official Anglicanism was directed as much to its aberrations in morals as to its deficiencies in dogma. In 1930, the Lambeth Conference formally abandoned what up to that moment had been the universal teaching of all Christians, Protestants as well as Catholics, and gave limited approval to birth control. That same summer, in the church of St-Magnus-the-Martyr in the City of London, praised by T. S. Eliot in *The Waste Land* for its 'inexplicable splendour of Ionian white and gold', the Anglo-Papalist Rector, Henry Fynes-Clinton, had the following statement read out from the pulpit: 'The Rector desires to express publicly and solemnly his abhorrence and entire repudiation and disassociation from the lamentable sanction given in certain circumstances by the Bishops in the Lambeth Conference to the deadly sin of contraception'. Noble though it was, the Anglo-Papalists' condemnation of the Lambeth decision exposed the frailty of their ecclesiology, as the principal Catholic participant in the conversations, Archbishop Goodier, did not fail to point out: 'The faith or the morals of one generation cannot contradict the faith or the morals of another [. . .] The Church that teaches morals which have never been the morals of Jesus Christ declares herself formally heretical.' The Anglo-Papalists were right to reject Lambeth, but wrong to imagine that the ecclesiastical body which Lambeth represented, and to which they themselves belonged, could be essentially Catholic and only accidentally estranged from the See of Peter.

One hundred years on, *Reunion All Round* seems less like knockabout satire and more like sober prediction. Anglicanism and the official Protestant bodies tolerate almost every species of heterodox theology and disordered morality. The Anglicans, who once claimed to follow St Vincent of Lérins in holding only what all Christians at all times and in all places have believed, now teach what has never been believed anywhere by anyone, even on the far left of heresy: first birth control, then the remarriage of the civilly divorced, and now the ordination of women and the openly homosexual. A man can deny the Virgin Birth and Bodily Resurrection of Christ and end up as Lord Bishop of Durham. There is even a 'Sea of Faith' group for Anglican atheists. The chief consequence of twentieth-century ecumenism would seem to be the even greater distancing of the Reformation communities from the Catholic Church. The hopes of the Anglo-Papalists are in ruins. Or are they? In 2009, by the *motu proprio Anglicanorum coetibus*, Pope Benedict XVI established a Personal Ordinariate for Anglicans reconciled with the Catholic Church, which would seem to fulfil the aspirations of the long neglected Anglo-Papalists of the 1930s. As Archbishop Augustine Di Noia, OP has recently said, in the Ordinariate we see a work of the Holy Spirit and an answer to the Church's prayers for Christian unity. Reunion has come to pass, not 'all round', but for those brave souls who relinquish the material comforts of the Anglican Establishment in order to profess the Catholic faith, in the divine integrity of its truth, with and under Peter.

Fr John Saward
23 September 2015

PREFACE

Like the proverbial dog walking on its hind legs, the content and consequences of the Malines Conversations are held to be of less significance than the fact that they occurred at all. The Conversations were a series of informal conferences between English Anglicans on the one part and French and Belgian Catholics on the other, hosted by Cardinal Mercier in the Belgian cathedral city of Malines between 1921 and 1925.

Active persecution had given way to polemics, but otherwise relations between Catholicism and Anglicanism were practically non-existent. Malines represented a unique, if brief and transitory, clearing of the clouds between the Reformation and the sunnier ecumenical climate prevailing after Vatican II. At least, that is the received wisdom. One author writes, 'Perhaps the most remarkable feature was that the Conversations occurred at all, at a time when it was almost unheard of for Roman Catholics to talk to members of any other church'.[1] Another Church historian presents them in similar terms: 'they were the first direct discussions between Anglicans and Catholics in over three hundred years. They also preceded a process of dialogue between the Anglican and Roman Catholic Churches which was reopened following the Second Vatican Council (1962–65).'[2]

To the extent I had heard of the Malines Conversations, that would have been my understanding also—until I undertook research in connection with a biography of Cardinal Bourne, Archbishop of Westminster at the time. One should not underestimate the opposition to the Conversations from both Protestants on the one side and hostile Catholics, such as Cardinal Merry del Val, the English Jesuits and the English Catholic Press, on the other. Nor was the average Catholic in the pew troubled by ecumenical concerns. As a tiny minority, they could hardly avoid contact with non-Catholics. But formed in their own schools and parishes, Catholics were actively discouraged from engaging with those outside their own communion.

And yet ... Was it as clear cut and hermetically sealed as this interpretation would suggest? Doubts arose as I read files in the Westminster Archdiocesan Archives, doubts confirmed by a couple of stray references in works on Malines. The latter first. Described as 'the irony of ironies', the talks between Anglicans and Catholics did not end in Belgium in the 1920s but, known to the Archbishops of Canterbury and Westminster, continued in London in the early 1930s. Given the complete secrecy in which these Conversations were conducted, John Dick and Bernard Barlow make a few understandable errors in outlining the details, regretting that nothing further is known about them.[3]

My own research in the Westminster Archives showed that these Conversations had taken place with the knowledge and approval of the English Catholic hierarchy, but their confidential nature was such that, while the identity of the Catholic participants was alluded to, the identity of the Anglicans was deliberately concealed. Other than a memorandum detailing the concessions the Anglicans hoped for should Reunion with Rome prove possible, there was little information on the context or content of the Conversations. Completing my Bourne biography, I concluded that there was no more to be said about these London Conversations than the few lines written by Malines scholars a generation earlier. But I wondered.

I returned to the Bodleian in Oxford which holds the papers of the man who chaired the Conversations; more material than at Westminster, but the same obvious desire to maintain strict confidentiality. The chairman impressed on the participants the need to destroy correspondence—an injunction, fortunately, he did not feel himself bound by. Again, there was the same frustrating lack of references to the identity of the Anglicans involved—until in a moment of fortuitous carelessness, one of the Catholic correspondents mentioned a name. I had been given an entrée.

The next significant advance occurred in the West Country. All the Catholic participants in these London Conversations were members of religious orders which tend to be rather good at retaining documents. I was made very welcome at Downside

Preface

Abbey, but was assured that no relevant papers existed. Within minutes of my arrival at the Archives, I had laid my hands upon a large brown envelope marked: 'Concerning Ecumenical Contact with Anglicans in Early 1930s'. Although the material it contained came to an abrupt, and unexplained, break at one point, it was the breakthrough I had been seeking. It contained copies of many of the papers delivered, the identity of the participants was made clear and, most surprisingly, I discovered that the Conversations continued much longer than the four months originally believed. This proved the key to much else. Knowing now what I was searching for, I was able to unearth further papers delivered at the Conversations in such unlikely places as the Lambeth Palace Library and the Dominican journal, *Blackfriars*.

The Anglicans continued to prove elusive. The possessions of celibate clergy are often dispersed or destroyed after their death. I am grateful to those nephews, nieces and grandchildren who assisted my investigation. Aware that 'Uncle X' was 'extremely High' and probably very learned, they were delighted and bemused that someone was interested in his activities eighty years on. I hoped for the emergence of a trunk of dusty letters stored in some attic finally seeing the light of day after three generations. It was not to be. But material came in piecemeal. Hours spent sifting uncatalogued material at Pusey House in Oxford, files located at the Beda College in Rome in consequence of a random enquiry, built up the fuller picture. Against all the odds, it became possible to piece together a reasonably complete and accurate account of what had occurred in such secrecy in the early 1930s. I am convinced that the story deserves to be told.

I am conscious that these London Conversations do not fit the established ecumenical narrative as it has been received over the last fifty years. They were controversial at the time, and remain so. The method adopted and assumptions made will challenge many today, as they did then. Given the apparent lack of enthusiasm and progress for ecumenical matters in recent years, I ask only that we give these Conversations and their participants a hearing, to consider whether, perhaps, there might be something to be learnt. The Anglican Conversationalists were loudly insistent that they stood in a continuous line of thought within the Church of England in respect of their relations to Rome. A number were distinguished historical scholars, and it was to history they turned to justify their position. I have attempted to set the London Conversations within a historical context stretching from the Oxford Movement to the early twenty-first century.

A note on terminology. The subject of this book is 'ecumenism'. Yet the term was not used in this context in the period in question. (Its introduction to the English language is attributed to the Dominican, Henry St John, a decade or so later.) The protagonists of this work spoke or wrote rather about 'unity' or 'reunion'. (More petulant Catholics objected to the latter term, claiming that the Anglican Communion could not be *re*-united with the Catholic Church to which it had never been united.) For the avoidance of confusion the term 'Catholic' is here used in reference to Roman Catholics, while acknowledging that most Anglicans mentioned in these pages undoubtedly understood themselves to be 'Catholic', albeit not in visible communion with the Holy See.

There was far less material available for writing this work than I had to plough through for the Bourne biography, but it involved much more effort in tracking it down. I was given unfailing and generous assistance along the way. In particular I wish to thank the following: Michael Black at Blackfriars Library, Oxford; Colin Harris at the Bodleian; the staff at the Borthwick Institute, York; Dom Lambert Vos of Chevetogne Monastery; Abbot Geoffrey Scott and Alison Day at Douai Abbey; Abbot Aidan Bellenger at Downside; Barbara Martire at the Graymoor Archives and Record Center; the staff at the Jesuit Provincial Archives; the staff at the Lambeth Palace Library; Gerrit Vanden Bosch at the Malines Archdiocesan Archives; Fr Barry Orford and Anna James at Pusey House; Fr Nicholas Schofield and William Johnstone at the Westminster Archdiocesan Archives; Sheila Campbell for information concerning her grandfather, Fr William Monahan; Fr Christopher Colven for sharing his reminiscences of the vanished world of Anglo-Papalism and picking up errors in reading the draft text; Fr Edward and the late David Corbould for information relating to Fr Robert Corbould; Anne Gurini for searching for any surviving

Preface

papers of her grandfather, Spencer Jones; Michael and Veronica Hodges for once more so generously making their home available to write up the fruits of my research; Fr Brooke Lunn for sharing his recollections of his friend and mentor, Fr Henry Fynes-Clinton, and his hospitality at the Charterhouse; Fr Athanasius McVay for his thoughts concerning Bishop Michel d'Herbigny; Bishop Stephen and Mary Pedley for recollections of Mary's uncle, Leslie Simmonds; Fr Graeme Rowland and Fr Mark Woodruffe for matters relating to the Catholic League; Fr John Saward, Fr Andrew Pinsent and Richard and Hannah Murray for their hospitality in Oxford; Mgr Roderick Strange and Ryan Day for their help in tracking down the papers of Mgr Henry Pierce in the dusty recesses of the Beda College; the grandchildren of Thomas Whitton; Michael Yelton for supplying copies of obscure Papalist tracts.

This book has been, as they say, very much a personal journey. I was first led through the doors of St Stephen's, Gloucester Road in South Kensington, one Sunday morning at the end of 1990 by a College friend, Richard Murray. I resisted. I was aware of its reputation as being 'virtually Catholic'. Forcefully exposed to High Mass, my reaction was complex. Everything militated against the familiar Prayer Book Anglicanism of rural Lincolnshire, and Durham and Chester Cathedrals. And yet . . . I was compelled to return. It was not just the beauty of the liturgy, music and furnishings, which I had encountered elsewhere in Anglo-Catholicism. Yes, it was more fun than the rather dour expressions of Anglicanism I had known earlier. But there was something more as well. That something more was 'Roman'.

I did not appreciate it at the time, but I had been introduced to Anglo-Papalism. The two years spent on this project have enabled me to understand properly for the first time its origins and significance. I have come to esteem the Anglicans we meet in these Conversations and to regard them as my spiritual grandfathers. Like their Catholic counterparts, I am challenged at times by their logic and their conclusions. But they were impressive, courageous and often holy men. They eased my path to full communion with the Catholic Church, and provided colour and amusement along the way. For that I am grateful.

I understand better now the roots and route from which I came. This recognition is best expressed by someone else who had entered the doors of St Stephen's, Gloucester Road two generations earlier:

> We shall not cease from exploration
> And the end of all our exploring
> Will be to arrive where we started
> And know the place for the first time.[4]

Fr Mark Vickers
7 April 2016

Notes

[1] M. Yelton, *Anglo-Papalism: An Illustrated History 1900–1960* (Norwich: Canterbury Press, 2005), pp. 35–6.

[2] B. Barlow, OSM, *'A brother knocking at the door': The Malines Conversations 1921–1925* (Norwich: Canterbury Press, 1996), p. 178.

[3] J. A. Dick, *The Malines Conversations Revisited* (Leuven: Leuven University Press, 1989), p. 189; Barlow, *The Malines Conversations*, p. 209.

[4] T. S. Eliot, 'Little Gidding', V.

'THE ULTRA-CATHOLIC'*

'I am an Ultra-Catholic—No 'Anglo-', I beseech you!
You'll find no trace of heresy in anything I teach you.
The clergyman across the road has whiskers and a bowler,
But I wear buckles on my shoes and sport a feriola.

My alb is edged with deepest lace, spread over rich black satin;
The Psalms of David I recite in heaven's own native Latin,
And, though I don't quite *understand* those awkward moods and tenses,
My *ordo recitandi*'s strict *Westmonasteriensis*.

I teach the children in my school the Penny Catechism,
Explaining how the C. of E.'s in heresy and schism.
The truths of Trent and Vatican I bate not one iota.
I have not met the Rural Dean. I do not pay my quota.

The Bishop's put me under his 'profoundest disapproval'
And, though, he cannot bring about my actual removal,
He will not come and visit me or take my confirmations.
Colonial prelates I employ from far-off mission-stations.

The music we perform at Mass is Verdi and Scarlatti.
Assorted females from the choir; I wish they weren't so catty.
Two flutes, a fiddle and a harp assist them in the gallery.
The organist left years ago, and so we save his salary.

We've started a 'Sodality of John of San Fagondez',
Consisting of the five young men who serve High Mass on Sundays;
And though they simply will not come to weekday Mass at seven,
They turn out looking wonderful on Sundays at eleven.

The Holy Father I extol in fervid perorations,
The Cardinals in curia, the Sacred Congregations;
And, though, I've not submitted yet, as all my friends expected,
I should have gone last Tuesday week, had not my wife objected.'

* E. L. Mascall, *Pi in the High* (London: The Faith Press, 1959), p. 39.

✤ 1 ✤

'A serious misunderstanding'

The Primate of All England

The Archbishop of Canterbury was puzzled by the letter he received in November 1927:

> I have a delicate and important matter to put before your Grace, dealing with a serious misunderstanding in which you have most unwittingly become involved in connection with the Roman Hierarchy of which I feel certain you would like to be informed, and to clear away. And I have a message for you, which I cannot write about.[1]

Sir James Marchant requested an interview.

Randall Davidson had occupied Lambeth Palace since 1903. Of Edinburgh Presbyterian stock, he might have appeared a rank outsider and an unlikely candidate to head the Anglican Establishment at its zenith. In fact, his social credentials were impeccable: Harrow and Oxford, chaplain and son-in-law to another (Scottish) Archbishop of Canterbury. A trusted advisor to Queen Victoria on ecclesiastical matters, royal preferment saw him move seamlessly from the diocese of Rochester to Winchester then Canterbury.

A cautious Scot, in no area was his caution more manifest than in his (limited) dealings with the Catholic Church. Davidson was a pragmatist who defined himself by a policy of comprehensiveness. He had a corresponding distaste for the doctrinal absolutes of Catholicism. He saw no place for *Roman* Catholicism in Great Britain: 'Believing as I do that the Church of England is in this country the true representative of the Catholic Church as it comes down to us from the past, I can hardly be expected to look favourably upon the establishment in England of another society claiming that position.'[2] Temperamentally, he opposed everything he believed that the Vatican stood for. Back in the 1890s he confessed, 'I do dread the Roman *way* of doing things'.[3] Davidson's opinion of Rome had not abated by the following decade when his predecessor's son turned papist. 'Terribly, perilously false'[4] was his pronouncement.

Davidson was weary of attempting to steer the Established Church in the unfamiliar world that emerged from the Great War. The Archbishop's moderation, whether on matters of morality, industrial relations or international affairs, was challenged as frequently by members of his own communion as by others, but a sense of duty drove him on. Liturgy was not his preferred subject. The more extreme Anglo-Catholics had chafed for decades under the constraints of the Book of Common Prayer. Initially, they interpreted it in a Catholic direction. Later they imported wholesale the ceremonies and devotions of the Catholic Church. It was those relating to worship and reservation of the Eucharist which produced the direst Protestant accusations of idolatry. There were limits to even Davidson's toleration. A tortuous process led to proposals for Prayer Book Revision. In return for conceding certain Catholic liturgical options, the more controversial unauthorised practices were to be prohibited — such prohibitions to be enforced. The compromise pleased no one. Church approval finally obtained, Parliament had also to agree the changes. (The Commons rejected the Revised Prayer Book on 15 December 1927 — and again six months later.) These were the matters preoccupying the Archbishop when Marchant's letter arrived.

'A queer customer'[5]

Who was James Marchant? A question his contemporaries asked frequently. His origins and ecclesiastical allegiance were obscure. Born in East London in 1867, he was raised and confirmed an Anglican. In his youth he worked in Barking as the Bishop of St Albans' lecturer in Christian Apologetics before deciding that the Church of England was too restrictive of his beliefs and ministry. After a short stint with the Congregationalists, he became an English Presbyterian and was ordained minister for their church in

'A serious misunderstanding'

Sir James Marchant

Chatham. There, working with the Anglican Bishop of Rochester, he instituted a crusade against the vice rampant in the town.[6] Like other Nonconformists in the aftermath of the First World War Marchant developed a taste for a more traditional ritual and spirituality, while remaining wary of doctrinal certainties and denominational commitments. By the early 1930s he was defining himself as an *'Evangelical-Catholic*. But not Anglo-Catholic as the extremists hold.'

Continuing to function and speak as an ordained minister, Marchant became increasingly involved in social work. He was Clerical Secretary of Barnardo's Homes for three years from 1903. His moral campaign in Chatham had attracted the favourable attention of the King and the Government, and was in part responsible for the establishment of the National Council of Public Morals, of which he was Director and Secretary for many years. The Council was a quasi-governmental body charged with producing reports on such subjects as the cinema and the declining birth rate. It was for his services to this organisation that he was knighted in 1921. This social work gave Marchant access to the great and the good. He first met Cardinal Bourne while working for Barnardo's. The Archbishop of Westminster furnished him with introductions to Catholic children's homes in Europe and to the Vatican Library. Meanwhile Marchant developed his contacts in the Established Church through the various Anglican bishops who served as members and presidents of the National Council of Public Morals.[7]

Marchant wrote copiously on social and religious issues, editing several spiritual anthologies. The publishing house, Longman, employed him as its theological reader. This gave him *carte blanche* to pursue his own prolific correspondence with all manner of Church leaders of the day, not just members of the Anglican and Catholic hierarchies, but also the more esoteric and self-appointed figures on the fringes of religious life. He adopted a recognisable pattern. In his professional capacity, he would write to a national religious figure, commissioning a work or a review. Given the smallest opening, he would enter a lengthy and detailed dialogue, sharing his ecclesiological views, expounding proposals for the Reunion of Christians, seeking assistance in their realisation. Marchant's interest in Christian unity dates from at least the time of the First World War. His contacts with those active in that field increased significantly from 1919 when Theodore Woods, Bishop of Peterborough (and later Winchester), became a member of the National Council of Public Morals. Woods was charged, especially after the 1920 Lambeth Conference, with promoting the work of Reunion both at home and abroad.

Although he edited a book on Christian Reunion in 1929[8] with contributions from Woods and other national and international Church leaders, Marchant included not a word of his own on the subject. His optimism, however, is apparent from his letter to the *Tablet* at the time:

> the Church of Christ, One, Holy, Catholic and Apostolic, is rising before the Christian world as a fair and entrancing vision beckoning away from small sects, changing opinions and half-truths.

'A serious misunderstanding'

He gave instances of steps towards Reunion among Nonconformists in Britain and the Empire:

> Anglo-Catholics at home have widened in certain aspects the outlook of the Anglican Church, and have adopted Catholic ceremonies and practices, which have weakened old prejudices.

It was, he felt, all tending in a certain direction.

> In a few generations more the non-Episcopal Churches will be united and will face the Episcopal Churches eager to find some solution of the final difficulties. Then united at last they will face the supreme issue, union with the Catholic Roman Church, and that in an atmosphere purified by the ceaseless prayers of generations of the faithful. For the Catholic Roman Church, holding rigidly, as she declares, to the Faith once and for all delivered to the saints, prays without ceasing for the healing of the open sore of separation [. . .] Deep fissures still divide us, vital problems of Faith and Order seem intractable, but the patience of God is infinite.[9]

Was there substance to any of this? Was Marchant sincere? What motivated him? Many were deeply suspicious. Davidson's successor wrote, 'I find it very difficult to know how far this man is pursuing obscure efforts and intrigues of his own'.[10] In promoting his projects, Marchant flattered and told people what they wished to hear. He presented matters in such a way as to make himself indispensable and provide for his own ongoing involvement. Such methods were to prove problematic.

Surprisingly, Catholics were more generous in their assessment. The *Tablet*, not noted at the time for giving the benefit of the doubt to Protestants, told its readers, 'Nobody who has met him in the flesh and has held converse with him touching holy things will deny that Sir James Marchant is a man of deep spirituality and lofty idealism'. The man was mistaken, but well-intentioned.[11] And that is probably accurate. It is difficult to charge Marchant with malice. He entertained grand and often fanciful ideals of Church unity, complicated by naivety and his own desire for recognition. He possessed a great gift for drawing people together, but, in his multifarious schemes, he could often lose sight of his ultimate objective and be less than transparent in his strategy for achieving it.

'The wicked Cardinal'

Sir James presented himself at Lambeth Palace at 10.30 am on 22 November 1927. Some background information is required.

The existence of the Malines Conversations was made public at Christmas 1923 when the Archbishop of Canterbury revealed that a group of Anglican theologians led by the High Church layman, Lord Halifax, had been meeting their Belgian and French Catholic counterparts for discussions in Belgium hosted by Cardinal Mercier. The Conversations were an exploration in a friendly spirit of the other's position to determine a possible basis for Reunion. Starting in December 1921, four Conversations were held up to May 1925. (A fifth occurred in October 1926, after Mercier's death, but was concerned mainly with drawing up reports of the proceedings.) The Conversations had a semi-official status, approved and encouraged by both Rome and Canterbury. They moved rapidly from a debate of the underlying theological differences to the formulation of practical proposals for the Reunion of Rome and the Church of England. This presumption of the ultimate outcome made Davidson extremely nervous. Attempting to pilot Prayer Book Reform through the Church Assembly and Parliament, the last thing he needed was the suggestion that he was secretly negotiating a betrayal of the very principles of the Reformation.

The Malines Conversations ended for various reasons: they had reached a natural hiatus, the unrepresentative nature of the Anglican delegation and their unrealistic expectations, a change of heart on the part of the Vatican, the death of Cardinal Mercier, the hostility of English Catholics. Most of the Malines participants assumed that foremost among their enemies was Francis, Cardinal Bourne. That assumption was wrong—and highly unfortunate.

Bourne had been Archbishop of Westminster since 1903, and Bishop of Southwark before that. A Londoner by birth, his father was an Oxford Movement convert from Anglicanism, his mother an Irish Catholic. Industrious and organised, he was a former seminary rector with pronounced views on priestly formation. His natural reserve was increased by the hostility he encountered when appointed Bishop at too young an age and his prolonged conflict with his brother Bishops over proposals for the multiplication of dioceses. Yet, Bourne's education at St Sulpice in Paris had given him an openness to new learning and a determination to present the truths of the Catholic Church in a medium comprehensible to the modern world.

From his earliest days in Westminster Bourne had been willing to work with Anglicans and Nonconformists in support of such shared concerns as Sunday observance, temperance and the resolution of industrial disputes. As the 1920s progressed, however, the Cardinal felt the gulf between the two communions was widening, especially on moral issues such as divorce and contraception. Added to this, Bourne consistently rejected Anglican claims to continuity with the pre-Reformation Church. Occasionally, disputes became acrimonious and public as at the 1,300th anniversary celebrations of the conversion of Edwin, King of Northumbria, and the founding of York Minster by St Paulinus. The Anglican Archbishop of York, Cosmo Lang, claimed unbroken succession of faith and office between Paulinus and himself. Bourne was having none of it. Preaching at York on Easter Sunday 1927, the Cardinal cited their respective beliefs regarding the Mass, Our Lady and papal authority. 'I claim, then, that we, and we alone in England, who belong to the Latin Church, who call ourselves Catholics, and are styled by others "Roman Catholics", believe and worship as Edwin and Paulinus believed and worshipped.'[12] Non-Catholics failed to distinguish Bourne's public assertion of Catholic claims whenever he felt these challenged from his personal willingness to enter dialogue and cooperation when he judged this possible without detriment to the truth.

Lord Halifax visited Cardinal Bourne in November 1921 to advise him of the imminent Conversations at Malines. Finding the Archbishop of Westminster 'altogether sympathetic', the peer expressed himself 'entirely satisfied' by their meeting.[13] Bourne knew Mercier from his student days in Louvain, and was happy for him to host such discussions. Halifax promised to keep the

Cardinal informed of progress. His failure to do so was undoubtedly an oversight, but the consequences were disastrous. The next Bourne heard about the Conversations was twelve months later when Mercier wrote, informing him of papal approval and asking for the English Cardinal's prayers. He added: 'I need not say that I should be deeply grateful for any advice and suggestions that you would like to give me. Living in daily contact with the Anglican Church you will be able to help me with information and clarification from which I should be very happy to profit.'[14] Bourne replied: 'I think these informal conferences may well be encouraged, though in my opinion it will be *a very long time* before anything definite can emerge from them.'[15] Bourne also enclosed a copy of an article from the *Tablet*, outlining Anglican divisions and critical of Halifax. Unfortunately, Mercier passed this on to the Malines participants. Rather than accept Bourne's genuine sympathy, moderated by a necessary note of realism, the conversationalists chose instead to demonise him.

Bourne, however, continued his benign attitude towards the Conversations. In Rome in the spring of 1924 when Mercier issued a Pastoral Letter on the subject, Bourne intervened to correct an inaccurate and potentially damaging translation in the *Osservatore Romano*. He advised the *Tablet* on the line it should take: 'Give it the most sympathetic and cordial treatment, and quote largely from it.'[16] In his own Pastoral Letter the English Cardinal again displayed considerable understanding tempered with realism:

> In the first place our attitude is, and must be, one of intense sympathy manifested both in constant and more fervent prayer for the restoration of England to the unity of Christendom [...] and in a readiness to explain and elucidate in every way those teachings of the Catholic Church which are still so often misunderstood and misrepresented by our fellow countrymen.

Bourne made a generous offer: 'There is no sacrifice of place or position that we are not prepared to make in order to attain so great an end — how there is no Bishop among us who would not gladly resign his see and retire into complete obscurity if thereby England could be Catholic again.' He expressed himself satisfied

'A serious misunderstanding'

that such talks should occur 'in France, or in Belgium, or here at home, or in any other country'. In his opinion 'such contact, with the help and guidance of the Holy Spirit, must be productive of good, even though no actual result may be immediately attained'. He simply stipulated that 'such union must be based on absolute truth and sincerity. There can be no question of compromise built up on the acceptance, or rejection, or mere toleration of a certain number of religious opinions. It can only come from the wholehearted and sincere acceptance of divinely revealed truths.'[17]

A change in Bourne's attitude was provoked by both the excesses of the conversationalists themselves and the hostile designs of their opponents. In autumn 1925 the English Jesuit, Francis Woodlock, alleged that the secrecy surrounding the Malines Conversations was allowing it to be said that a different, doctrinally minimalist form of Catholicism was being taught in Belgium and France to that held in England. Rather than prudently ignoring the insinuation, Cardinal Mercier demanded space in the English Catholic Press to air his grievances. Bourne became involved. There followed an angry exchange of letters between the two Cardinals characterised by neither charity nor accuracy. Bourne accused Mercier of ignoring him in matters of fundamental importance to the English Catholic Church, while confiding in the Anglicans. Mercier responded: 'Your Eminence gave me no testimony of sympathy, no word of encouragement [. . .] Rather the impression Your Eminence always gave me was that you wished our Conversations ill; that, as you see it, all the efforts of Catholics should be concentrated on individual conversions, and that to such conversions our meetings at Malines are more a hindrance than a help.'[18]

The two men effected a reconciliation as Mercier lay dying of cancer, but the damage was done. Bourne had an audience with Pope Pius XI on 14 December 1925 when he raised the subject of the Malines Conversations. We know his concerns: the proposal that the existing English Catholic hierarchy be abolished in the event of agreement for Reunion between Rome and Canterbury; the reopening of the question of Anglican priestly orders which the Vatican had ruled invalid a generation earlier; the undermining of Catholic doctrine such as papal infallibility.[19]

This spat between the two Cardinals seemed to justify those who viewed Bourne as an inveterate obstacle to Anglican-Catholic unity. That was Halifax's decided opinion: 'I am told on good authority that [the Pope] is still as anxious as ever to further the cause of Reunion, but that Cardinal Bourne and other English Catholics have been making hostile representations to him.'[20] The Archbishop of Westminster *was* irritated by the ongoing contact Belgian Benedictines maintained with Anglicans. Bourne felt these Belgian monks were predisposed to accept the arguments of Anglicans rather than those of their English co-religionists. He feared they were discouraging converts by leading them to assume that the ruling against the validity of Anglican Orders would be reversed. The Cardinal used his contacts in Belgium and Rome to end this ecumenical endeavor, leading one of Halifax's Catholic correspondents to inveigh against *le méchant Cardinal*.[21]

And yet at the same time Bourne remained surprisingly open to the prospect of further conversations between Catholics and Anglicans. Mercier's death seemed to galvanise him. Perhaps it was the thought that he was inheriting his dead friend's mantle, possibly he felt guilty that he had been manipulated by the opponents of Malines. Were the Malines Conversations to continue, Bourne proposed sending representatives: his auxiliary, Bishop Manuel Bidwell, and Canon Edward Myers. Just four months after Mercier's death the Cardinal was receptive to Halifax's suggestion of a meeting between Anglicans and English Catholics under the chairmanship of the Catholic elder statesman, Viscount FitzAlan. The Cardinal met twice with FitzAlan to discuss the proposal and, although nothing came of it, offered to send Bishop Bidwell, Lord Lovat and the convert, Algernon Cecil.[22] The Cardinal felt a meeting in England between Englishmen more likely to be productive, freed from the unrealistic notions of Anglicanism entertained by French and Belgian Catholics.

'A more acceptable way'

Marchant recognised the Cardinal's genuine desire to heal the divisions of English Christianity and his antipathy to foreign

'A serious misunderstanding'

intervention. He astutely adopted both stances as his own. Sir James opened his campaign, writing on 25 July 1927 to Cardinal Bourne, whom he knew from his time with Barnardo's Homes and also more recently in connection with his publishing work. The Cardinal was inclined to view him as a lost soul, but someone on a genuine spiritual quest who, with prayer and courtesy, might be brought into the Catholic Church. Marchant was not inclined to disabuse him of his misapprehension.

Marchant proffered his services as one long interested in the cause of Reunion. What he had in mind was 'to bring together a group of devout, catholic-minded scholars to consider the objections to submission to the Catholic Roman Church [...] It would *not* be a reunion Committee.' (Initially, he envisaged Nonconformists as well as Anglicans participating in such discussions.) Adeptly, and affecting great deference, he sought the Cardinal's support, without which he knew no serious English Catholic would entertain his scheme. 'I have always felt that the *first* thing to do would be to approach Your Eminence and to submit the suggestion for your consideration, and thus to discover, if one may, whether such an object would be likely to have your sympathy [...] Perhaps this suggestion will be wholly unacceptable, but it may lead to a more acceptable way, and better Malines!'[23]

The letter Marchant wrote to *The Times* on 3 October was clearly intended for the Cardinal's eyes. He warned off the Belgian Benedictines from any intervention 'in the English conversations [...] which no foreigner, however sympathetic, can adequately understand. They may pray for us, but we must work out our own salvation, and there is sufficient good will and knowledge in the English hierarchy for this high purpose [...] No country long enjoys foreign encouragement to its religious duty.'[24] Lord Halifax claimed to detect papist casuistry behind the letter, which he declared 'inspired directly or indirectly by Roman sources'.[25] Sir James required no instruction in sophistry. The thought and the execution were his alone.

Marchant offered further enticements, writing directly to the Cardinal two weeks later. 'An important Bishop [...] one of my oldest and most influential friends in the C of E' had been pressing an urgent invitation on him. Important conversations were to be held. Marchant was not sure what line to take. He would appreciate the Cardinal's advice. He added seductively, 'There is more behind the invitation that I can refer to'.[26] Marchant was almost certainly referring to the Bishop of Winchester. While Woods was personally committed to the Reunion of Christendom and laboured hard for this object on behalf of the Anglican Communion for over a decade, his approach was one hardly likely to commend itself to Bourne. Woods was an Evangelical, far more comfortable in his relations with Nonconformists, Presbyterians and Lutherans. His preference was for comprehensiveness and cooperation rather than detailed theological discussion to resolve doctrinal differences. There was to be no dramatic conversion or denouement to interest the Catholic Church as Marchant hinted.

The letter, however, had the desired effect on Bourne. Sir James obtained his 'interview with the Cardinal [which] went off satisfactorily'. The mysterious suggestion of conversations with Woods was dropped. Instead, he pursued his original motive—conversations between Catholics and non-Catholics. Relying on Marchant's version of events, it is always a little difficult to know exactly what was said, but it is clear that the Cardinal gave encouragement to the proposal. In the light of the outcome of Malines, others immediately recognised the significance of this: 'Of one thing I am sure—that in establishing relations with the English Hierarchy you have secured one of the most important conditions of success.'[27] Reassured by the Cardinal's reaction, Sir James wrote his opaque letter requesting a private meeting with Archbishop Davidson.

'A long and intimate talk'[28]

And so Sir James Marchant came to be seated before the Archbishop of Canterbury's study fire one late November morning. Davidson's caution meant he kept detailed memoranda of his meetings, especially with those like Marchant of whom he was suspicious.

Sir James explained that he knew Cardinal Bourne through the publishing world and had had the opportunity to observe 'the deep distress felt' by the Cardinal at his exclusion from Malines and the wounding assumption that he 'would be adverse to any approaches towards mutual explanations between Romans and Anglicans in England'. Sir James did not refrain from pathos to strengthen his case. 'The Cardinal's eyes were filled with tears when he spoke to me of his longing to see more friendly relations established and his constant prayer for reunion.' We cannot know what gloss the publisher applied when he claimed that the Cardinal had asked him to clarify matters with the Archbishop should the opportunity present itself. Sir James stated that he was acting on his own responsibility, rather than as the Cardinal's emissary. 'I have felt it my plain duty to put these facts before you in case you might like to take any action or to communicate with Cardinal Bourne on the subject.'

Davidson was not the type to be swept along by this sudden rush of enthusiasm for Christian Reunion. He remarked the picture of the Cardinal painted by Marchant was not one he recognised. He had seen nothing to make him think that Bourne shared Mercier's understanding and generosity towards Anglicans. Indeed, Bourne had 'throughout maintained that the conversion of individuals and the bringing of them into the fold is the only policy he could further in England, and his addresses and references to Anglicanism have never indicated, so far as I have observed, any desire for corporate conversations or approaches or for ultimate corporate reunion save by absorption'. Davidson had heard nothing from the Cardinal on the matter.

Marchant conceded the substance of the Archbishop's criticisms as they concerned the past. 'He thought Cardinal Bourne from his somewhat rigid and even hard way of expressing himself on these matters had been largely misunderstood, but he repeated that he had no commission to say this to me and was speaking of his own impression only; that impression was to the effect that Cardinal Bourne was changing his attitude a little and was departing from the sort of rigidity which found expression in his utterances—for example, at York a few months ago.'

If, as the Archbishop suspected, the publisher was looking for confidences and indiscretions from the Scot, he had chosen the wrong man. Davidson was no fool. He had the measure of Marchant and was undoubtedly correct when he recorded: 'Sir James rather hinted, though he did not say so, that he would like to be the bearer of some message to the Cardinal from myself.' The Archbishop protected himself by repeating that he had heard nothing from the Cardinal and he did not understand Marchant to be the Cardinal's authorised representative. But, should the Cardinal care to submit written proposals or request an interview, then this would be met 'with respect and cordiality'.[29]

Davidson's record of the meeting emphasizes Bourne's, or at least Marchant's, desire to correct mistaken impressions of the Cardinal's supposed hostility to Malines. But Marchant had confided to a trusted few the real purpose of his visit: to promote 'the idea of conversations in England'.[30] More was said than Davidson cared to admit. The Archbishop's natural wariness was exacerbated by the sensitivities surrounding the climax of Prayer Book Revision, which he did not want derailed by gossip concerning another set of secret negotiations with Rome. But there was some detailed discussion of possible conferences. For example, the Archbishop vetoed the inclusion of Nonconformists in any such talks as a hopeless complication.[31]

The Athenaeum

No sooner was Sir James out of Lambeth Palace than he began writing to others about his interview with the Archbishop. The correspondence supports the contention that Marchant and Davidson had indeed discussed the possibility of conversations in England between Catholics and Anglicans. Indeed, attention now focused on potential participants, although, on the Catholic side at least, it tended to be a question of who should be excluded. The Cardinal's preference for Bishop Bidwell to chair any conversations was felt to be problematic as was the inclusion of certain English Jesuits, who enjoyed reputations as 'conspicuous controversialists'.[32]

Marchant's letter to the Cardinal aimed to tantalise. He mentioned only the fact of his meeting with Davidson, adding, 'I have a report to give you which I feel you would be most pleased to hear'.[33] This explains comments made by the Cardinal to Catholic writers a couple of days later which might otherwise have puzzled his audience: 'The whole purpose of the Malines Conversations was to receive explanations. The Anglicans wanted explanations and the Church was ready to given them. We are always ready to do the same thing here.'[34] Marchant met Bourne at noon on 30 November. As with his interview with the Archbishop of Canterbury, the outcome of that meeting caused 'pleasure and surprise' among his correspondents. They attributed its success entirely to Sir James: 'Your courage and tact and *faith* are having a wonderful reward.'[35] No doubt Marchant put a positive interpretation on Davidson's position, but Bourne was genuinely open to conversations—provided they were conducted on what he deemed to be the correct basis. The Cardinal was more than willing 'to depute two or three competent persons to enter into discussion with [Anglicans chosen by Davidson] to see if in this way explanation of points of difference might lead to closer mutual understanding'.[36]

Thus encouraged, Marchant continued his shuttle diplomacy, chancing his luck once more with the Archbishop of Canterbury: 'I have a direct message of *importance* to deliver to you personally, from Cardinal Bourne. Would you kindly give me an interview at your convenience?'[37] This time, however, Davidson wanted to exclude all possibility of misunderstanding or manipulation. Bypassing the self-appointed intermediary, he wrote directly to the Cardinal. If Bourne had something to say, then he would be glad to hear from him personally.[38]

To the Archbishop's surprise, it did not prove a chimera. Bourne did have something to say. In fact, he wrote at some length to Davidson. He recounted how Marchant had told him about the Lambeth meeting of 22 November and how the Archbishop had 'expressed some satisfaction at the possibility of friendly, but essentially private, talks on such questions between those whom I represent and those for whom Your Grace is the official spokesman'. The Cardinal was eager to pursue the possibility and suggested he and the Archbishop meet after his return from an impending visit to Rome.[39]

The two men met on 16 February 1928 on the neutral territory of the Athenaeum, the clergy's London club of choice to which Davidson had proposed Bourne for membership eight years earlier. They discussed the Cardinal's supposed hostility to the Malines Conversations, a hostility which Bourne entirely repudiated. Then the Cardinal stated that he was 'practically ready to arrange for any talks we like between Anglicans and Roman Catholics in England, although he is not very hopeful that much would eventuate from them'.[40] That throughout was Bourne's authentic attitude towards Reunion talks: a willingness to explore all options, qualified by a hard realism regarding the possibility of success.

Leaving the Athenaeum, Davidson was probably more enlightened as to the position of the English Catholics than Bourne was regarding the Anglican stance. There was no response to the Cardinal's offer. The Church of England was smarting under the terms of the papal Encyclical Letter, *Mortalium Animos*, of the preceding month. The change in Vatican attitude since the early days of the Malines Conversations appeared to have been made official. Pope Pius XI seemed to exclude the very possibility of ecumenical dialogue:

> The Apostolic See can by no means take part in these assemblies, nor is it in any way lawful for Catholics to give to such enterprises their encouragement or support. If they did so, they would be giving countenance to a false Christianity quite alien to the one Church of Christ. Shall we commit the iniquity of suffering the truth, the truth revealed by God, to be made a subject for compromise?[41]

For Davidson, the matter was of secondary interest. All his energies had been invested in Prayer Book Reform. When this was defeated in Parliament for a second time, aged eighty, he informed the King that he intended to become the first Archbishop of Canterbury in history to retire, with effect from 12 November 1928.

All Marchant's schemes and the Cardinal's openness appeared to have amounted to nothing.

'A serious misunderstanding'

Notes

[1] Sir James Marchant to Archbishop Randall Davidson, 15 November 1927, LPL, Davidson Papers, 466/293.

[2] Davidson to Arnold Mathew, 20 January 1908, cited G. K. A. Bell, *Randall Davidson: Archbishop of Canterbury*, 3rd edn (London: Oxford University Press, 1952), p. 1018.

[3] Davidson to Viscount Halifax, 24 April 1895, cited Bell, *Randall Davidson*, p. 236.

[4] Davidson to Robert Hugh Benson, 16 September 1903, cited Bell, *Randall Davidson*, p. 413.

[5] Rev. A. C. Don to Bell, 31 March 1931, LPL, Bell Papers, 211/31 (copy).

[6] E. S. Woods and F. B. MacNutt, *Theodore, Bishop of Winchester: Pastor, Prophet, Pilgrim* (London: SPCK, 1933), p. 281.

[7] Marchant to Archbishop Cosmo Lang, 28 February 1932, LPL, Lang Papers, 112/161 (copy); Lang, Memorandum, 12 March 1932, LPL, Lang Papers, 112/169–70; *Who was Who, 1951–60* (London: A. & C. Black, 1961).

[8] J. Marchant, ed., *The Reunion of Christendom: A Survey of the Present Position* (London: Cassell & Co., 1929).

[9] Marchant to Editor, *Tablet* (24 Aug. 1929), pp. 244–5.

[10] Lang to Davidson, 22 November 1929, LPL, Lang Papers, 97/209 (copy).

[11] Editorial, *Tablet* (26 Nov. 1927), p. 689.

[12] Francis, Cardinal Bourne, Homily, 17 April 1927, *Tablet* (23 April 1927), pp. 555–7.

[13] Halifax to Portal, 29 November 1921, Portal Papers, Paris, cited Barlow, *The Malines Conversations*, pp. 59–60.

[14] Désiré, Cardinal Mercier to Bourne, 30 November 1922 (copy), MAA, Malines Conversations, 1922, B II 1, cited R. Aubert, 'Cardinal Mercier, Cardinal Bourne and the Malines Conversations', *One in Christ*, 4 (1968), pp. 372–9, at p. 375.

[15] Bourne to Mercier, 4 December 1922, MAA, B1, cited Barlow, *The Malines Conversations*, p. 90.

[16] Bourne to Ernest Oldmeadow, 6 February 1924, AAW, Bo. III, 124/4/2.

[17] Bourne, Pastoral Letter, 20 January 1924, read on 2 March 1924.

[18] Mercier to Bourne, 7 December 1925, AAW, Bo. III/124/4/2.

[19] Bourne, *Aide-memoire* for audience with Pius XI, 14 December 1925, AAW, Bo. III, 124/4/1.

[20] Halifax to Fr Hippolyte Hemmer, 18 September 1927 (draft), LPL, Davidson Papers, 466/251.

21 Robert Gordon George to Halifax, undated (August 1928?), BIY, Halifax Papers, General Ecclesiastical, 1926–34, A4/271/2.

22 Viscount FitzAlan to Bourne, 2 May 1926 and Bourne to FitzAlan, 4 May 1926, AAW, Bo. III/124/4; FitzAlan to Halifax, 7 May 1926, BIY, Malines Papers of Lord Halifax, Box 8/9.

23 Marchant to Bourne, 25 July 1927, AAW, Bo./ALN.

24 Marchant to Editor, *The Times*, 3 October 1927.

25 Halifax to Davidson, 10 October 1927, LPL, Davidson Papers, 466/254.

26 Marchant to Bourne, 20 October 1927, AAW, Bo./ALN.

27 Abbot Leander Ramsay to Marchant, 3 November 1927, OUL, Marchant, 315/44.

28 Marchant to Bourne, 22 November 1927, AAW, Bo./ALN.

29 Davidson, Memorandum of interview, 22 November 1927, LPL, Davidson Papers, 466/309–13.

30 Abbot Cuthbert Butler to Marchant, 22 November 1927, OUL, Marchant, 299/9.

31 Butler to Marchant, 24 November 1927, OUL, Marchant, 299/11; Bourne to Davidson, 6 December 1927, LPL, Davidson Papers, 466/330.

32 Butler to Marchant, 24 November 1927, OUL, Marchant, 299/10.

33 Marchant to Bourne, 22 November 1927, AAW, Bo./ALN.

34 Bourne, Catholic Writers' Day, 25 November 1927, *Tablet* (3 Dec. 1927), p. 727.

35 Butler to Marchant, 1 December 1927, OUL, Marchant, 299/14.

36 Bourne to Davidson, 6 December 1927, LPL, Davidson Papers, 466/329.

37 Marchant to Davidson, 2 December 1927, LPL, Davidson Papers, 466/327.

38 Davidson to Bourne, 3 December 1927, LPL, Davidson Papers, 466/328 (copy).

39 Bourne to Davidson, 6 December 1927, LPL, Davidson Papers, 466/329–30.

40 Davidson, Memorandum, 16 February 1928, LPL, Davidson Papers, 466/381.

41 Pope Pius XI, *Mortalium Animos*, 6 January 1928.

✧ 2 ✧

Catholic Reunion

Edinburgh and Beyond

Ecumenism began in Edinburgh in 1910. That gross oversimplification is often repeated. One overview of a centenary of ecumenical endeavour notes 'the 1910 Edinburgh Missionary Conference [is] usually identified as the beginnings of the twentieth-century ecumenical movement'.[1] Between the Protestant denominations a thaw had already begun. For some years students from differing Nonconformist traditions and Low Church Anglicans had been accustomed to study and pray together in British universities and colleges with scant regard for confessional divides. The experience of the Student Christian Movement altered perspectives and provoked questions. This was combined with a growing appreciation that missionary activity was being impeded by denominational differences. How could non-Christian peoples be successfully evangelised when offered competing messages? Understandably, they asked which Christ, which Church, they were being asked to accept. Against this backdrop 1,200 delegates from Protestant missionary societies around the world gathered in Edinburgh in June 1910. As the Conference drew to a close, a missionary to the Far East rose to his feet and appealed for an end to the denominational differences which were proving such an obstacle to evangelisation.

That one comment struck a chord. The Edinburgh Conference led to an increasing coordination of Protestant missionary activity, resulting in the foundation of the International Missionary Council in 1921. Another delegate heard that impassioned call too, and left the Conference determined to work for change. Bishop Charles Brent was a missionary Bishop in the Philippines whose churchmanship was far higher than most of his fellow delegates. Returning to the United States, he persuaded his fellow Episcopalian bishops to promote the cause of Christian unity. The First World War delayed their endeavours, but only served to increase their desire for unity. A preparatory meeting in Geneva in 1920 led to the first Conference of Faith and Order at Lausanne in August 1927.

It was an extraordinary achievement. Bishop Brent presided over more than 400 delegates, representing 108 different Christian bodies. The Catholics were the only significant absentees. The delegates considered the nature of the Church and issues relating to the creed, sacraments, ministry and unity. The Orthodox and the Anglo-Catholics were wary of according equality of status to the various Christian bodies represented. It fell to the Orthodox to assert the impossibility of doctrine and Church practice being determined by vote and compromise. Yet many were surprised by the measure of agreement achieved. Only on the issue of unity did Anglo-Catholics succeed in preventing the matter being put to the vote, with the Report being referred instead to a Continuation Committee.

Simultaneously with the development of the Faith and Order Movement, Archbishop Nathan Söderblom of Uppsala pioneered a coordinated approach towards the application of Christian principles to international and social affairs. The Life and Work Conference in Stockholm in 1925 was attended by more than 500 delegates. The decision was taken in Utrecht in 1938 to unite the two Movements. And so, delayed by the Second World War, the World Council of Churches was formally inaugurated in 1948. Reflecting its origins, it attempted to encompass two distinct approaches towards unity. A more 'Catholic' approach, promoted by the Orthodox and Anglo-Catholics, held out for Corporate Reunion, complete agreement on all fundamental issues of doctrine and Church life, a sharing of creed and ministry. Nothing less, they argued, would fulfil Christ's prayer at the Last Supper that all might be one. Many Protestants had little interest in details of doctrine and ecclesiology. Their objective, rather, was a loose federation of Christians, wishing each other well, cooperating where possible, even enjoying intercommunion, but agreeing to differ in their tenets and practices.

It was the Stockholm and Lausanne Conferences, rather than the Malines Conversations, which were the real object of papal ire in the 1928 Encyclical. The unity sought by these 'pan-Christians', the Pope maintained, was no unity at all. 'They conceive the visible Church as nothing more than a federation of the various Christian communities, even though these may hold different and mutually exclusive doctrines.'[2] No Catholic was permitted to engage in such talks lest it compromise the Catholic Church's claim to be the only Church founded by Christ and to possess alone the authority to transmit and interpret revelation.

Statements such as those contained in the Encyclical are responsible for the assumption that, until its enlightenment at the Second Vatican Council in the 1960s, Rome had nothing to offer the search for Christian unity save for unremitting and unconstructive hostility. A review of early twentieth-century ecumenism focuses on the 1910 Edinburgh Conference and the Faith and Order Movement. The Malines Conversations receive not a mention. There is, of course, the obligatory reference to papal negativity as exemplified by *Mortalium Animos*.[3] Even Pope Benedict XVI bought into this mind-set when he wrote:

> The ecumenical movement had gradually come into being in the nineteenth century, initially as a result of the missionary experience of the Protestant churches [...] Ecumenism, in this sense, was first and foremost a phenomenon of world Protestantism [...] Eastern Orthodoxy was the first to join it, albeit in the beginning with cautious provisos. The Catholic Church [...] [was generally absent] until the Second Vatican Council flung the Church's doors open to the search for the unity of all Christians.[4]

The contention of this work is that, even if less prominent, there was another, more authentic approach to Christian unity and that this approach was not confined to the Catholic Church.

Association for Promoting the Unity of Christendom

The Anglican clergy whom we will encounter later were adamant that there had always existed within the Church of England a school of thought which never accepted as legitimate or desirable the break with Rome at the Reformation. They adduced copious historical evidence to demonstrate that such a division was forced upon an unwilling English Church by the Crown. Reunion with Rome, they argued, was the only means of remedying the serious failings of Anglicanism and re-establishing normal ecclesiastical life in England. But even proponents of this view had to concede that such a school of thought, even if it did not die out entirely, lay dormant for much of the eighteenth century as spiritual stupor becalmed the Established Church.

The reawakening began with the birth of the Oxford Movement in 1833. This started as a call to arms against the perceived State encroachments upon the liberty of the Church. Seeking spiritual and moral renewal, the Movement turned to history and the Church Fathers to justify Anglican claims. Such studies led John Henry Newman and others to convert to Catholicism. But the majority who accepted the principles of the Oxford Movement remained loyal to the national Church. They too had to determine their relationship to the Church as she existed prior to the Reformation and to Rome as she existed in their own day. Were such divisions in Christendom permanent and irreconcilable?

Many avoided the discomfort of such questions by adopting 'the branch theory' according to which there were three 'branches' of the Church of (more or less) equal validity. Thus, the Church of England was the only legitimate form of historic Christianity in this country, as Catholicism was in much of Western Europe and Orthodoxy in the East. Accepting that each branch was equal, separate and self-contained absolved one from the responsibility to mend the breaches or even to seek contact with Christians of other Communions.

One man who did not feel himself thus absolved was Ambrose Phillipps de Lisle. From a family of Leicestershire gentry, de Lisle

Catholic Reunion

converted to Catholicism in his teens but, unlike many converts, he never forgot his former co-religionists. He was excited by the possibilities for Reunion which the Oxford Movement seemed to present and, to this end, he corresponded with many High Church Anglicans.

De Lisle accepted that most Anglicans were not about to abandon the Church of England in the immediate future. Rather he felt, through study and prayer, the object of Reunion ought to be kept to the fore in the minds of all men of goodwill. Working with Anglicans and other Catholics, de Lisle founded the Association for Promoting the Unity of Christendom (APUC) on 8 September 1857. Membership required only a commitment to pray for unity in a manner commensurate with the principles of the individual's own church. Catholic priest members agreed to offer Mass quarterly for the intention of unity. The movement grew rapidly. By 1864 it had 8,000 members: 1,000 Catholics (many of those from overseas), 300 Orthodox and the vast majority Anglican. Catholic bishops expressed sympathy with the Association. While doubting de Lisle's realism, Cardinal Wiseman looked benignly on his efforts. Even Pius IX extended his blessing to the work of APUC.

Moderate and harmless as its methods appeared, APUC had its enemies in England and in Rome. There were fears that it would result in a decrease of individual converts. Unwisely, articles were published critical of English Catholicism and the discipline of clerical celibacy. At their 1864 Low Week meeting the English Catholic hierarchy referred the matter to the Holy See. Rome prohibited Catholic membership on the basis that APUC was committed to the branch theory, holding Catholicism, Orthodoxy and Anglicanism to be equally valid. Registering his protest, de Lisle submitted to the ruling and resigned from APUC. There then followed, what was for the 1860s, the extraordinary step of 200 Anglican clergy in the movement petitioning the Holy Office in Rome to reverse the original ruling, arguing that the Vatican had been mistaken in condemning APUC for holding the branch theory. Urged on by Henry Manning, who had succeeded Wiseman as Archbishop of Westminster, Rome rejected the Anglican appeal in November 1865.

APUC continued as a predominantly Anglican body. It had never been its intention to develop a practical programme for Reunion. And yet the fact that an association with such an object should be established within a generation of the Oxford Movement and attract the attention and blessing of the supreme authority in the Catholic Church was itself extraordinary. And APUC's aim had been Catholic Reunion—not some Protestant concept of a federation of Christian bodies, united in goodwill but agreeing to differ in the essentials of doctrine and discipline. APUC looked forward to Corporate Reunion, the visible unity of Christendom in matters of belief and practice.

Sixty years later, the Benedictine historian, Abbot Cuthbert Butler of Downside, paid tribute to its significance:

> This was the earliest of the Reunion movements in the English Church after the Oxford Movement had spread its influence through wide circles; and as such hankerings after the ideal of Unity have been asserting themselves again and again ever since in the High Church circles of the Church of England, the story of APUC has to this day a living interest, and deserves to be told here as the story of the first and most noteworthy of such Reunion movements, wherein certainly the high-water mark was reached.[5]

Apostolicae Curae

Born in 1839, as a young man, Lord Halifax had known de Lisle. Charles Lindley Wood, second Viscount Halifax, was the grandson of a Prime Minister (Earl Grey), the son of a Chancellor of the Exchequer and a friend of the Royal Family. Eschewing a political career, he dedicated his long life to the lay leadership of the Anglo-Catholic party in the Church of England, serving for decades as President of the English Church Union. Whether they agreed with him or not, contemporaries never doubted Halifax's essential sincerity and sanctity.

From his time at Oxford, Halifax was committed to Christian unity, a unity which, for him, was unthinkable without the Apostolic See. He later wrote: 'In regard to Reunion with Rome [...] I cannot believe that it is as difficult as it is thought.'[6] While always acknowledging his integrity and perseverance, many felt that Halifax shared de Lisle's lack of realism when it came to matters of Reunion. If he was unrealistic, Halifax's achievements were nevertheless impressive.

His practical efforts for Reunion resulted from a chance encounter with a French priest, Fernand Portal, on the island of Madeira in the winter of 1889. The English aristocrat and the seminary professor struck up an unlikely friendship and continued to correspond. Portal persuaded Halifax to pursue the reunionist cause, having him write on the validity of Anglican Orders for the French Catholic Press. On his part, writing under a pseudonym, Portal wrote a two-part article, *Les Ordinations anglicanes*, inviting the conclusion that the Catholic Church should accept that Anglican clergy were indeed validly-ordained priests. Portal waxed lyrical and optimistically:

> In a world hostile to the teaching of Our Lord and Saviour, His followers realise instinctively the need for closer union to support the coming struggle between believers and non-believers [...] In England prejudices are disappearing, the Established Church asserts her independence of the civil authority, the influence of the Oxford Movement continues to grow, and the Church is recovering the fullness of the faith. The inevitable, providential end of this evolution is Rome.[7]

If Reunion was dependent simply on the goodwill of these two men, then success was assured. Halifax was also correct in the methods to be employed: 'The first thing necessary is to get to know each other; the second that we really do want union with all our heart, and without making any sacrifices to the truth, to judge as leniently as possible all that has been said and done in the past or is being said and done now, by either side. Above all, many explanations are needed.'[8]

Matters progressed rapidly, much more rapidly than Halifax and Portal had foreseen. Visiting England in the summer of 1894 as Halifax's guest, Portal was introduced to the world of Anglo-Catholicism. He also met the Archbishops of Canterbury and York. Portal expressed himself puzzled by Archbishop Frederick Temple:

He is a holy man and learned, but he seems to think that in his position he must be very cautious, a feeling probably explained by what he said to me in connection with our movement, 'Reverend Sir, we have to remember that many of our fellow churchmen to whom we must be loyal do not agree with us on these matters'.[9]

The Frenchman's bewilderment at Canterbury's caution was indicative of a fault line which would continue to bedevil the efforts of reunionists: their persistent failure to appreciate the need of religious leaders to take into account the views of constituencies—in this period always numerically far more significant—other than their own.

Portal found himself summoned to Rome for secret talks with Cardinal Rampolla, Leo XIII's Secretary of State, and an audience with the Pope himself. The Pope shared Portal's desire for Reunion with the Church of England along the lines of the overtures he had made the Orthodox, offering to respect local custom. And so Portal returned to England in September 1894 with a letter addressed by Cardinal Rampolla to himself, but, in reality, designed to test Anglican willingness to enter into discussions. But, without any official approach on the part of Rome, and conscious of the far less sympathetic utterances of Cardinal Vaughan closer to home, Canterbury and York were suspicious and refused to be drawn.

Halifax sought to advance the cause of Reunion with an effusive speech to the English Church Union in Bristol in February 1895. 'Rome', he said, 'was the symbol and centre of the unity of the Church. Canterbury was the daughter of Rome, bound to her by the closest ties of faith and assistance'.[10] Halifax sent copies to Anglican bishops and others and, carrying the favourable responses, set off for Rome. Thus encouraged, Leo XIII issued his letter *Ad Anglos* on 20 April 1895, inviting all Englishmen to pray for Reunion.

Halifax and Portal sought bilateral negotiations between Rome and Canterbury on the subject of Reunion. Instead, with no substantive Anglican response to *Ad Anglos*, the Vatican decided its only option was unilateral action. In March 1896, Leo XIII appointed a Pontifical Commission of Enquiry, comprising only Catholics, into the question of the validity of Anglican Orders. Not without controversy, the Commission upheld Rome's continuous position and, in the Bull *Apostolicae Curae* issued on 13 September 1896, the Pope ruled Anglican Orders 'absolutely null and utterly void'. There was Anglican anger at what they perceived as Catholic impertinence on pronouncing on a matter which did not concern them. If that was Rome's position, then even the consideration of any possibility of Reunion was off the table, the Archbishop of Canterbury maintained at the 1897 Lambeth Conference.

The prospects for Catholic Reunion seemed dead, with no hope of resurrection. Virtually no one would have shared Halifax's continued optimism expressed to his friend: 'We tried to do something which, I believe, God inspired. We have failed, for the moment; but if God wills it, His desire will be accomplished, and if He allows us to be shattered, it may well be because He means to do it Himself. This is no dream. The thing is as certain as ever.'[11]

The Society of St Thomas of Canterbury

So, the twentieth century opened with an impasse. The Anglican Establishment ruled further contact impossible while the Catholic Church refused to lift the condemnation contained in *Apostolicae Curae*. The Catholic Church maintained that her doctrine was immutable; change could not be contemplated without betraying her very nature and the commission entrusted to her by Christ Himself. One man proposed a creative solution to an intractable problem — but he found it difficult to gain an audience. The 1896 censure of Anglican Orders is covered at great length in histories of the ecumenical movement. Many also devote a few paragraphs to Ambrose de Lisle and APUC. But the alternative approach described below is curiously absent from virtually every account of the search for Christian unity. Sometimes the omission is due to genuine ignorance. Sometimes there is a decision that, in terms of numbers and consequences, its significance was minimal. However, might the omission also be due to the fact that this approach fails to fit within the narrative of ecumenism held by both Catholic and Anglican establishments for half a century?

In 1900, APUC arranged a series of sermons to be delivered in the Anglican parish church of St Matthew's, Westminster on the principal saints' days that year. Inspired by Lord Halifax's speech on Reunion with Rome given in Bristol in 1898, a Gloucestershire clergyman, Spencer Jones, asked to preach on 29 June, the Feast of St Peter the Apostle.[12] No one who heard that sermon doubted that a new line had been struck. Halifax, who had been in the congregation, rushed into the vestry, placed his hand on the preacher's shoulder and told him: 'Now you must publish that; you said some strong things that you may like to reconsider.'[13]

In a much extended form, Jones published his sermon in 1902 as *England and the Holy See: An Essay towards Reunion*, with an introduction by Halifax. Jones clearly stated that the views expressed were his own, that he spoke for neither APUC nor the English Church Union. He had no illusions as to the controversy of his position. He resigned as a diocesan delegate in the House of Clergy in the Canterbury Convocation. According to his friends, his 'manifest yet humble priestliness fitted him for higher rank than the priesthood', but 'his devotion to the truth' ensured that any possibility of 'clerical preferment' disappeared the instant his book was published.[14] Following publication, Jones received letters which were 'violent, sometimes even virulent'.[15] Yet this work remained for decades the standard text of 'the Roman school' within the Church of England. It was translated into German and reviewed across Europe and America.

Jones accepted from the outset that: 'Rome cannot formally change; that is, she cannot contradict her formal dogmatic *ex cathedra* definitions.'[16] But while Rome could not change, change was characteristic of the Church of England and it was, therefore, incumbent on Anglicans to change.[17] This represented a development beyond Halifax's own thought. However much the peer desired Reunion with the Holy See, he felt change and compromise was necessary on both sides, and he wrote to Jones: 'I think you do not quite see how much Rome has to and can learn.'[18] For the clergyman, the conditions imposed by Halifax were to consign unity to the realms of fantasy. For most Anglicans, Jones's premise was not a basis for Reunion, but rather abject submission. He and those who came after him were to be accused of dishonesty and betrayal. His consistent response was that he was remaining true in the deepest sense to the Church of England, whose Catholic identity had been compromised by the State at the Reformation. Yes, Reunion required Anglican acceptance of the full doctrinal position of the Catholic Church, but there were issues that pertained to discipline, rather than doctrine, where Rome could, and should, change.

To proceed along such lines, Jones argued, required humility. It required a willingness to approach old controversies afresh, to sweep away prejudice and to recover a Catholic interpretation of disputed questions, principal among them Christ's intention in founding the unity of His Church upon the person of St Peter. Anglicans were inclined to say 'while Rome is what she is reunion with her is impossible. But the answer to this, so far, is that before we pronounce judgment we have to be sure we know what it is we are judging, and that in regard to Rome the majority of people are without this knowledge.'[19] He sought in his book to cast light upon a correct understanding of papal infallibility, Marian dogmas, Tradition, the interpretation of Scripture and indulgences. (Tellingly, Jones passed over the recent Catholic pronouncement on Anglican Orders.)

Progress could only be made where there was personal contact. Jones acknowledged his own debt to the Dominicans, Jesuits and other Catholics whom he had come to know.[20] Our Lord's own plea for the unity of His disciples that the world might believe simply could not be ignored. 'On these grounds I consider that Conferences on Reunion present themselves no longer merely as wise but also as a necessary step; and they are, I think, to be welcomed as supplying evidence of the revival in our midst of the true instinct of unity.'[21]

Jones claimed that the publication of *England and the Holy See* resulted in two hugely important practical consequences for the cause of Catholic Reunion. The first was a decision taken at a meeting in London on 17 February 1904 of forty Anglican clergy in sympathy with his book. The Eastern Churches Association had been founded forty years earlier to promote understanding and unity between the Church of England and the Orthodox. Jones had no difficulty with this, but he stated the obvious corollary: 'It seems only natural, then, on the face of things, that there should also be a Western Church Association [...] Indeed, since charity starts at home, the Western Church would seem to have a prior claim upon our attention.'[22] Anglican fascination with the Orthodox Church increased as British imperial interests expanded in the Eastern Mediterranean. At such a safe distance, Orthodoxy never posed a threat to Anglicanism on its home turf, as Rome might. Jones and those who followed him were suspicious of these overtures to the East. The Reunion of Christendom, he argued, could never be founded

> upon impossible attempts to unite Canterbury and Constantinople in opposition to the Holy See as such, but upon the willingness of Constantinople and Canterbury alike to acknowledge once again as they both did in times preceding their schism, and on the testimony of the Ecumenical Councils, the primacy of the Holy See, *de jure divino*.[23]

The Church of England was founded by Rome, the Mother Church of the West, and it was to the West that Englishmen must look primarily to promote the cause of Reunion.

So came into being the Western Church Association, more commonly known as the Society of St Thomas of Canterbury, whose patronage its members sought. The purpose of the Society was Reunion with Rome, its methods were prayer and study. In particular, Jones maintained that the opening up to the public of many archives in the late nineteenth century permitted a reassessment of the true causes of the Reformation. His own research, and that of others, conclusively exploded the Whig myth that the Protestant Reformation in England had been a popular and a progressive event. Anglicanism needed to recover a sense of its continuity with the Anglo-Saxon and medieval Church, to appreciate the violence to her true self, suffered at the hands of the English Crown in the sixteenth century. Jones did not underestimate the risks he was undertaking: 'If it should prove to be our lot, in however small a measure, to do the work of pioneers, we must expect to be misunderstood at the outset and to be called names.'[24]

The Society met twice a year, initially in Holborn Town Hall, later at the Caxton Hall. Jones avoided the troubles encountered by APUC by limiting membership to Anglicans. However, from the outset, it was intended that Catholics should be present and participate as welcome guests. Jones himself delivered the first lecture. Thereafter, speakers alternated between Anglicans and Catholics. In fact, the Catholics seemed to attract greater publicity. Those who addressed the Society included Abbots Gasquet and Chapman, Frs Vincent McNabb, Robert Hugh Benson and Adrian Fortescue, and Hilaire Belloc. Meetings lasted all day and could attract an audience of 120 from across the country. Members were expected to take their duties seriously. Speakers circulated lengthy reading lists in advance of lectures.

The quality of talks and discussion was high. The Society gradually wound down after a generation or so, having served Jones's intended purpose: to reduce 'the distance between our members and Rome'.[25]

Church Unity Octave

The other important outcome of the publication of *England and the Holy See* identified by Jones was the result of his book being read 3,500 miles away by an Episcopalian clergyman named Paul Wattson. In 1898 Fr Wattson and Mother Lurana White had founded in New York State a religious community, the Society of the Atonement, living the Franciscan life within the Anglican Communion. Two years later they committed the Society to the cause of Corporate Reunion with Rome, publishing a periodical, the *Lamp*, to propagate their vision. But Wattson was only too aware of his isolation within his own Communion. 'As far as I know,' he wrote, 'I am the only Anglican ecclesiastic in 30,000 who holds these views.'[26]

Reading *England and the Holy See* assured Wattson that there was at least one other Anglican clergyman who thought as he did. The two men entered into correspondence, resulting in a lifelong friendship and their collaboration in 1907 in the authorship of the book *The Prince of the Apostles: A Study*. In the same year Jones made another suggestion to Wattson. Drawing on his own experience in 1900, he called for sermons to be preached wherever possible on 29 June each year on the subject of 'the Apostolic See and the Roman Primacy'. The American tweaked the suggestion: the observance of an annual Church Unity Octave with eight days of prayer from the Feast of St Peter's Chair on 18 January to the Feast of the Conversion of St Paul on 25 January. Wattson recalls: 'I did not waste any time in starting the ball rolling and sent out letters to Anglican clergymen and Catholic prelates and prominent pastors, inviting them to unite with us in such an Octave in January 1908.'[27]

Wattson had also argued for Corporate Reunion between Canterbury and Rome, claiming that individual conversions would only delay the catholicising of the Anglican Communion and, therefore, the ultimate realisation of Reunion. But by the end of 1907 he was sharing his doubts with Jones:

> This is due I think to a gradually maturing conviction that only a portion of the Anglican body will corporately unite with the Holy See at first and that adhesion of the larger portion will come at a later day [. . .] Is there any additional reason you can bring forward why we are justified in remaining for the present in the Anglican Communion and exercising our ministry after having accepted *ex animo* the dogmatic position of Rome?[28]

The argument was compelling, and one which Jones and his followers always struggled to answer. Wattson, at least, was convinced by the logic of his assertion. On 30 October 1909 he and his community were received into the Catholic Church.

Wattson's conversion seemed only to strengthen the appeal of the Church Unity Octave. Both the American and the Englishman were determined to continue the work they had begun and not to allow the fact they were now in different communions to impede their collaboration in the work of unity. Wattson described his community's conversion as the first fruits of the prayers offered during the Octave. If prayer brought conversions, then Rome was more than willing to endorse it. Pope Pius X approved the Octave in 1909; in 1916, Benedict XV commended its observance to the universal Catholic Church.

The Catholic League

Within the Church of England promotion of the observance of the Octave was taken up during the First World War by a new organisation, the Catholic League. Formed in July 1913 by two Anglican clergymen, Richard Langford-James and Henry Fynes-Clinton, the League immediately courted controversy. Both Langford-James and Fynes-Clinton were forced to resign after the bishops objected to the invocation of the saints and the singing of the *Salve Regina* at the Service of Inauguration. Fynes-Clinton, however, chose to regard the episcopal sanction as having lapsed upon his moving parish the following year. For the next half century he was the dominant figure within the League and a host of associated bodies.

The League published a quarterly bulletin, the *Messenger*. The first edition sought to define its purpose:

> It is somewhat difficult to describe exactly *the motives* which should be the predominant ones in our Catholic League. The *main objects* of the League may be stated in the precise terms of our formal declaration: that we desire to promote brotherhood and union among Catholics, to deepen their spiritual life and to encourage the spread of the Catholic Religion.[29]

(As used here 'Catholic' referred to the Church of England; Fynes-Clinton had an antipathy to the term 'Anglo-Catholic', always understanding himself to be part of something wider than the Anglican Communion.) At the outset the League claimed twenty branches. Initially, the focus was liturgical and spiritual. Feasts were celebrated with due ceremony, Mass, fasting and the rosary promoted, processions and retreats organised.

This side of the Atlantic, the Church Unity Octave received little attention and less organisation in the decade following its inception. The Catholic League took out a Press advertisement in 1914 calling for observance of the Octave, but it was circumspect in its language. There was no reference to Rome. It was simply an invitation each day during the Octave to pray the *Veni Creator* and Prayer for Unity and receive Holy Communion for that intention. It took the Pope's endorsement of the Octave in

1916, raising it from the status of a private devotion to an official observance of the Universal Church, and a heartfelt plea the following year from the Society of the Atonement to the English Church Union, to galvanise the League to a more strenuous promotion of the Octave.[30]

In January 1917, the League asked all its members 'to join in intercession for reunion during these days, and for the return of England to Communion with the Apostolic See'.[31] Subsequently, Reunion was explicitly identified as the League's primary objective, 'Reunion' being understood in a fully Catholic sense:

> There is today much peril in schemes of Protestant federation. These involve a denial of the Divine Authority of the Apostolic Hierarchy, and of the supernatural claims of the historic Catholic Church [...] The only remedy against these dangers is the visible reunion of the Catholic Episcopate.[32]

Together with its adoption in 1920 of the Creed of the Council of Trent as its profession of faith, this placed the Catholic League at the very extremes of the Church of England.

Under the auspices of the League, a Church Unity Octave Council of 58 clergy and laity was established in 1926 to further this work, with Jones as President and Fynes-Clinton as Chairman. The Council published literature, distributed material and advertised in the Church Press annually, asking Anglican clergy to commit to observance of the Octave, it being clearly understood the unity for which they were praying was exclusively union with Rome. Each year the Octave was kept in churches across London and the provinces and perpetual prayer was maintained in Anglican religious houses, but the culmination was always High Mass in Fynes-Clinton's City church of St Magnus-the-Martyr. Great fun was had by all with high liturgy, glorious litanies and 'exquisite music'. But how effectively was the cause of Reunion being promoted? In 1930, the Octave could still muster only 79 priest supporters in England. Then suddenly it experienced rapid and exponential growth—807 three years later, and still increasing.[33]

The Lambeth *Appeal*

The running in the cause of Reunion described above was made by the *avant-garde*, a relative few on the fringes of Anglicanism. It is time to return to the mainstream.

The Lambeth Conference is the meeting every ten years (give or take) of all the bishops of the international Anglican Communion at the London residence of the Archbishop of Canterbury. Not an executive body, such meetings were nevertheless felt to be increasingly desirable to promote contact and coherence as the Anglican Communion expanded with the British Empire over the course of the nineteenth century.

Randall Davidson presided over the 252 Bishops who met at the Sixth Lambeth Conference in 1920. Meeting so soon after the end of the First World War, no one questioned the prevailing subject matter of the Conference. The Anglican bishops summarised their deliberations in an Encyclical Letter:

> In order to accomplish its object, the Church must itself be a pattern of fellowship. It is only by showing the value and power of fellowship in itself that it can win the world to fellowship. The weakness of the Church in the world of today is not surprising when we consider how the bands of its own fellowship are loosened and broken.
>
> The truth of this had been slowly working into the consciousness of Christians before the war. But the war and its horrors, waged as it was between so-called Christian nations, drove home the truth with the shock of a sudden awakening. Men in all Communions began to think of the reunion of Christendom, not as a laudable ambition or a beautiful dream, but as an imperative necessity. Proposals and counter-proposals were made, some old, some new. Mutual recognition, organic union, federation, absorption, submission — these phrases indicate the variety of programmes put forward. Some definite proposals came from the Mission Field, where the urgency of the work of evangelisation and the birth of national Churches alike demand a new fellowship [. . .] The great wind was blowing over the whole earth.[34]

The largest Committee ever appointed by a Lambeth Conference, chaired by Archbishop Lang of York, considered the Reunion of Christendom. Two subcommittees reported on relations to and Reunion with episcopal and non-episcopal churches respectively. The subcommittee concerned with the non-episcopal churches noted the 'dramatic and impressive' moves towards Reunion with Anglicanism since the Lambeth Conference had last met in 1908, urging that 'great freedom [. . .] be left to local negotiators'.[35]

The subcommittee charged with relations to and Reunion with episcopal churches had a broad remit. It reported not only on the prevailing situation as it pertained to the Church of Sweden, the Old Catholics, the Moravians and 'the Reformed Episcopal Church', but also the Eastern Churches. Great attention was paid to the Orthodox, not least because the Ecumenical Patriarch in Constantinople had sent a special delegation to the Lambeth Conference. Hopes ran high that the Orthodox and the Anglicans might be 'steadily moving towards the goal of ultimate reunion'.[36]

Only in respect of Catholicism had the subcommittee no resolution to propose to the Conference, but it recognised that its report would be incomplete without any reference to the largest Christian Communion. So it adopted the text of the 1908 Conference that there could be

> 'no fulfilment of the Divine purpose in any scheme of reunion which does not ultimately include the great Latin Church of the West, with which our history has been so closely associated in the past, and to which we are still bound by many ties of faith and tradition.' But we realise that—to continue the quotation—'any advance in this direction is at present barred by difficulties which we have not ourselves created, and which we cannot of ourselves remove.'

Apostolicae Curae clearly still rankled. Yet an olive branch was proffered: 'Should, however, the Church of Rome at any time desire to discuss conditions of reunion we shall be ready to welcome such discussions.' The report listed encouraging signs in the Catholic Church: the establishment by the religious orders of houses of study in Oxford and their willingness to engage in the intellectual life of the Universities, the hierarchy's readiness to share a common platform on social matters and the personal relations enjoyed between chaplains of different denominations in the trenches.[37]

Anglicans saw themselves as 'a Bridge Church', enjoying a privileged position which enabled them to effect reconciliation between episcopal and non-episcopal churches, between the communities of the Reformation and the ancient communions of East and West. But their unique standpoint brought challenges as well as opportunities. Critics were not slow to point out the apparently irreconcilable inconsistencies which might arise depending upon whom Anglicanism was addressing at any given time.

The Anglican bishops could seem to be attempting to have it both ways. On the one hand their Encyclical Letter seemed to support Catholic Reunion. 'Some vague federation' of Christians was inadequate. The only acceptable goal was 'a united and truly Catholic Church', all Christians 'united in the fellowship of one visible society whose members are bound together by the ties of a common faith, common sacraments and a common ministry'. Words that might have been written in the Vatican. More questionable to the Catholic mind was the insistence on 'diversity' over 'uniformity' so 'that the Church can become all things to all men'.[38] One of the predominant influences at the 1920 Lambeth Conference and beyond was Arthur Headlam, Regius Professor of Theology at Oxford and later Bishop of Gloucester. For Headlam, unity did not exist owing to human sinfulness; it had to be sought and created.[39] For a Catholic, unity had always existed within the visible society founded by Christ and presided over by the Pope on earth; it had to be recognised and accepted.

The greatest achievement of the 1920 Conference was its *Appeal to All Christian Peoples*, a heartfelt plea for unity. It began and ended with touching humility:

> We acknowledge this condition of broken fellowship to be contrary to God's will, and we desire frankly to confess our share in the guilt of thus crippling the Body of Christ and hindering the activity of His Spirit.[40]

To further the cause of Reunion, if terms were otherwise agreed, Anglican bishops and clergy announced their willingness to undergo whatever form of commissioning might be necessary to make their ministry acceptable to others.[41] (Although it might not have been formulated with that purpose in mind, others were not slow to suggest that here was a potential solution to the dilemma posed by *Apostolicae Curae*.) Following Anglican precedent, the *Appeal* suggested such unity might be based on a 'whole-hearted acceptance' of Scripture, the Nicene Creed, the sacraments of Baptism and Holy Communion and a common ministry grounded in the historic episcopacy.[42] Again, an encouraging start for those who believed in Catholic Reunion, but then largely vitiated by the Conference's resolving to welcome Nonconformists to Anglican pulpits and Holy Communion.[43]

The Irish Dominican, Vincent McNabb, was generous in his response to the *Appeal*. For him, it was 'the most authentic promise of dawn that has yet appeared in the dark night legacied to us by the sixteenth century'. He would not allow the Church of England 'to accept all the sin of disunion'. He found the Anglican offer to enter discussions with Rome unutterably moving and he was convinced that the offer would resonate elsewhere too. 'It is nearly three hundred years since words such as these passed between the Mother-Church and its beloved Daughter-Church [. . .] The Shepherd who guides his flock where Peter laid down his life for the sheep, will not hear this Voice of the English without feeling his Shepherd heart moved to its depths.'[44]

Cardinal Bourne's pronouncement was less generous, but more representative of Catholics:

> A little more than a year ago they were gazing, sympathetically, yet pitiably, upon a gathering which took place at Lambeth. The Anglicans met there in a spirit of prayer, yet Catholics knew that their deliberations must end in pathetic failure [. . .] It was now generally admitted that the hopes then raised as to reunion had been frustrated, and many minds, as a result of that failure, were turning towards the Old Church that spoke today with the same voice as she spoke a thousand years ago.[45]

If that sounds harsh, it was not a viewpoint reserved exclusively to the Roman Communion.

Catholic Reunion

Those on the Catholic wing of the Church of England were unhappy, not with the *Appeal* itself, but with its practical consequences. Most Anglicans were far more comfortable with the prospect of Reunion with the Nonconformists. Discounting Rome and Orthodoxy, the Bishop of Norwich wrote: 'I feel that approaches towards reunion in England are the thing that matters; *near home* counts for more than things at a great distance.'[46] On 30 November 1921, Free Church delegates met Anglican bishops at Lambeth to explore the possibility of unity in light of the *Appeal*. These discussions foundered on the question of the reordination of Nonconformist ministers, but the twenty-two joint conferences over the next four years were a constant source of anxiety to Anglo-Catholics.

The Catholic League registered its opposition: 'A wonderful opportunity of establishing very close relations, even some intercommunion, with the Ancient Catholic Churches of the East was sacrificed to dreams of "Home reunion" with those who deny the doctrines of the Church and Sacraments.'[47] Simultaneously, the Jesuit Leslie Walker received overtures from 'the more advanced section of the Anglican Church' enquiring as to the Catholic response 'should this section—clergy and laity—*as a body* approach Rome with a view to submitting themselves to her authority'. These Anglicans felt their position untenable owing to 'the un-Catholic proposals of Lambeth' and 'the increase of friendliness with the Nonconformists'. Should Rome be open to the possibility of a Uniate Church for such Anglicans, with provision for married clergy and vernacular liturgy, it was felt 'that several hundred of the clergy *and their congregations* would embrace the offer'.[48] Cardinal Bourne read of the approach with 'deep and sympathetic interest', and referred the matter to his Canon Theologian, Canon James Moyes, a member of the 1896 Papal Commission which had considered the validity of Anglican Orders. While professing to meet the Anglican approach 'in the full spirit of apostolic charity', Moyes was so disparaging of the prospects of disciplinary concessions and so insistent on the need for absolute 'submission', that nothing further came of the proposal.[49]

Malines

It is not intended to give here a comprehensive account of the Conversations which took place in Malines between 1921 and 1925. A thorough record and analysis can be found in Bernard Barlow's book, *'A brother knocking at the door': The Malines Conversations*. It is necessary, however, to understand some of the issues which arose at Malines and some of the consequences which would have relevance for future relations between Catholics and Anglicans.

The Anglican bishops at Lambeth had felt perfectly safe in welcoming the possibility of discussions with Rome on 'conditions of reunion'. The terms of *Apostolicae Curae* and the attitude of the Vatican and the local Catholic hierarchy seemed to preclude even the possibility of such discussions. Archbishop Davidson faced an unanticipated contingency, therefore, when Lord Halifax informed him in October 1921 that he was visiting Belgium with Fr Portal to ask Cardinal Mercier to host Reunion conversations between Anglicans and Catholics. Halifax's disclosure placed the Anglican Establishment in a quandary. There was no real enthusiasm for discussions, still less for union, with Rome as they understood Rome's theology and practice to be. Yet to veto such discussions would expose the Lambeth offer as insincere. Furthermore, the hierarchy were concerned how Anglo-Catholics would react to such a veto. The Archbishop of York reminded Davidson: 'Many are suspicious about the *Appeal* because it seems to be moving entirely in the Protestant direction.'[50]

When Mercier agreed to host such talks, Portal wrote to his friend, 'As you said, we are beginning again'.[51] Had the *Appeal* breathed new life into a hope which had seemed to die a generation earlier? Halifax felt it provided him with a mandate to resume the search for Catholic Reunion: 'The Lambeth *Appeal* opens a new chapter: its opportunity is great.'[52] Copies had been sent to the Pope, Bourne and Mercier. The timing was fortuitous, but Mercier later strongly denied that the Malines Conversations were simply his response to the *Appeal*. His interest in Reunion pre-dated the 1920 Lambeth Conference. Touring the United States in 1919 to thank the American people for their aid to war-ravaged

Catholic Reunion

Belgium, the Cardinal had addressed the Episcopalian General Convention and drawn criticism from Rome for referring to Episcopalian bishops as his 'brothers in the Christian Faith'. Mercier wrote to Benedict XV:

> Does not charity demand that we make it easier for those souls in search of unity to find the way to the true Church of Our Lord Jesus Christ? [...] I offer to make such an attempt [...] I would try to invite to Malines, *one after the other*, groups of theologians of each of the principal dissident churches, in particular the Anglican and the Orthodox. I would keep them for a number of days—put them in contact with a Catholic theologian of sound doctrine and a loving heart. In the intimacy of a tête-à-tête the penetration of souls can, with the grace of God, be much deeper.[53]

The Pope ignored the suggestion, but when Halifax and Portal arrived in Malines they found they were pushing an open door.

So on 6 December 1921, six participants assembled at the Archiepiscopal Palace at Malines for a two-day conference. On the Anglican side, in addition to Halifax, were Dr Walter Frere and Dr Armitage Robinson. Frere, the Superior of the Community of the Resurrection and a future Bishop of Truro, also stood in the Catholic tradition within the Church of England. Robinson was more difficult to categorise. The Dean of Wells, and a former Dean of Westminster, Robinson was happier immersed in early patristic texts than contemporary Church politics. It helped that he was a personal friend of Archbishop Davidson. The third Catholic was Mgr Joseph-Ernst Van Roey, Mercier's Vicar-General and successor. Halifax had planned the agenda to emphasize what united, rather than divided, the two groups. He began by arguing that the Thirty-Nine Articles of the Church of England were capable of an interpretation consistent with the teaching of the Council of Trent. Halifax also dwelt on the eirenic intentions of the Lambeth *Appeal*. On the second day there was a more wide-ranging discussion on the decrees of the First Vatican Council, sacraments, doctrine and jurisdiction. No conclusions were reached. That was not the intention. But the participants were pleasantly surprised by the experience. The discussions had been amicable, Catholics and Anglicans could see what they shared, and everyone was delighted by Mercier's hospitality and charm.

The same six participants returned to Malines for a Second Conversation on 13–14 May 1923. Again, Halifax prepared the agenda. To the Cardinal's surprise, Halifax concentrated, not on outstanding doctrinal differences, but on the practical consequences of Reunion, matters such as the extent of the Pope's jurisdiction in England, patriarchal status for the Archbishop of Canterbury, and the retention of married clergy, vernacular liturgy and communion under both kinds. No wonder, when he learned of the proceedings, Davidson was alarmed. The conversationalists were assuming that Reunion was a done deal and arranging for the exact manner in which Davidson's authority might be rectified by papal action. Not what he had intended! Halifax had already rehearsed his reasons for a pragmatic approach:

> There would be a real advantage of discussing the question of those rights recognised by the Holy See vis-à-vis Canterbury rather than the theological question of the extension of the Pope's power. It is the practical questions which will interest the English more than the theological questions.[54]

The tendency to concentrate on history and the practical consequences of Reunion characterised future discussions. One can appreciate Halifax's desire to avoid polemics. No doubt he was right; the English are a practical people easily bored by academic debate, but an unwillingness to address doctrinal issues separating the parties ultimately was not helpful.

Responding to pressure from Mercier to increase the scope of the conversations and hoping to counterbalance Halifax, Davidson nominated two additional Anglicans to the Third Conversation, which took place on 7–8 November 1923: Bishop Charles Gore and Dr Beresford Kidd. Both were committed Anglo-Catholics. Gore, the founder of an Anglican religious community and a former Bishop of Oxford, redeemed himself in the eyes of the Anglican Establishment by being a notoriously anti-Roman aristocrat and enjoying an earlier reputation for Modernism. Kidd was the Warden of Keble College, Oxford and a noted Church historian. Their inclusion was matched by the addition of two more Catholics: the

French Church historians, Mgr Pierre Battifol and Fr Hippolyte Hemmer. This time, at Davidson's insistence, doctrinal differences were discussed, focusing on papal claims. As expected, Gore was prepared to concede least, but the discussion, if at times animated, remained good-natured.

The Fourth Conversation was delayed given the ill-health of some participants and Anglican difficulties surrounding Prayer Book Reform, but eventually the same ten men met again on 19–20 May 1925. The relationship between the papacy and the episcopacy dominated the first day as papers were delivered which had been circulated in advance. Gore attempted to distinguish between fundamental doctrines, upon which all would be required to agree, and non-fundamental doctrines, upon which there could be legitimate diversity among reunited Christians. The conference concluded with Battifol giving the Catholic response to Gore's presentation.

But the most remarkable contribution to the Fourth Conversation, indeed to the whole series, was that delivered unannounced by the Cardinal on the second morning. Although he did not reveal its authorship, Mercier had commissioned the paper, 'The Anglican Church united not absorbed', from Dom Lambert Beauduin, a Belgian teaching at the Benedictine house of studies at Sant'Anselmo in Rome.[55] Beauduin argued that, prior to the Reformation, the English Church had enjoyed a high degree of autonomy from Rome and the Archbishop of Canterbury had effectively exercised a patriarchal role. Therefore, following Reunion, Canterbury, as a Cardinal-Patriarch, could be responsible for the internal organisation of the English Church largely free from Roman interference. England would have its own liturgy; canon law and clerical celibacy would not apply. The existing English Catholic hierarchy would be suppressed.

Beauduin's paper created astonishment. Frere remarked: 'All this took our breath away, especially as it seemed to lead up to a proposal for a Canterbury patriarchate.'[56] Mercier agreed to give copies to the participants. The paper was to have far-reaching consequences. It gave great hope to the more committed reunionists in the Church of England. If a Cardinal of the Roman Church were prepared to contemplate such concessions then Reunion might indeed be a practical proposition in the near future. One can see Beauduin's paper informing the proposals which were to be advanced in future discussions.

But the consequences were not uniformly positive. The proposals explain Cardinal Bourne's changed attitude towards the Conversations. He was hardly to be expected to concur to his own abolition, and that of his brother bishops, without consultation. But it went further than that. Beauduin's historical presuppositions were contentious. They undermined Bourne's profound conviction that the pre-Reformation Church was completely at one with Rome and that the current English Catholic hierarchy, and they alone, enjoyed continuity with that Church. Someone must have given Bourne a copy of Beauduin's paper. We know Bourne took particular exception at Beauduin, citing mediaeval sources, describing the Archbishop of Canterbury as *'quasi alterius orbis papam'*, 'almost the Pope of another part of the world'.[57] The English Archbishop took his objection directly to the Pope. These grievances account for Bourne's deep antipathy towards Beauduin and the Benedictine monastery dedicated to the work of Reunion he was to found at Amay.

Halifax and Portal were under no illusions as to the significance of Mercier's death from cancer on 23 January 1926: 'A terrible loss for all, a terrible loss for the Church; for us, absolute disaster.'[58] No Catholic of equivalent stature was willing to lend their patronage to the enterprise. Portal himself died in June 1926. So a depleted company assembled at Malines for one final conference on 11–12 October 1926. Its work was limited to agreeing a means of publishing the results of the Conversations. It was agreed that there should be two, complementary reports: the Anglicans would emphasize the differences still to be resolved, the Catholics would focus on the points of agreement. But events had moved on. A different attitude prevailed in the Vatican; Davidson was beset with Anglican internal difficulties. As nothing emerged, Halifax became increasingly frustrated, fearing that the results of the Malines Conversations would be lost to the world. To the irritation of many, he published the reports unilaterally, first in January 1928

Catholic Reunion

and then in a fuller form (including Beauduin's paper) in 1930.

The Malines Conversations were the first significant attempt at Anglican-Catholic Reunion since the Reformation. (APUC had really been a private initiative focused on prayer. While Halifax and Portal had hoped for bilateral talks in the 1890s, the result was a unilateral ruling from the Catholic Church on one specific issue.) So what were the issues raised by Malines and the implications for the future?

The question of the level of authorisation of participants by their respective communions raised itself immediately, and remained uncertain. Later we will see Marchant desperate to obtain some degree of accreditation for those whom he had lined up for subsequent talks. When Halifax notified Davidson of his intentions in 1921, the Archbishop of Canterbury could hardly prevent a peer of the realm visiting a distinguished Roman Catholic prelate overseas. But in what capacity did Halifax approach Mercier? Lang in York was as wary as his fellow Scot at Lambeth: 'It is obviously impossible that we should do anything which would imply that Halifax was a sort of accredited agent for any dealings between the Church of England and Rome [. . .] his zeal outruns his discretion, and as an agent he would be certain to commit his principals in ways that might be difficult afterwards to justify.'[59] Davidson sent a carefully drafted letter to Mercier:

> Lord Halifax does not go in any sense as ambassador or formal representative of the Church of England, nor have I endeavoured to put before him any suggestions with regard to the possibility of such conversations as might take place between Your Eminence and himself. Anything that he says therefore would be an expression of his personal opinion rather than an authoritative statement of the position or the endeavours of the Church of England in its corporate capacity.

But the Archbishop conceded that such purely private talks would be 'consonant' with 'the visions set forth in the Lambeth Conference *Appeal*'.[60]

When the subject matter was the Corporate Reunion of the Catholic and Anglican Churches, when the host was a Prince of the Roman Church, when the Anglican participants were as well-known as Halifax, Robinson and Frere, it was never feasible to claim this was an entirely private affair. As the Conversations proceeded, Davidson attempted to parry the question by asking that the Catholic participants first demonstrate their authorisation. The response surprised him. Benedict XV died shortly after the First Conversation. His successor elected on 6 February 1922 was Mercier's personal friend, the Archbishop of Milan, who took the name Pius XI. Mercier was, therefore, able to tell the new Pope about the Conversations at his audience the day after the election. Pius XI replied: 'I see nothing but good from these meetings.'[61] The new Secretary of State at the Vatican was Pietro, Cardinal Gasparri, one of the members of the 1896 Pontifical Commission deemed more sympathetic to the Anglican case. Responding to Davidson's query, Gasparri was able to reassure Mercier: 'He [the Pope] authorises Your Eminence to say to the Anglicans that the Holy See approves and encourages your Conversations and prays with all his heart that the good God will bless them.'[62] While the Catholic participants were not official delegates specifically appointed by Rome with a particular mandate, they entered the Conversations with the assurance that their efforts were known of and approved by the Supreme Authority. Thanks to his Encyclical *Mortalium Animos*, Pius XI receives a bad ecumenical press. This needs to be corrected in the light of his action here and elsewhere.

Predictably, Mercier then asked the Anglicans at the start of the Second Conversation as to *their* authorisation. They replied that they came with the authorisation of the Archbishops of Canterbury and York. Mercier pondered why that authorisation was not more formal. Portal felt Anglican participation was envisaged by the Lambeth *Appeal*.[63] Davidson had told the other Anglican bishops about the Conversations. He nominated Gore and Kidd to the Third Conversation, but was not prepared to go beyond 'friendly cognisance' of the Conversations. Mercier failed to appreciate fully the difficulty Davidson encountered from Protestant sentiment and the devolved nature of Anglican governance. Even an Archbishop of Canterbury could not speak for the Church of England, still less for the wider Anglican Communion.

To be fair to Davidson, he did not flinch from accepting his responsibility in the light of criticism once the Conversations became public. His outright opposition to the talks

> would have belied the *Appeal* which the Lambeth Conference had made in the widest possible terms 'to All Christian People' for the furtherance of a wider unity of the Church of Christ on earth [...] I have always believed that personal intercourse is of the highest value for the better understanding of matters of faith or opinion whereon people are in disagreement [...] To me the quenching of smoking flax by the stamping out of an endeavour to discuss, thus privately, our differences would, I say unhesitatingly, have seemed to be a sin against God.[64]

Despite the Archbishop's principled defence of his position in this instance, both sides, especially the Anglicans, were reluctant to commit officially in the first faltering steps taken towards Reunion.

Given that they sought the union of both Churches in their entirety, were the participants representative of their respective Communions? The question is of particular relevance to the Anglicans who understood themselves as encompassing a broad spectrum of theological opinion. And the answer there has to be a resounding 'No'. With the exception of Robinson, all the Anglicans were firmly in the Anglo-Catholic camp. Robinson claimed to represent the Anglican mainstream. His family background was Evangelical but, in truth, he was more *sui generis*, a learned, but singular, scholar. An English Jesuit warned Mercier: 'Private individuals do not represent the Church for which they claim to speak, but are almost invariably eccentric in one direction or another.'[65] At Malines, it was invariably in *one* direction. Halifax was not unaware of the anomaly, and the inclusion of other Anglicans was discussed. It was felt better, however, to continue the Conversations with more sympathetic Anglicans, who might act as pioneers until the position of Anglicanism generally advanced in their direction. Again, this issue bedevilled future discussions. Was Corporate Reunion ever a realistic possibility when one was only ever talking to an unrepresentative minority of Anglicans? Should one be considering as an alternative an accommodation between Rome and the Catholic wing of the Church of England?

In the 1920s one does not have to ask whether the Catholics were representative of their Church. The differences between the Belgian and English Cardinals were not ones of theology, but rather style and temperament. Mercier was more optimistic about the possibility of Reunion; Bourne would have claimed to be more realistic. Ninety years of history tend to vindicate the Englishman. Mercier was no liberal. He forthrightly rejected any suggestion that other Christian bodies could in any sense be placed on a level of equality with the Church of Rome. He shocked Halifax in April 1924 by asking him to make his personal submission to the Catholic Church. At the end of the Fourth Conversation, Gore was complaining that, despite a surprising flexibility in disciplinary matters, the Catholics were absolutely 'unconcessive' 'on the heading of dogma'.[66] The one area in which the Catholics were unrepresentative—a point picked up by Marchant—was the lack of an English Catholic participant. The omission was unfortunate.

Another obstacle to progress at Malines and beyond was a lack of clarity as to the objective. All would have subscribed to a long-term desire to promote Corporate Reunion. But more immediately? When Davidson wrote, 'Halifax quite sees that such discussions would be rather for the promoting of good feeling than for the actual accomplishment of any defined plan',[67] he was attempting to reassure himself that no practical consequences would arise from the Conversations. Possibly, perhaps, at some point in the future, the two Churches might come to some understanding. Yet Mercier

> never visualised Reunion, as most Anglicans would visualise it, in the form of an honourable agreement between two Churches of commensurable standing; to him it was more the reconciliation of a body of schismatics with the Catholic Church [...] It should be corporate, because the process of individual conversion would be far too slow; but if corporate Reunion flagged, it was for individuals to make their separate peace with Rome.[68]

Catholic Reunion

The Conversations with which we shall be concerned were expressly formulated to be on a different basis to those at Malines. Yet, given Malines constituted the only precedent, they could not help being influenced by what had happened there. It is worth listening, therefore, to the assessment of Malines by our later Anglican Conversationalists:

> And what, after all, did Malines achieve? Nothing—and that first step which counts for everything. For the first time in 300 years Rome and Canterbury had each, at least semi-officially, spoken to each other of peace. As [Halifax] had written to Davidson of Reunion twenty years before [...]: 'There are defeats which are the necessary steps to victories; present failures which spell future success' [...]
>
> Malines [...] supplied just that semi-official lead from the Hierarchies of both sides which could raise the duty of seeking Unity in the minds of the faithful and inspire their prayers by kindling their imaginations.[69]

The Confraternity of Unity

With the Malines Conversations concluded, Catholic Reunion seemed to have stalled. A few fringe societies listened to scholarly papers, indulged in colourful liturgy and urged the necessity of prayer. And there matters may have rested had it not been for two developments.

A generation earlier Spencer Jones's promotion of Catholic Reunion had its parallel in the efforts of Paul Wattson in the United States. It seemed providential that the end of the Malines Conversations should coincide with reunionist stirrings on the other side of the Atlantic. They began in the rooms of a curate at the notoriously High church of St Mary-the-Virgin in New York. Henry K. Pierce was born in 1881 into a wealthy family in Ohio and educated at Dartmouth College. Upon graduation, he joined the family business providing marble for hotel and theatre lobbies. Already attracted by Anglo-Catholicism, the death of his parents provided Pierce with the freedom and resources to pursue his priestly vocation. Having studied at the General Theological Seminary in New York, he was ordained as an Episcopalian in 1920 to serve at St Mary-the-Virgin. Even as a theological student Pierce had discussed with others the possibility of founding an Anglican Oratory.

Pierce was a standard-bearer in the early skirmishes of the culture wars. A contemporary recalled:

> His upbringing and his natural inclinations made him conservative in every sense of the word [...] both in his home and elsewhere the 'grand manner' of nineteenth-century culture always surrounded him. He loved what he described as 'good books, good living and good religion'.[70]

As a curate he published a pamphlet attacking Modernism: 'The Modernist is a sceptic or an agnostic *within the church* [...] the religion he offers is not the Christian religion.'[71] This enmity towards Modernism formed a consistent *leitmotif* of his religious thought. The following decade he was describing Modernism as 'merely agnosticism which illogically clings to certain outward forms of Christianity'.[72]

Pierce was not alone in deploring the Modernist denial of orthodox Christian teaching on faith and morals, and Anglo-Catholicism's apparent inability to defend that orthodox teaching. He met with three other Episcopalian curates in his rooms towards the end of 1926. The only hope for the survival of the authentic faith within Anglicanism, they felt, was 'corporate reunion with the Roman See'.[73] Thus came into being the Confraternity of Unity. They advertised their existence and their aims in the Press. Of the forty replies, half were hostile, advising the founders to take themselves off to Rome immediately.[74] They justified their continued presence within Anglicanism, arguing: 'We cannot repudiate the Church of England because we know we have the hierarchy and the sacraments, and we are not guilty of formal heresy. We cannot ignore the papacy, or imagine that Catholic unity can emerge without the Pope as the Head.'[75] Their work, they maintained, was essential to prevent Anglicanism compromising its claim to catholicity and apostolicity by some fatal accommodation with Modernism or Protestantism which would preclude future Reunion not only with Rome but also with the Orthodox East.

Catholic Reunion

Initially, the Confraternity imported and distributed reunionist material from England, then branched out with its own periodical, the *Bulletin*. The bibliophile Pierce ensured it was an elegant and scholarly production. To promote their work, the founders travelled overseas, meeting sympathetic Anglicans in Oxford, addressing Fynes-Clinton and his friends in London. Given the similarity of their aims, the Catholic League was happy to announce a formal association of the two bodies: 'We welcome cordially this ally in the work of the Counter-Reformation.'[76] Bowyer Campbell, Secretary of the Confraternity, also went to Belgium, visiting Beauduin's Monks of Unity at Amay. He was exultant at the response he met with, feeling 'at last the Confraternity had gained a point of contact with the Roman Communion'.[77] The Americans and Belgians agreed to cooperate in promoting Catholic Reunion.

Curates, however, have little security. Pierce recalled: 'We knew that we trod dangerous ground, but did not much care.'[78] Their advanced, pro-Roman position was too much even for their own Anglo-Catholic parishes, and they were forced to resign. Pierce and one of the other officers, Sheafe Walker, might not much care—they had independent means—but Campbell did, and had to resort to novel-writing to support himself. Freed from parish duties, the Americans now directed their energy and enthusiasm exclusively to the reunionist cause. The three of them made Oxford the base for their activities and breathed new life into the movement in England. Halifax, the veteran reunionist, remained aloof. Campbell noted that the ageing viscount 'never emerged from the purely academic position in which he had always moved'.[79] Jones, however, made common cause with them. After all, Pierce maintained, the CU platform was 'nothing more than the Spencer Jones position, taught these thirty years, made clear and explicit—a position without which all this talk of reunion is fatuous'.[80]

The Confraternity went from strength to strength. English priests and laity enrolled as members. On 26 May 1929 there was a large attendance in London for the first general meeting of the CU. An English secretariat was established at St Saviour's, Hoxton in London. 'But the centre of activity, for conferences, correspondence, editing, publishing, etc., was at Oxford', where the Americans resided 'for the purpose of mutual conference, study, writing our Cause, and forming contacts with English priests sympathetic to the point and view of the Confraternity'. The print run for the *Bulletin* grew from 500 for the first edition in November 1927 to 3,000 by 1930. Lengthier tracts were produced. Progress was being made; there was a sense of confidence and purpose:

> The Confraternity of Unity proclaims that the Counter-Reformation is still unfinished. Even though we should gain the whole Anglican Communion to a belief in sacramental doctrine and practice, yet we should feel there was something lacking. We will never be satisfied with a mere variety of Catholicism that separates us, as though we were Protestants, from the main body of the Catholic Episcopate outside our own ranks [...]
>
> The Confraternity proposes to drag the deeps of the Anglican Communion in order to bring to the surface and into one net all who long for and desire the return of our Communion to the Apostolic See. Then we propose to batter at the Anglican conscience until all are converted to the only programme for unity that can bring together all the scattered sheep of Christ, namely, the Roman claims in all their majestic grandeur and divine assurance of security and permanence.[81]

The 1930 Lambeth Conference

In the years immediately following the First World War, the initiative in the Church of England seemed to lie entirely with Anglo-Catholicism. Time and effort would bring the desired result of Catholic Reunion. What could prevent such an outcome? The answer lay partly in the background to, and the deliberations of, the 1930 Lambeth Conference.

Once more Christian unity was high on the agenda. But, for the Confraternity of Unity and others, it was the wrong kind of unity. They feared a 'Lambeth Plot':

> At that [1930] Conference influential English Churchmen [...] of the modernist and 'evangelical' variety are planning a campaign to commit our communion to a scheme for intercommunion or actual union with the Protestant sects. The essence of the

scheme consists in this: that the Anglican communion shall cease to insist on the apostolic succession and shall recognise the ministry of Baptists, Presbyterians, Congregationalists, etc. as of equal validity with that of our own priesthood.[82]

The Conference attempted to reassure Catholically-minded Anglicans. It spoke of the 'paramount duty to seek unity among Christians in every direction'. It purported to reject entry 'into any scheme of federation, involving interchangeability of ministries, while differences on points of order that we think essential still remain, for this would seem to us both to encourage and express an acquiescence in essential disunion'.[83]

Despite this effort to put their minds at rest, there was much to disturb our reunionists. The Conference tentatively approved the creation of a new Church of South India, uniting Anglicans with non-episcopal bodies such as the Methodists, Presbyterians and Congregationalists. To High Churchmen this constituted a betrayal of Anglicanism's claim to understand itself as part of the Catholic Church holding the historic creeds and ministering valid sacraments. Contrasting with the critical tone it employed with respect to developments in the Church of Rome, the Conference noted 'with satisfaction and gratitude the great measure of agreement on matters of faith' attained in the conferences with the Free Churches. The Committee on the Unity of the Church looked forward to 'full organic union' with Nonconformity. Resolution 42 of the Conference (albeit subject to limitations) permitted Anglicans to receive Holy Communion from ministers of other communions, including those not episcopally-ordained.

Even contact with other episcopal churches was not necessarily a source of encouragement. The Conference's approval of discussions with the Old Catholics led to intercommunion between the two Communions within two years. Agreement with such recent schismatics, even with valid orders, was viewed as a retrograde step. The attendance of Orthodox delegates at Lambeth and the Conference's resolution to seek theological discussion with representatives of the Ecumenical Patriarch appeared more encouraging. But not, as some feared, if the objective was the creation of a 'non-papal' Catholicism. Christ had founded his

Church on Peter, and Peter had been the first Bishop of Rome. Unity which excluded Rome had no basis in Scripture or Tradition. Seeking to present Rome as one church among many is 'like trying to persuade a mother that she was no longer really the mother but only one of the children'.[84] The CU commissioned Jones to reassert these views in his book *Catholic Reunion*. A copy was sent to every bishop attending the Conference.

Modernism had initially exercised the Catholic Church. Debate had raged as to whether it constituted the attempt to state eternal truths in a manner comprehensible to the modern world, or whether in reality it was the denial of revealed truth. Of course, those accused of Modernism fell into both categories, but the disciplinary measures introduced by Pope Pius X effectively suppressed Modernism in the Catholic Church at least for the while.

It emerged within the Anglican Communion from an unlikely quarter. The first two generations of the Oxford Movement were thoroughly conservative in doctrinal matters. Charles Gore (later one of the participants at Malines) caused great distress to more traditional Tractarians, like Halifax, when he sought to reconcile High Church theology with modern critical scholarship in the book he edited in 1889, *Lux Mundi: A Series of Essays in the Religion of the Incarnation*. Attempting to assert the full humanity of Christ, Gore developed his *kenotic* theory, by which Christ willingly laid aside His divinity at the Incarnation. To others, this impugned Christ's divinity and represented an abnegation of orthodox Christian teaching. Gore's own faith remained deeply devotional and sacramental, and he was to become highly critical of the genie of 'liberal Catholicism' he had released. Gore was to be among Davidson's fiercest critics, urging him to take action against those Anglicans who denied the historicity of miracles and doctrines such as the Virgin Birth.

But the Church of England appeared infinitely accommodating of Modernism. A particular bugbear of the 1920s and beyond was Ernest Barnes, Bishop of Birmingham, an early advocate of eugenics and contraception. Engaging in a bitter dispute with those in his own diocese who reserved the Eucharist, Barnes's opposition to Anglo-Catholics went beyond issues of principle. The Bishop had a highly-developed capacity to cause offence. Anglo-Catholics, he perversely maintained, were racially inferior, being of Iberian origin. He insulted their most deeply held convictions: 'There are among us today men and women whose sacramental beliefs are not far from those of the cultured Hindu idolater. They pretend that a priest, using the right words and acts, can change a piece of bread so that within it there is the real presence of Christ.'[85]

As the Lambeth Conference drew near, the Anglican Establishment recognised that the loyalty of some Anglo-Catholics to the Anglican Communion was being stretched to breaking point. Archbishop William Temple of York wrote to Lang at Lambeth:

> Of course we have to face the fact that a considerable Anglo-Catholic section is contemplating secession as a genuinely practical idea. I don't know that any of them want it, and most heartily shrink from it, but they are certainly thinking about it.[86]

When the Conference began, the point of greatest controversy concerned neither doctrine nor Christian unity, but rather morality. The Anglican bishops at the 1930 Lambeth Conference followed the recommendation of the Committee chaired by Bishop Woods of Winchester and, rejecting universal Christian tradition and their own position reaffirmed at the previous Conference, gave limited approval to the practice of artificial contraception. The more Roman-tending Catholics within Anglicanism were horrified—both by the resolution itself, and even more by its effect of undermining the claim of the Church of England to teach Catholic truth. On holiday at the time, Fynes-Clinton caused the following statement to be read from the pulpit at St Magnus-the-Martyr: 'The Rector desires to express publicly and solemnly his abhorrence and entire repudiation and disassociation from the lamentable sanction given in certain circumstances by the Bishops in the Lambeth Conference to the deadly sin of contraception.'[87] Jones in Gloucestershire shared the sentiment, but counselled against too strong a reaction. His response was typical of many of those opposed to the general drift of Anglicanism—hope that somehow things will be reversed, and deny, in any event, that the Church of England has any power to change anything anyway.

The Americans in the Confraternity of Unity did not do nuance. Pierce told the CU Council that 'Lambeth had blessed mortal sin [...] In former days the Anglo-Catholic party could be counted on to defend the Faith. That is no longer so: there is only our minority.'[88] Campbell was equally clear that a watershed had been passed: 'The pronouncements of the Conference meeting in London in the summer of 1930 finally and fully killed whatever confidence I had clung to in the Anglican Communion.'[89] 'Their minority' met and drafted letters to the Press and protests to the bishops. Lambeth's approval of artificial contraception, they claimed, would

> serve only to widen the breach between ourselves and the many millions of our fellow Christians throughout the world [...] unless protests of this kind are forthcoming we are confident that many will feel constrained, as a matter of duty, to withdraw from the Anglican Communion.[90]

In London, Fynes-Clinton outlined his scheme for a grand Catholic alliance with Cardinal Bourne and the Jesuits to combat 'moral heresy'. As his audience suspected, nothing came of it.[91]

There was, therefore, a febrile and pessimistic atmosphere among Catholic reunionists in the Church of England in the days following the 1930 Conference. Under the heading 'Lambeth Betrayal', the Catholic League cited its grievances: the South India scheme, permission given to the non-ordained to perform acts reserved to the priest, artificial contraception. 'Our fears that the Bishops would not stand firm on matters of vital principle have been fully justified.'[92] No one knew how matters would develop from here.

Notes

[1] D. Geernaerts, SC, 'Achievements of ARCIC and IARCCUM', in J. A. Radano, ed., *Celebrating a Century of Ecumenism: Exploring the Achievements of International Dialogue* (Geneva: World Council of Churches, 2012), p. 122.

[2] Pope Pius XI, *Mortalium Animos*, 6 January 1928.

[3] Radano, *Celebrating a Century of Ecumenism*.

[4] Pope Benedict XVI, *Many Religions — One Covenant: Israel, the Church and the World* (San Francisco: Ignatius Press, 1999), pp. 90–1.

[5] C. Butler, *The Life and Times of Bishop Ullathorne* (London: Burns, Oates & Washbourne, 1926), vol. I, p. 334.

[6] Halifax, 'Introduction', in S. J. Jones, *England and the Holy See: An Essay towards Reunion*, 2nd edn (London: Longman, Green & Co., 1902.), p. xv.

[7] H. Hemmer, *Fernand Portal (1855–1926): Apostle of Unity* (London: Macmillan & Co., 1961), pp. 32–3.

[8] Halifax to F. Portal, 11 July 1894, cited Hemmer, *Fernand Portal*, pp. 33–4.

[9] Portal, cited Hemmer, *Fernand Portal*, p. 40.

[10] J. G. Lockhart, *Charles Lindley, Viscount Halifax* (London: Centenary Press, 1935–6), vol. I, p. 60.

[11] Halifax to Portal, 21 September 1896, Portal Papers, Paris.

[12] At the time, the Church of England did not keep the feast of the double dedication of Ss Peter and Paul on 29 June.

[13] S. J. Jones, 'Lord Halifax and Reunion with Rome', 6 June 1939, *The Pilot*, 71 (July 1939), 1–9.

[14] V. McNabb, OP, 'Tribute to Father Spencer Jones', *The Pilot*, 117 (May 1943), p. 36.

[15] S. J. Jones, 'Steps to Reunion', Part II, *Reunion*, 1/2 (July 1934), p. 37.

[16] Jones, *England and the Holy See*, p. 11.

[17] *Ibid.*, p. 21.

[18] Halifax to Jones, 11 January 1904, PHA/Rea/CU1/32.

[19] Jones, *England and the Holy See*, p. 187.

[20] *Ibid.*, p. 25.

[21] *Ibid.*, pp. 167–8.

[22] S. J. Jones, *Rome and Reunion: The Inaugural Lecture to the Members of the Society of St Thomas of Canterbury* (London: Longman, Green & Co., 1904), pp. 1–2.

[23] S. J. Jones, 'England and the Holy See in the Middle Ages', in A. H. Mathew, ed., *Ecclesia: The Church of Christ* (London: Burns & Oates, 1906), p. 182.

24 Jones, *Rome and Reunion*, p. 78.

25 S. J. Jones, *The Counter-Reformation in the Church of England* (London: Skeffington & Son, n.d.), p. 125.

26 P. J. F. Wattson, cited C. Angell, SA, and C. LaFontaine, SA, *Prophet of Reunion: The Life of Paul of Graymoor* (New York: Seabury Press, 1975), p. 54.

27 Wattson to Jones, 21 June 1934 (copy), GARC, Wattson, 821–2-14.

28 Wattson to Jones, 30 November 1907 (copy), PHA/Rea/CU1/43.

29 *Messenger*, 1 (Dec. 1913), p. 1.

30 'The Church Unity Octave Golden Jubilee', *Reunion*, 6/51 (Dec. 1958), pp. 57–9.

31 *Messenger*, 13 (Jan. 1917), p. 2.

32 *Messenger*, 19 (July–Sept. 1918).

33 Jones, 'Steps to Reunion', Part III, *Reunion*, 1/3 (Nov. 1934), p. 72.

34 Encyclical Letter, *Conference of Bishops of the Anglican Communion: Encyclical Letter from the Bishops with the Resolutions and Reports* (London: SPCK, 1920), p. 11.

35 Report of the Sub-Committee on Relations to and Reunion with Non-Episcopal Churches, *Conference of Bishops of the Anglican Communion*, pp. 139, 142.

36 Report of the Sub-Committee on Relations to and Reunion with Episcopal Churches, *Conference of Bishops of the Anglican Communion*, p. 147.

37 *Ibid.*, pp. 144–5.

38 *Ibid.*, p. 12.

39 R. Jasper, *Arthur Cayley Headlam: Life and Letters of a Bishop* (London: Faith Press, 1960), p. 142.

40 *An Appeal to All Christian Peoples*, III, *Conference of Bishops of the Anglican Communion*, p. 27.

41 *Ibid.*, VIII, p. 29.

42 *Ibid.*, VI, p. 28.

43 Resolution 12, *Conference of Bishops of the Anglican Communion*, p. 29.

44 V. McNabb, 'Canterbury and Rome', *Blackfriars*, 1/7 (Oct. 1920), pp. 381–9.

45 F. A. Bourne, Catholic Truth Society Conference, Leicester, 26 September 1921, *Tablet* (1 Oct. 1921), p. 444.

46 Bishop Bertram Pollock of Norwich to Marchant, 14 January 1921, OUL, Marchant, 315/10.

47 *Messenger*, 28 (Oct.–Dec. 1920).

48 L. J. Walker, SJ, to Bourne, 30 October 1920, AAW, Hi. II/184.

49 Canon J. Moyes, Memorandum, AAW, Hi. II/184.

50 Lang to Davidson, 10 October 1921 (copy), LPL, Lang Papers, 59/138–9.

51 Portal to Halifax, 4 November 1921, cited Lockhart, ii, p. 271.

52 Halifax, Memorandum, 'Outline of Points', First Conversation, 6 December 1921, BIY, Halifax, Malines Papers, A4/272/1.

53 Mercier, Memorandum to Benedict XV, December 1920, cited R. Aubert, 'The History of the Malines Conversations', *One in Christ*, 1 (1967), pp. 57–8.

54 Halifax to Portal, March 1923, Portal Papers, cited Barlow, *The Malines Conversations*, p. 95n.

55 Mercier and Beauduin had shared the same spiritual director, the great Irish Abbot of Maredsous, Bl. Columba Marmion.

56 W. Frere, CR, *Recollections of Malines* (London: Centenary Press, 1935), p. 56.

57 L. Beauduin, OSB, 'The Anglican Church United not Absorbed', cited Barlow, *The Malines Conversations*, p. 238; Bourne, *Aide-memoire* for audience with Pius XI, 14 December 1925, AAW, Bo. III, 124/4/1.

58 Portal to Halifax, 14 January 1926, cited Lockhart, ii, p. 327.

59 Lang to Davidson, 10 October 1921 (copy), LPL, Lang Papers, 59/138–9.

60 Davidson to Mercier, 19 October 1921, MAA, cited Barlow, *The Malines Conversations*, p. 54.

61 Mercier, Memorandum, *Voyage à Rome*, MAA, cited Barlow, *The Malines Conversations*, p. 74.

62 Pietro, Cardinal Gasparri to Mercier, 25 November 1922, MAA, B1, cited Barlow, *The Malines Conversations*, p. 88n.

63 Barlow, *The Malines Conversations*, p. 96.

64 Davidson, Speech to the Upper House of Convocation, 6 February 1924, cited Barlow, *The Malines Conversations*, pp. 228–30.

65 Walker to Mercier, 13 June 1922, MAA, B1/6, cited Barlow, *The Malines Conversations*, p. 80.

66 Bishop Charles Gore to Halifax, 25 May 1925, BIY, Halifax Malines Papers, A4 271/5, cited Barlow, *The Malines Conversations*, p. 158.

67 Davidson, Memorandum, 1 November 1921, LPL, Davidson 186/1, cited Barlow, *The Malines Conversations*, p. 57.

68 Barlow, *The Malines Conversations*, p. 305.

69 *The Pilot*, 70 (June 1939), p. 3.

70 C. A. C. H., 'Monsignor Henry Pierce', *Beda Review* (March 1963), p. 7.

71 H. K. Pierce, *The Message of Modernism* (New York: League for Catholic Action, 1926), p. 3.

72 H. K. Pierce, 'The Confraternity of Unity', *The Bulletin of Catholic Unity*, 12 (Easter 1931), p. 1.

73 S. Walker, *The Confraternity of Unity; A Brief Explanation of its Aims and Methods* (Oxford: Baxter Press, 1929), p. 3.

74 T. B. Campbell, OUSR Minute Book, vol. I, p. 161, PHA.

75 *The Bulletin of Catholic Unity*, 6 (Ascensiontide 1929), p. 9.

76 *Messenger*, 59 (July–Sept. 1928).

77 Campbell, Notes on the Confraternity of Unity, March 1939, PHA/Rea/CU3.

78 Pierce to Jack, 1 March 1940, PHA/Rea/CU3.

79 Campbell, Notes on the Confraternity of Unity, March 1939, PHA/Rea/CU3.

80 Pierce to L. C. Gillam, 7 February 1934, PHA, Harris Papers.

81 Pierce, 'Notes on Bowyer Campbell's Sketch of the Origin of the Confraternity of Unity', 29 April 1939, BCA, Pierce Bequest, CU Founding and Letters; *Bulletin*, 7 (Ss Peter and Paul 1929).

82 *Bulletin*, 5 (Epiphany 1929), p. 8.

83 *Lambeth Conference 1930: Encyclical Letter from the Bishops with the Resolutions and Reports* (London: SPCK, 1930), pp. 54, 113.

84 S. J. Jones, *Catholic Reunion* (Oxford: Confraternity of Unity (Blackwell), 1930), p. 73.

85 J. Barnes, *Ahead of his Age: Bishop Barnes of Birmingham* (London: Collins, 1979), pp. 142, 175, 193.

86 Archbishop William Temple to Lang, 22 February 1930, LPL, Lang Papers, 7/20.

87 *Gloucester Citizen* (18 August 1930), p. 2.

88 Pierce to CU Council, 17 February 1933 (copy), PHA/Rea/CU3.

89 Campbell, http://www.catholicauthors.com/campbell.html (accessed on 21 February 2014).

90 'Open Letter to the Lord Bishop of Monmouth, President of the Newport Church Congress', 17 September 1930, Oxford, signed by Revv. Acheson, Campbell, Harris, Joblin, Jones, Monahan, Nattrass, Orr, Pierce, Shaw and Woodhouse, BCA, Pierce Bequest/Cuttings.

91 B. E. Joblin to Pierce, 7 October 1930, PHA/Rea/CU2/529.

92 *Messenger*, 67 (July–Sept. 1930).

✛ 3 ✛

'The best men in the Church'

'The big intention'[1]

We left the Cardinal Archbishop of Westminster and the Archbishop of Canterbury at the Athenaeum in February 1928. The few in the know felt that Sir James Marchant had achieved the near impossible in bringing the two men together. Bourne offered 'to arrange for any talks we like between Anglicans and Roman Catholics in England'.[2] But Davidson was not persuaded. He had no natural inclination to pursue relations with the Catholic Church. The experience of Malines and the subsequent papal encyclical simply strengthened that reluctance. Prayer Book Revision brought sufficient trouble of its own. He was an old man, approaching eighty. He was not to be drawn into another controversial venture for which he saw no prospect of success.

The following month, Marchant was telling the Benedictines at Downside of the difficulties encountered by his 'proposed conferences'. The Abbot responded sympathetically, advising, 'You will need all your patience before the end—or rather the beginning'.[3] Fortunately, Marchant possessed patience in abundance. He used his position in the literary world to continue to court senior Catholics. He commissioned a contribution from Bourne for his book on Reunion, deploying again his armoury of flattery. He suggested how the Cardinal might demonstrate that

> the Church in urging her unique claim is not 'narrow' but is following the way of right reason and, above all, *of true charity* [...] If I may be allowed to say so, Your Eminence is always so clear, simple, concise, that I feel sure your Introduction would clear away many misunderstandings.[4]

The following year, at Marchant's request, the Cardinal presented a copy of his anthology on the Madonna to the Pope himself.[5]

Sir James viewed Davidson's retirement as an opportunity to chance his luck once more with the Anglican Establishment. He wrote to the outgoing Archbishop asking whether he might leave a memorandum for his successor 'about the proposal, one day, to hold conversations on English soil with the full knowledge and approval of the English authorities, so that he may be cognisant of the matter when, in due course, it is brought before him'. Davidson could not see how this would commit himself or his successor to any unfortunate entanglement, and so agreed.[6]

Davidson's successor at Lambeth was another Scot, Cosmo Lang, Archbishop of York since 1908. (He was the prelate who baptized the future Queen Elizabeth II in 1926.) As Archbishop of Canterbury, Lang broke new ground, giving a passable impression of an Anglo-Catholic. Eschewing his Presbyterian roots, Confession and daily Eucharist formed part of his spiritual life. He assuaged many troubled Anglo-Catholic consciences, assuring them they were an essential and valued constituency of the Established Church.[7] Yet, like Davidson, Lang was committed to Anglican comprehensiveness. His conciliatory approach to the Free Churches in the negotiations following the 1920 Lambeth Conference surprised many. Capable of praising Anglo-Catholics, simultaneously he warned that they were only one part of the national Church.[8] Even to hint that Protestantism or Modernism might be the equivalent to Catholic truth could never be anything other than anathema to the members of the CL and CU.

Lang had been at Lambeth less than three weeks when a letter arrived from Marchant in terms similar to those which his predecessor had been wont to receive. He referred to Davidson's promise to leave a memorandum for his successor 'about the suggestion of new conversations on our own soil between chosen and unofficial representatives'. Marchant sought to arouse Lang's curiosity:

> The inner story of how the new suggestion arose, and how groups here and there in secret have prayed for guidance in bringing Cardinal Bourne and the Archbishop to meet, you

yourself would like to hear, and they would wish me to relate to you, so that you may be fully aware of the spiritual significance of what has so far happened, and may, when the time comes, be ready to consider the matter with fuller knowledge.

Atypically, Marchant misjudged his man, suggesting that the Archbishop of Canterbury might use the centenary of Catholic Emancipation to join in a national apology to Cardinal Bourne for past Protestant wrongs.[9] Lang saw no need for such an apology. Marchant's letter appears to have gone unanswered.

The two men spoke in August 1929, but again with no enthusiasm on Lang's part. Three months later Marchant was still pursuing the Archbishop, even if he had lowered his expectations:

> Do you think that in quite an informal and friendly way a few Anglicans might meet a few Romans to talk over the position of Rome and to elicit explanations? I feel sure Your Grace could not *initiate* such a meeting, but would you go so far as not to discourage it, to allow it to come to your knowledge and to at least make sure that the wrong men did not come into it? [. . .] I can but throw myself upon Your Grace's mercy. If and when such a meeting takes place I shall, of course, disappear. Meanwhile may I feel that you do not discourage the effort?[10]

Lang made no effort to disguise his irritation with Marchant's persistence when he sought Davidson's advice. Lang's opposition to such conversations was practical rather than principled. He saw no value to the proposal 'unless it were publicly known, and if it were publicly known the misunderstanding and controversy aroused would be far greater than any notice that the Pope would be likely to take of it'.[11]

Having consulted Davidson, Lang sent Marchant his considered response. He listed his objections to any conversations of an official character:
1. The attempt had already been made at Malines. The Archbishop felt that similar conversations in England had even less chance of success.
2. He resented the terms of *Mortalium Animos*. What was the point, he asked, of 'encouraging conversations which can only lead up to

a door firmly closed, not to say banged, by His Holiness's Encyclical'? He failed to see that the Catholic Church was interested in any form of unity save on the basis of 'complete submission'. 3. The 1930 Lambeth Conference was little more than six months away, and he did not wish to pre-empt its deliberations on questions of Christian unity.

Lang had no objection to talks between individuals who met in a purely private capacity. But he categorically rejected any possibility of discussions between authorised representatives: 'I am not prepared to take part in countenancing or having cognisance of conversations of this kind [. . .] I am not disposed to give even a qualified official recognition to them.'[12]

Marchant had other irons in the fire. He was simultaneously flirting with another exotic Nonconformist, Dr William Orchard. Originally ordained a Presbyterian, since 1914 he had been the minister at the Congregationalist King's Weigh House Chapel in Mayfair.[13] There was more substance to Orchard than Marchant. A serious scholar, he was increasingly attracted to the mystical and sacramental traditions found in the historic churches. Large crowds were drawn by his combination of evangelical preaching and Catholic ritual in a Free Church setting. He advertised his curious creed in the national Press: 'I teach the whole Catholic faith. I believe that faith is reasonable [. . .] We employ all Catholic sacraments with the traditional Catholic ceremonial, with the sacrament of the Eucharist, confession and such rites as Benediction.'[14] His article in Marchant's book on Reunion indicated his drift in a Catholic direction, speaking of 'a growing sacramental hunger' and the necessity that 'a living, progressing Church [. . .] possess dogmatic authority'.[15]

Fear of having to surrender his intellectual freedom held Orchard back from Rome for the moment. Compromised, as he held it to be, by Modernism and its connection to the State, Orchard doubted whether the Church of England could offer the sacramental and doctrinal security he craved. Nevertheless, encouraged by the *Lambeth Appeal*, he and Marchant pondered unconventional solutions. On Orchard's behalf, Marchant investigated the possibility of Orchard being jointly ordained by the

Anglicans and the Orthodox, and allowed to remain *in situ* without the requirement to use the Anglican Prayer Book.[16] Marchant hoped the two of them might be bishops in this hybrid creation. Even Anglican flexibility had its limits. Orchard's proposals were finally rejected by the Established Church in June 1931.[17] At the same time Marchant was also effecting introductions for Orchard among the Catholic community, subsequently professing horror when Orchard followed his actions to their logical conclusion and converted to Catholicism in 1932. Little wonder some questioned Marchant's consistency and sincerity.

Lang was confident that he had excluded all ambiguity in his last letter to Marchant. The publisher required, however, only the slightest of loopholes, and he believed he had found this. The Archbishop of Canterbury had said that he had not wished to anticipate the work of the 1930 Lambeth Conference. Very well; with the Conference over, Marchant felt at liberty to write once more. At exactly the same time as he was exploring novel suggestions for a new independent church in Mayfair, Marchant was pursuing Lang again in support of Anglican-Catholic conversations. Sir James wondered whether the Archbishop might feel able to

> take any further step, for instance in getting in touch with Cardinal Bourne, or if you do not feel that you should go so far as that I think that you said in your letter, which is not before me as I write, that, whilst you could not formally approve of private informal conversations taking place [. . .] I hope now you will be able to say that if such conversations are initiated they have your blessing.[18]

Then ensued silence from Lambeth Palace. Marchant might have surmised that Lang's patience had finally snapped and was now ignoring this irritating correspondent.

In fact, Lang was seriously ill and away from his duties for four months. When he finally replied to Marchant in May 1931, however, his response was not substantially different from that seventeen months earlier. He had no objection to conversations between private individuals — and indeed would be interested to learn of any results. But the attitude of the Pope and Cardinal Bourne precluded his initiating anything more formal.[19] In addition to the reasons he gave Marchant, it should be remembered that Lang had taken great exception to Bourne's travelling to York in 1927 to refute his claims to Anglican continuity with the pre-Reformation Church. He had written at the time: 'I have great respect for Cardinal Bourne and his office, and I write in all courtesy; but I cannot think that the cause of unity or of charity is advanced by a sermon such as that he preached in York on Easter Day.'[20]

Received opinions need to be revised. A recent biography claimed that during Lang's primacy, 'There were no talks about church unity between the Church of England and the Roman Catholic Church [...] The Roman Catholic Church continued to hold aloof from other denominations.'[21] There were talks about church unity, but it was not the Catholic Church which held aloof.

While officially-authorised Anglican participants for the envisaged conversations were lacking, attention turned to who the Catholics might be. Cardinal Bourne had already indicated his willingness to send Bishop Bidwell (together with Canon Edward Myers and others) to represent him either in the continuation of any conversations in Malines or new conversations in England. Bourne intimated to Marchant in autumn 1929 his continuing preference for Bidwell.[22] Manuel Bidwell was Anglo-Spanish, the archetypal Church bureaucrat. Having worked in the Vatican, he returned to England as Bourne's Chancellor and was consecrated auxiliary bishop for the Diocese of Westminster in 1917. He may have enjoyed Bourne's confidence, but he was a source of frustration to others. The Australian publisher, Frank Sheed, recalled that Bidwell was 'a master of the art of stopping anything happening'.[23] One priest recounted that he could never look at Bidwell 'without thinking that his head was exactly like an egg, and longing for a spoon to crack it with'.[24] It is difficult to see progress being made had Bidwell been involved. God intervened. Bidwell died in his fifties on 11 July 1930.

English Jesuits in the 1920s and '30s were generally conservative, especially concerning relations with non-Catholics. Their periodical, the *Month*, made it a point of honour to publish regular articles refuting Anglican claims. Marchant's friends were concerned lest any of these writers might be proposed for conversations: 'It is essential to keep out conspicuous controversialists, as Fr Woodlock and Fr Keating: if any Jesuit had to be on, I should suggest Fr Thurston, a learned all round man, not mixed up in the Anglican controversy like the other two.'[25] (Collaborating with Cardinal Merry del Val[26] in Rome, Woodlock had been instrumental in provoking Bourne's hostile reaction to the Malines Conversations which was a significant factor in their demise.)

Cuthbert Butler

The man who counselled caution against the inclusion of English Jesuits, and who was himself suggested by Bourne as a fellow participant with Bidwell, was Cuthbert Butler, former Abbot of Downside. Although Butler was known and respected by Bourne, his nomination for this role is far more likely to have originated with Marchant. The two men had been in contact since at least 1926. Marchant had sought Butler's advice on details of Catholic Church history and the Abbot offered his assistance.[27] Marchant pursued his accustomed strategy. Initially, the two men corresponded on literary matters. It was not long before Marchant had Butler acting as a sub-editor and reviewer, and was commissioning articles on Catholic doctrine.[28] In return, Butler introduced the publisher to the community at Downside. By November 1927, Marchant was confiding in Butler his hopes and his every action regarding the proposed Anglican-Catholic conversations. Butler offered his advice and was praying for success at the very times Marchant was meeting with Bourne and Davidson. Under no illusions as to the obstacles to be overcome, Butler clearly shared Marchant's hopes. He expressed his 'great surprise and great joy', congratulating Marchant on his success in bringing together the Cardinal and the Archbishop. Butler appreciated the sensitivities of their correspondence, destroying Marchant's letters on receipt.[29] (Fortunately, Marchant did not reciprocate.) In gaining Butler's sympathy and collaboration, Marchant had secured more for the success of his scheme than probably he appreciated.

Cuthbert Butler

Born Edward Butler in Ireland in 1858, his ancestry was largely English. His grandfather was a convert to Catholicism, his father was professor of mathematics at Newman's new university in Dublin. Educated at Downside, Butler entered the Benedictine novitiate at Belmont at the age of 18, assuming the name Cuthbert. He returned to Downside where Gasquet was Prior. Butler's monastic vocation was inseparable from his career as a scholar, although never to the detriment of his life of prayer. He spent six years at Benet House, Downside's house of studies in Cambridge, becoming in 1896 the first Catholic priest to take a BA degree at the University since the sixteenth century. Butler was elected Abbot of Downside in 1906, holding office until 1922. As a result of his historical and spiritual writing, 'his name came to stand to educated readers, Catholic and non-Catholic alike, as a guarantee for sound scholarship and robust common-sense'. He was a frequent preacher at Westminster Cathedral and speaker for the Catholic Evidence Guild. Frugal in his personal needs and habitually careless of his appearance, he was nevertheless a striking character. 'He would never have passed for an ordinary man. Indeed he recalled nothing so much as one's conception of an impoverished nobleman.'[30]

Unstinting in his praise of Butler's scholarship, his fellow Benedictine, David Knowles, was damning in his assessment of the Abbot's interpersonal skills. Butler, he maintained, lacked personal sympathy and was no judge of character. 'He lacked also the capacity for "making" conversation [...] it was as if an iceberg had drifted up.'[31] That was not the experience of others. Possibly Butler was more expansive outside his own community. The lay theologian, Friedrich von Hügel was effusive in his thanks to Wilfrid Ward for effecting the introduction: 'I owe you a debt of gratitude for drawing my attention to Father Butler, the Benedictine [...] I like his mind and heart very much. There is a breadth and warmth and peaceful activity about him which does one much good.'[32] They became good friends and Butler in turn extolled von Hügel's work when he was regarded with suspicion by others.[33]

It was in this environment of liberal Catholic scholarship that Butler flourished. He was no Modernist. Rather his outlook was formed by his father's veneration for his employer, Newman. Butler's weighty volumes, *The Life and Times of Bishop Ullathorne* and *The Vatican Council: The Story told from the Inside in Bishop Ullathorne's Letters*, were in large measure a defence of the moderation of Wiseman, Newman and Ullathorne against the ultramontanism of Manning, Faber and W. G. Ward. Given the events and subjects were very much within living memory, Butler wrote robustly with an eye to his own day. An anonymous reviewer (Marchant?) of the Ullathorne biography comments on this:

> His very style wins our confidence. It is blunt, straightforward, even at times careless and rugged. The Abbot has no taste for epigram or ornament. He seems to say to us: 'Here is the plain judgment of a plain man', and we yield to his transparent honesty and candour [...] He has wide views and deep views, but no fanaticisms [...] [Ullathorne is presented as] a happy synthesis of solid Catholic belief and British common sense. The biographer is in this the counterpart of his subject.[34]

His honesty and style appealed to the Anglicans with whom we are concerned. One CU officer wrote to another: 'Let me recommend

Dom Cuthbert Butler's *Vatican Council*, if you have not already read it. It gives abundant information in the most readable way. I have enjoyed it like a good novel.'[35]

The Anglicans also appreciated Butler's engagement with modern critical scholarship. In June 1930 he published *Religions of Authority and the Religion of the Spirit*, a series of essays written a generation earlier. They revealed a mind both intellectually rigorous and solidly Catholic. Butler nailed his colours firmly to the mast:

> For myself, I do not hesitate to say that, with Catholic Faith on the right hand, and English common sense on the left, I am willing to throw myself frankly and fearlessly into the full current of modern criticism, in the conviction that truth has nothing to fear from the most searching scrutiny.[36]

He delighted our Anglicans by refuting the liberal Anglo-Catholic critique of the early papacy using the scriptural scholarship of an earlier generation of Anglicans.[37] Butler gratified that audience still further by opining on the most suitable venue in which Modernism might be refuted: 'No more favourable atmosphere for the pursuit of these higher ecclesiastical studies could be found than in our old University towns.'[38] At Cambridge, Butler read voraciously all contemporary thought on the New Testament and the early Christian corpus, and wrote himself a history of eastern monasticism. But, for our purposes, more important than his studies were the contacts made there with non-Catholics. Butler happily participated in the Association for the Study of Christian Doctrine founded by the Regius Professor of Divinity.[39]

It was in Cambridge that he also met a Fellow of Christ's College, Armitage Robinson. Sharing a passion for early Christian texts, the two Irishmen became scholarly collaborators and firm friends. Their friendship was further cemented after 1911 when Robinson became Dean of Wells and a regular visitor to Downside.

After Robinson's death, Butler revealed how the Dean had confided to him his role in the Malines Conversations. Robinson was not an Anglo-Catholic, but had agreed to attend the Conversations 'chiefly with the object of keeping the thing in touch with the realities' of the English Church. Robinson's appreciation of St Paul's theology of the Church as the Body of Christ led him to deplore 'the divisions of Christendom as a dismemberment of the Body; above all he deplored the Reformation and the English breach with Rome'. Robinson never expected Malines to produce immediate results, but he was charmed by Cardinal Mercier and he rejoiced in the fact that for 'the first time since the Reformation that Catholics and Anglicans had met, not in controversy, but in friendly talk over differences, with explanations and elucidations'. From the very first Conversation, Robinson took Butler into his confidence, told him all that was happening and shared his 'excitement and enthusiasm'.[40]

When Marchant made contact, therefore, the Benedictine was already well versed in the aspirations and immediate history of those who worked for Reunion. He brought with him Robinson's sympathy, but also his realism. Butler reminded Marchant of the very definite limits to potential Catholic concessions:

> Of course any compromise of any defined Catholic doctrine, [the decrees of the First Vatican Council] or anything else, is out of the question. All that could be hoped for is that things might be put in such a way as to remove misconceptions and exaggerations, and render the Catholic doctrines acceptable or tolerable to a considerable section of High Church people: the C of E as a whole, with its great strong Protestant wing, is, humanly speaking, hopeless—to say nothing of the Modernists.
>
> Such things as vernacular liturgy, Communion under both kinds, clerical celibacy, and other matters of discipline, might be conceded for the sake of so great a good: but not any point of defined Catholic Faith.[41]

Gaining Butler's participation in any such conversations was a major achievement. After his retirement as Abbot in 1922, he was close at hand, living at Ealing Priory in West London.

Alban Goodier

Marchant proudly announced to Archbishop Lang the Catholic team he had assembled:

> Two of the Roman members I have known for a number of years; they are good scholars and certainly represent a different type to those we are accustomed to think of. I think they are regarded by the Pope and the Cardinal as being the best men in the Church.[42]

The first of the two was Butler, the second was Archbishop Alban Goodier. They were very different men. Intellectually, socially and spiritually, Butler was self-assured. Although an Archbishop, Goodier was not. Fortunately, each enjoyed a mutual respect for the other.

Goodier never seemed quite at ease in the company of non-Catholics—nor of most Catholics for that matter. His background was insular. He was born in 1869, the son of a grocer and draper, into the enclosed world of Lancastrian Catholicism. To the best of his knowledge, there was not a drop of non-Catholic blood in his veins. Goodier described his upbringing to Marchant:

> In my childhood I was taught to avoid non-Catholic companions [...] The pre-Emancipation spirit was still upon my father and mother. I took it for granted that non-Catholics, of whatever denomination, but especially Nonconformists, disliked my faith, indeed hated it [...]
>
> I tell you this that you may see how high a wall has been built around us old English Catholics from our infancy, so that we, too, find it hard to enter the minds of those outside the Church. [...] I am tempted to have only two categories, Catholics, in mind or in spirit, and anti-Catholics [...] because of my upbringing as a child, I find it very hard to appreciate those who are, or who profess to be, neither one nor the other.[43]

Not the most promising preparation for one required to treat with extreme and flamboyant Anglicans who claimed to be as Catholic as Goodier himself.

The 1920 Lambeth Conference rightly noted the importance for Reunion of Catholic religious orders establishing houses of

'The best men in the Church'

Alban Goodier

studies in Oxford and their members entering into the academic and social life of the ancient universities. Three of our four Catholic participants were Oxbridge-educated, relating easily to their Anglican counterparts. Goodier was the exception. His education was solely within the Society of Jesus, which he joined on finishing school at Stonyhurst. Another Jesuit recognised these limitations:

> he should have profited by going [to Oxford]: his London extern B.A. degree left him practically a self-trained man; he was not nourished by the Oxford atmosphere (which still existed), and his scholarship was not as disciplined as perhaps it should have been.[44]

Goodier taught both at Stonyhurst and the novitiate at Manresa House in Roehampton at a time when the Jesuits were a formidable intellectual body. Yet one is constantly aware of Goodier's self-doubt.

That insecurity was not helped in his early years by the fact that he felt his doctrinal orthodoxy to be questioned. This was the period of the Modernist Crisis when Pius X sought to purge the Church of those who undermined revealed religion. Drastic action was required, but many innocent souls suffered as a consequence. Goodier was not a Modernist, but this period proved a considerable trial to him:

> his temperament made scholastic philosophy and theology and legal minutiae distasteful to him; he liked what was humane, ascetical and even mystical [...] he was on the rack, being tugged by loyalty to men and to orthodoxy this way and that. This may have sufficed to arouse distrust of him in certain minds; I think he allowed the notion that he was 'suspect' to prey upon him.[45]

Whatever suspicions might have been entertained, they did not prevent ecclesiastical preferment.

Goodier was sent to St Francis Xavier College in Bombay in November 1914 to replace German Jesuits classified as enemy aliens within the British Empire upon the outbreak of war. He blamed his predecessors for the anti-British sentiment he found among his students. A loyal British subject himself, he did little to gain his charges' affection, defending the Raj's action in the Amritsar Massacre of 1919. That same year Goodier was the wrong man in the right place when Bombay required a new Archbishop. It was not a happy appointment. While he developed the charitable outreach of the Diocese, 'from the outset he was surrounded by real suspicions, religio-political intrigue (which disgusted him) and misrepresentations'.[46] He became embroiled in a protracted dispute with the Patriarch of Goa, who claimed jurisdiction over all priests ordained in Goa regardless of their subsequent location. At Pius XI's request, and no doubt very much to his own relief, Goodier resigned from Bombay as a condition of the resolution of the conflict.

Returning home in 1926 as a retired Archbishop still only in his mid-fifties, Goodier might have been regarded as a failure. Fortunately, Cardinal Bourne had a reputation for allowing his fellow clergy second chances and giving sufficient space to those

'The best men in the Church'

who did not fit into the normal routine of diocesan and parish life. In this case, it proved a genuine inspiration. Goodier functioned as Bourne's auxiliary in the Diocese of Westminster. He took up residence and responsibility at St Mary's, Cadogan Street in Chelsea, giving him a central London base, while curates undertook the mundane parochial work. The arrangement enabled Goodier to develop the work for which he was widely appreciated at the time and is still remembered today. Goodier possessed a fluency and directness of language which appealed to many and made him a popular communicator of the truths of the faith. The Archbishop gave lectures and preached frequent retreats, but, above all, he wrote many spiritual works.

The Public Life of Our Lord Jesus Christ was dedicated to Cardinal Bourne 'in gratitude, in esteem, with deep affection'.[47] The work made no pretence to scholarship. It was a heartfelt attempt to harmonise the four Gospels to present the Person of Christ *as He truly was*. It won Goodier a devoted following, and he followed it with a book on the Passion with which he had a lifelong preoccupation. The printed word allowed Goodier to bare his soul in a manner in which he would never have contemplated in person: 'Love, real and objective, and the insights and interpretation which come of love, are the only key to the Passion, certainly far more than learning; for love alone opens our eyes that we may know Him.'[48]

As with Butler, it was his literary output which drew Goodier to Marchant's attention. The publisher was attracted by the Archbishop's direct and personal presentation of the life of Christ, and by spring 1930 was discussing the possibility of a new book. Goodier hoped that concentrating upon the Person of Christ and the Christian's participation in His life might serve to emphasize the beliefs which united Catholics and Anglicans. These fundamentals, he wrote,

> should provide us all with common ground; and once we are on common ground, but only then, we can hope to understand the meaning and significance of each other's terms. Then we shall find, I do trust, how much many of us mean and believe the same thing, and the grace of God must do the rest.[49]

Marchant immediately noted Goodier as an ally in the cause of Reunion. He might have come to a different assessment had he read an essay the Archbishop wrote that same year:

> The best of England, and the oldest, is everywhere Catholic [...] The rest has come later, and is only an accretion; the communion table where once stood the consecrated altar, the cross of brass, where was once the tabernacle and the crucifix, the meaningless candlesticks, the Book of Common Prayer for the missal, all these of which England every day becomes more ashamed and which she endeavours to discard.

He rejoiced at the fact that he was born into a Catholic family. All alternatives to Catholicism, he implied, involved 'pretensions or deceptions or concealments'.[50]

Martin D'Arcy

There were four Catholic participants in the Conversations with which we are concerned. Marchant admitted that only two, Butler and Goodier, were known to him personally. The identities of the third and the fourth were almost certainly determined by Goodier.

Only 32 at the time, Martin D'Arcy had already established for himself the reputation of directing his brilliance and charm to the challenge of making converts to Catholicism, especially among the upper echelons of society. (Evelyn Waugh, whom he received into the Church in September 1930, recalled D'Arcy's 'blue chin and fine, slippery mind'.[51]) The son of an Irish barrister, he too had joined the Jesuits on finishing school at Stonyhurst. Goodier was the Prefect of Juniors when D'Arcy arrived at Roehampton. There was mutual admiration and respect. The socially-accomplished Irishman and the dour Northerner immediately hit it off, and remained friends for life.

After Roehampton, D'Arcy was sent in 1912 to Campion Hall, the Jesuit house of studies in Oxford, to study Classics, gaining a First in Greats. He returned to teach at Stonyhurst before being assigned to the Jesuit parish of Farm Street in Mayfair in 1926, just in time to renew his acquaintance with Goodier, back from

'The best men in the Church'

Martin D'Arcy

Bombay. The next few years were spent between London and Oxford, where D'Arcy taught from 1927.

D'Arcy mixed easily with non-Catholics in the University. Taken to tea at the Mitre, the Episcopalian, Campbell, noted that the Jesuit could benefit from a haircut, but his manners were faultless.[52] D'Arcy was a regular attendee at the Anglican-led undergraduate Society for Reunion, and created a similarly favourable impression there. He heard Spencer Jones speak on 'Rome and Reunion' in June 1928, and 'paid a graceful tribute to the reader of the paper'. That autumn term he contributed to a discussion on the papacy.[53] He was probably one of the 'two Jesuit Fathers' who attended a further talk on Reunion with Rome in March 1930 and who 'spoke in a most friendly tone'.[54]

D'Arcy recognised, and sympathised with, the strong desire for Reunion in the years following the First World War. Yet, while avoiding the polemical tone of some of his colleagues in the English Province of the Society, he fully shared their perspective:

> All over the world where Christianity is diffused there has arisen a desire for Christian unity. The Protestant bodies still hope that the Church may meet them half-way. If this means that the Catholic Church is asked to surrender any part of the message committed to it by the Son of God, they are doomed to be disappointed, and unfortunately for their own future the Protestant Churches are ceasing to have any treasure to defend.[55]

Contact with non-Catholics had as its objective conversion, not compromise.

Bede Jarrett

Writing to the Archbishop of Canterbury just days before the First Conversation, Marchant indicated 'that three devout and learned men — and I may say liberal-minded in the best sense of that word — belonging to the Roman Church would be quite happy to meet in friendly conversations'.[56] They were Goodier, Butler and D'Arcy. A week later a fourth man also attended.

The son of an Indian Army officer, Bede Jarrett was also educated at Stonyhurst. He was taught there by Goodier, to whom he confided his desire to be a priest. Unlike D'Arcy, he chose to pursue his vocation, not with the Jesuits, but with the then very unfashionable Dominicans. Indeed, it is to Jarrett that much of the credit is due for restoring the intellectual life of the English Dominicans in modern times. He himself was the first Dominican to study at Oxford since the Reformation, reading Modern History while living with the Benedictines. Without neglecting his studies, he was not averse to entering the University social life of tea parties and cricket matches. His attractive personality appealed to many; his capacity for friendship was legendary. 'It is rare for a man to grow up into a glorious maturity and still retain all the charm and grace of youth: that is what Father Bede somehow managed to achieve.'[57]

'The best men in the Church'

Bede Jarrett

Oxford awakened in Jarrett the desire for an intellectual apostolate to non-Catholics. As Prior of the Dominican house at Haverstock Hill, he founded an annual series of lectures at Caxton Hall in London aimed specifically at a non-Catholic audience.[58] His election in 1916 as Provincial of the English Dominicans—an office he was to hold for the next sixteen years—increased his scope to develop this ministry. In 1919 he purchased the *Catholic Review*, relaunching it the following year as *Blackfriars*, which rapidly established itself as one of the most serious journals of Catholic intellectual life in England. Jarrett himself considered his greatest achievement to be the return of the Dominicans to Oxford, 700 years after their first arrival. The refoundation of Blackfriars enabled the Order of Preachers to make once more a significant contribution to the life of the University, studying, teaching and being a presence among non-Catholics.

It was the enthusiastic response to the Lambeth *Appeal* by Jarrett's confrere, Vincent McNabb, in the pages of *Blackfriars* which led Lord Halifax to propose conferences in England between High Church Anglicans and the Dominicans. Jarrett was open to the possibility: 'I'm hoping we shall fix something up—but we'll get condemned by Rome and burnt.'[59] McNabb was delated to the Holy Office and his article referred to the Master-General of the Dominicans. Nothing came of the proposed conferences, except that it opened up a line of communication between the doyen of Anglo-Catholicism and the Provincial of the English Dominicans. Jarrett was characteristically generous in his praise of the elderly peer, expressing his personal admiration of Halifax's courtesy and unselfishness, his life consecrated to God.[60]

Halifax was not immune to flattery. When the time came in 1923 to consider expanding the number of participants in the Malines Conversations, Halifax proposed Jarrett's name to Mercier. The Belgian Cardinal knew nothing of Jarrett but welcomed the possibility that a suitable 'English Catholic, who would eventually act as a connecting link between us and Cardinal Bourne and the Catholic hierarchy in England, should be one amongst our number here'.[61] Mercier must have been surprised to have received Halifax's further letter just days later asking him to pause before issuing any invitation to Jarrett to join them in Malines. It is not clear whether Mercier ever received a satisfactory explanation for this sudden volte-face. Halifax's motives are, however, apparent from his correspondence with his fellow Anglican participants: he had received another letter from Jarrett. Halifax and Jarrett might share a mutual personal 'respect and regard', but the Dominican was too good a Catholic and historian to allow that to colour his opinions of Anglican claims.[62]

His own research led Jarrett to the conclusion that Anglican Orders were, at best, 'most terribly uncertain'. He asked Halifax: 'Is it not possible for you, with that immense courage you have always shown [. . .] to forego an earlier judgment and find your way [. . .] to the Faith in peace?'[63] Jarrett and McNabb seem to have coordinated their efforts, for McNabb also wrote at the same time:

Forgive me if I seem cruel—but if my reasoning be correct, you stand in this position—Rome tells you that to acknowledge the jurisdiction of the Pope and *not* to obey, is a grave sin; the Church of England will tell you that you are disloyal. There is no middle course. I beg of you, dear Lord Halifax, to consider that your first duty is to save your soul.[64]

Halifax preferred to receive courtesy rather than personal challenge from his Catholic correspondents.

Elsewhere too, Jarrett used his historical knowledge to refute Anglican claims to Catholicism and continuity with the pre-Reformation Church.[65] If Goodier was responsible for Jarrett's inclusion in our Conversations, then he chose wisely and well.

Notes

[1] Archbishop Alban Goodier to Marchant, 21 October 1930, OUL, Marchant, 299/168.

[2] Davidson, Memorandum, 16 February 1928, LPL, Davidson Papers, 466/381.

[3] Ramsay to Marchant, 24 March 1928, OUL, Marchant, 315/63.

[4] Marchant to Bourne, 5 May 1928, AAW, Bo./ALN.

[5] Bourne to Marchant, 30 April 1929, OUL, Marchant MS, English Lett 314/218.

[6] Marchant to Davidson, 7 September 1928 (copy), LPL, Davidson Papers, 466/396; Davidson to Marchant, 10 September 1928, LPL, Davidson Papers, 466/398.

[7] R. Beaken, *Cosmo Lang: Archbishop in War and Crisis* (London: I. B. Tauris & Co., 2012).

[8] Lang to Bishop Arthur Chandler, 10 July 1929, LPL, Lang Papers, 95/251.

[9] Marchant to Lang, 22 December 1928, LPL, Lang Papers, 97/214.

[10] Marchant to Lang, 12 November 1929, LPL, Lang Papers, 97/208.

[11] Lang to Davidson, 22 November 1929 (copy), LPL, Lang Papers, 97/209.

[12] Lang to Marchant, 22 November 1929 (copy), LPL, Lang Papers, 97/210–11.

[13] The chapel's curious name derived from its former location in the City of London. Today the building in Mayfair is the Ukrainian Catholic Cathedral.

[14] Rev. W. E. Orchard, *Sunday Express* (13 Sept. 1925).

[15] W. F. Orchard, 'A Vision of the Reunited Church', in Marchant, *The Reunion of Christendom*, pp. 278, 280.

[16] Marchant to Bell, 1 September 1930, LPL, Bell Papers, 212/1; 12 December

1930, LPL Bell Papers, 212/2.

[17] E. Kaye, *The History of the King's Weigh House Church: A Chapter in the History of London* (London: George Allen & Unwin, 1968), p. 137.

[18] Marchant to Lang, 29 December 1930, LPL, Lang Papers, 107/18.

[19] Lang to Marchant, 2 May 1931 (copy), LPL, Lang Papers, 107/21.

[20] Lang, *York Diocesan Gazette* (May 1927).

[21] Beaken, *Cosmo Lang*, p. 48.

[22] Marchant to Lang, 12 November 1929, LPL, Lang Papers, 97/208.

[23] F. J. Sheed, *The Church and I* (London: Sheed & Ward, 1974).

[24] M. Ward, *Unfinished Business* (London: Sheed & Ward, 1964), p. 99.

[25] Butler to Marchant, 24 November 1927, OUL, Marchant, 299/10.

[26] Rafael, Cardinal Merry del Val (1865–1930) had served as secretary to the President of the Commission investigating the validity of Anglican Orders and was influential in drafting the 1896 Bull. He went on to serve as Cardinal Secretary of State under Pope Pius X, and consistently opposed any attempt to rescind or modify *Apostolicae Curae*'s ruling against Anglican Orders.

[27] Butler to Marchant, 7 November 1926, OUL, Marchant, 299/3.

[28] Butler to Bourne, 27 June 1928, AAW, Bo./ALN; Bourne to Butler, 28 June 1928 (copy), AAW, Bo./ALN.

[29] Butler to Marchant, 22 November 1927, 24 November 1927, 28 November 1927, 1 December 1927, OUL, Marchant, 299/9–14.

[30] D. Knowles, OSB, 'Abbot Butler: A Memoir', *Downside Review*, 52 (1934), pp. 347–465.

[31] *Ibid.*, p. 434.

[32] F. von Hügel to W. Ward, cited M. Ward, *The Wilfrid Wards and the Transition* (London: Sheed & Ward, 1934), p. 304.

[33] M. Ward, *Insurrection versus Resurrection* (London: Sheed & Ward, 1937), p. 546.

[34] J. M., Review of Butler's *Life and Times of Bishop Ullathorne*, *Blackfriars*, 7/72 (March 1926), pp. 185–6.

[35] Campbell to Joblin, 9 October 1930, PHA/Rea/CU2/532.

[36] C. Butler, *Religions of Authority and the Religion of the Spirit with Other Essays Apologetical and Critical* (London: Sheed & Ward, 1930), p. 75.

[37] *Ibid.*, p. 178.

[38] *Ibid.*, p. 75.

[39] C. Butler, *Western Mysticism* (London: Constable, 1922), p. vi.

[40] C. Butler, 'Armitage Robinson: A Memoir', in *Downside Review*, 51 (1933), pp. 391–405.

[41] Butler to Marchant, 28 November 1927, OUL, Marchant, 299/12–13.

[42] Marchant to Lang, 14 May 1931, LPL, Lang Papers, 107/22.

[43] Goodier to Marchant, 11 March 1930, OUL, Marchant, 299/155–7.

[44] C. C. Martindale, SJ, Obituary, *Tablet* (18 March 1939), p. 362.

[45] *Ibid.*

[46] *Ibid.*

[47] A. Goodier, *The Public Life of Our Lord Jesus Christ* (London: Burns, Oates & Washbourne, 1930), 2 vols.

[48] A. Goodier, *The Passion and Death of Our Lord Jesus Christ* (London: Burns, Oates & Washbourne, 1933), p. xi.

[49] Goodier to Marchant, 16 March 1930, OUL, Marchant, 299/161.

[50] Goodier, 'Why I am a Catholic', in *Why I am and Why I am not a Catholic* (London: Cassell and Company, 1930), pp. 16, 23.

[51] E. Waugh, Diary, 8 July 1930 cited H. J. A. Sires, *Father Martin D'Arcy: Philosopher of Christian Love* (Leominster: Gracewing, 1997), p. 71.

[52] Campbell to Pierce, 16 February 1931, BCA, Pierce Bequest, CU Founding and Letters.

[53] PHA, OUSR, Minute Book, vol. I, pp. 156, 160.

[54] Pierce to Dom A. de Lilienfeld, OSB, 3 March 1930, PHA/Rea/CU2/261.

[55] M. C. D'Arcy, SJ, ed, *The Life of the Church* (London: Sheed & Ward, 1934), p. 326.

[56] Marchant to Lang, 29 December 1930, LPL, Lang Papers, 107/18–19.

[57] B. Delany, OP, 'Father Bede Jarrett, OP', *Blackfriars* (May 1934), pp. 310–12.

[58] S. Tugwell, OP, and A. Bellenger, OSB, *Letters of Bede Jarrett, Letters and Other Papers of the English Dominican Archives selected by Bede Bailey, OP* (Bath: Downside Abbey and Oxford, Blackfriars Publications, 1989), p. 29.

[59] Jarrett to Lady Margaret Domvile, 10 August 1920, cited Tugwell and Bellenger, *Letters of Bede Jarrett*, p. 47.

[60] Jarrett to Halifax, 5 November 1921 (copy), BIY, Halifax, Malines Papers, A4/271/1.

[61] Mercier to Halifax, 23 September 1923 (copy), BIY, Halifax, Malines Papers, A4/271/1.

[62] Halifax to Gore, 27 September 1923 (copy), BIY, Halifax, Malines Papers, A4/271/1.

[63] Jarrett to Halifax, 24 September 1923 (copy), BIY, Halifax, Malines Papers, A4/271/1.

[64] McNabb to Halifax, 27 September 1923, BIY, Halifax, Malines Papers, A4/271/1.

[65] Jarrett, 'Introduction' in J. Clayton, *The Historic Basis of Anglicanism* (London: Sands & Co., 1925).

✢ 4 ✢

'Our Anglican friends'[1]

'The right men will come in'

One of the most notable features of our Conversations was the strength and seniority of the Catholic team: an Archbishop, a respected and scholarly Benedictine Abbot, the dynamic Provincial of the English Dominicans and a Jesuit widely regarded as the rising star of his generation—all blessed by Cardinal Bourne, head of the Catholic Church in England and Wales. In many ways it was a more appropriate group than the Franco-Belgian one which had gathered at Malines. Sir James Marchant was happy enough disclosing the identity of the Catholic participants to the Archbishop of Canterbury. He was more reticent when it came to the Anglicans—and with reason. Marchant struggled, and ultimately failed, to convene an equivalent body of Anglicans. To a large measure this was the result of the antipathy of two Archbishops of Canterbury and the Anglican hierarchy as a whole to conversations with Catholics in the aftermath of Malines.

The Anglican Establishment's unwillingness to engage presented a serious problem. Whom were the Catholics to talk to? Marchant and his Catholic contacts proffered various suggestions. Butler wanted to involve at least some of the Anglican participants from Malines in the hope that this would bestow a certain significance on the new talks, allowing them to benefit from the Belgian experience. He recommended, with an implicit swipe at Halifax, his friend Armitage Robinson, the Dean of Wells, 'to keep the Anglican side *sane*'. Butler also proposed Dr Beresford Kidd, Warden of Keble College, Oxford, as a prominent Church historian sympathetic to Catholic claims.[2] Robinson had been a reluctant participant at Malines, and was not about to engage in a new venture in his seventies. Marchant met with Kidd in April 1928 to invite him to join 'in a patient enquiry into the whole position of the Catholic Church, with a view to finding out whether the difficulties which seem to stand in the way of the act of Faith are insuperable'. Sir James was uncharacteristically taciturn following that meeting, but it is clear 'that things did not go quite as well as [he] expected'.[3] Kidd declined involvement. He was not feeling particularly pro-Roman in the aftermath of Malines, preaching that conversion to Catholicism was tantamount to 'committing intellectual suicide'.[4]

Marchant was discovering that his Anglican contacts made from various committees and charities were not bearing the desired fruit. Bishop Woods of Winchester was not to be drawn. Sir James wrote to Lang: 'I must not presume to suggest names to Your Grace' — and proceeded to do precisely that. He felt that surely in Oxford, the spiritual home of High Church Anglicanism, he would find those who shared his zeal for Reunion. He volunteered the names of Henry Leighton Goudge, Regius Professor of Divinity at Oxford, and Thomas Strong, Bishop of Oxford.[5] Goudge was a Scripture scholar horrified by Lambeth's tolerance of contraception in 1930, but no friend of papal claims. Strong was too fond of compromise to entertain seriously Reunion with the Catholic Church. Indeed, he looked to the Orthodox to present a united anti-Roman front. The Archbishop was not to be drawn on the question of suggesting Anglican participants.

Marchant persevered, corresponding with anyone and everyone who might be interested in the cause of Christian unity. It was inevitable, therefore, that at some point he would make contact with representatives of the Roman School of Anglicanism. Pierce of the Confraternity of Unity received his first letter in October 1929. Marchant continued to pursue the American over the coming months:

> I should much like to meet you for I am going to arrange a private gathering of a few friends of reunion with the Catholic Roman Church which may issue in something else being done, and I should like to know you, or the movement you represent. When are you likely to be in town?[6]

'Our Anglican friends'

Despite the blandishments, nothing came of this. The travel commitments of the two men precluded their meeting. One suspects also that the Episcopalian mistrusted the involvement of a Nonconformist in talks designed to promote the union of Catholics and Anglicans.

The Anglo-Papalists

Where Marchant failed, the Catholic participants themselves found willing Anglicans to engage with them in theological conferences. 'The Romans expressed a desire, at first, to meet certain Anglicans who happened to have written books which they knew, and that made an easier contact for them.' Sir James had to admit that he 'did not personally know them' — quite a concession for one who prided himself on the comprehensiveness of his ecclesiastical connections. But, simultaneously, he was deliberately distancing himself from the Anglicans concerned. He would have been aware that not only were they not of the Establishment, but that they were suspect in the eyes of, and shunned by, that Establishment. It is very noticeable that, when he reports back to Lang on the initial Conversations, Marchant confidently parades the identity of the Catholic members — and reveals the name of not a single Anglican. He brushes hurriedly over the omission: 'As we become more at ease the right men will come in.'[7]

These Anglicans, not 'the right men', were Papalists, members of the movement which Pierce represented and which, to a large degree, Jones had founded three decades earlier. An Anglican Benedictine of a later generation set out their creed:

> We are those who [...] believe that the natural and lawful head of the Catholic Church on this earth is or should be the Pope; that it is most unfortunate that we are separated from him [...]; and that we most earnestly desire that this separation should come to an end.[8]

Papalists maintained that they held the same doctrinal position as the Roman Catholic Church, that there could be no Reunion with Rome save on the grounds of complete dogmatic agreement.

They accepted Trent, Vatican I and papal teaching. Their liturgy and devotions emulated contemporary Roman practice. They claimed to be a legitimate part of the Western Latin Church, even if in an irregular position as the result of changes forced upon an unwilling English Church by the State in the sixteenth century. Regularising their position was their urgent objective. They countered criticism, by holding that Reunion with Rome must be corporate—anything less would be to abandon the Church of England to Protestantism and Modernism. They felt justified in remaining in the Church of England until such corporate Reunion was achieved given, in their view, they held valid orders and exercised a valid sacramental ministry. Papalists held that Leo XIII's Bull *Apostolicae Curae* was not infallible teaching and was the unfortunate result of misinformation; it would be reformed in the fullness of time.

Based on the numbers supporting the Church Unity Octave by the 1930s, it is claimed that the over 1,000 Anglican clergy in England alone held the Papalist position. While the CUO never disguised its Romeward objective, it is far from certain that all its supporters were committed to practical and immediate Catholic Reunion rather than a more vague sympathy for Reunion with the historic churches of the East and West. It is difficult to quantify the numbers of Papalists because, as contemporaries pointed out, there was no 'Papalist party', rather a 'Papalist tradition' within the Church of England.[9] Nevertheless, Papalism could count upon the backing to a greater or lesser degree of several hundred clergy — possibly somewhere between 1 and 3% of the total. Crucially, by the late 1920s and early 1930s it seemed to be gaining momentum.

Papalists were realistic about the prospects of success of corporate Reunion with Rome. Writing in 1942, one Papalist believed that three conditions would first need to be satisfied:
1. The bishops themselves (or a considerable proportion of them) must be converted to the [Papalist position].
2. They must be liberated from the control of Parliament now exercised under the Royal Supremacy.
3. They must be able to carry with them a sufficient proportion of the clergy and laity.

He acknowledged that this might take a century to achieve.[10] Many wondered, however, whether they had a century at their disposal given the Anglican Establishment's propensity to compromise with Protestantism and Modernism, and thus shatter all claim to catholicity.

The Papalists took theology, liturgy and the spiritual life extremely seriously. It is among their more endearing characteristics, however, that they were not above self-parody. To achieve a more rounded view of the Papalist phenomenon, one should read Eric Mascall's 'The Ultra-Catholic'[11] in conjunction with what is written here.

Roman Catholics aware of their existence tended to view the Papalists with incomprehension. How could Anglicans claim to accept the primacy and jurisdiction of the Pope when he categorically denied the validity of their orders? A French commentator mused: 'It is difficult for cradle Catholics who have always lived in a Catholic ambience to understand how those Anglicans can remain long in perfect good faith in such an illogical position.'[12] Converts were among the Papalists' harshest critics. While recognising 'a fruitful ground for conversions', the Dominican, Henry St John, was disparaging of Papalism:

> Having little individuality of its own, it has become hardly more than a close imitation of ourselves, and some times of our worst selves, uneasily yoked with the spirit and organisation of the Church of England.[13]

Thomas Whitton, on the cusp of conversion, was equally unrelenting in his critique: Papalists

> overlook the obvious fact that they reject the fundamental dogma on which the Pope bases his religion, namely, the necessity of the visible unity of the Church. With this school of Anglicans the extraordinary situation has come about that they believe in the Pope more than in the Church.[14]

At times, the Irish Dominican, Vincent McNabb, appeared a lone voice among Anglophone Catholics in welcoming the 'Romeward Movement' in the Church of England.

History is indeed written by the victors. It has suited mainstream Anglicanism to ignore the role played by Papalism in the Church of England in general and ecumenical relations in particular. Canon Bernard Pawley was an Establishment Anglican, representing the Archbishop of Canterbury at the Second Vatican Council. He and his wife wrote what amounts to the official account of Anglican-Catholic relations since the Reformation. Papalists are dismissed as 'extreme dissidents'.[15] (They were simply the wrong kind of dissident; the Pawleys willingly chronicled the activities of far less representative Catholic dissidents.)

There has been a reaction. Michael Yelton sought to rehabilitate the Papalists, placing them in their proper context and acknowledging their achievements in his definitive work published in 2005.[16] Geoffrey Curtiss, of the Community of the Resurrection, had attempted something similar in more cursory form four decades earlier:

> We are beginning to see that Anglican Papalists have been unfairly judged [...] They are accused by English Roman Catholics of failure in logic and by many of their fellow Anglicans of disloyalty [...] Contrary to average opinion this small group is notable for its intellectual power as well as for its holiness. Perhaps of the books of Anglican theology of [the twentieth] century that have been most widely read abroad have been books by Papalists.[17]

It is because of their intellectual power manifest in some of those books that the Papalists were invited to our Conversations.

Dr Scott

This broad overview of Papalism fails to do justice to the sheer colour and eccentricity of individual Papalists. Scott was one of the most intriguing and intellectually capable. Like many Papalists, he exhibited an intense concern for self-image. Born Sidney Scott, he died Herbert Drane-Scott, D.Phil., FRHS, 'gentleman'. The 'Drane' was the result of a change of name by deed poll in honour of cousins whose portraits and silver he inherited.[18] He was known invariably as 'Dr Scott'.

'Our Anglican friends'

Dr Scott

Scott was born in 1876 in Ipswich, where his father was Sergeant-at-Mace, a minor Corporation official. His siblings were milliners, grocers, confectioners and workers in the shoe trade. The family worshipped at the mediaeval church of St Mary-le-Tower, recently rebuilt and in the Tractarian tradition. Perhaps it is there that his intellectual ability and religious leanings were first recognised. He studied Theology at Hatfield Hall, Durham, and was ordained in 1901. There followed a bewildering succession of curacies and school chaplaincies, suggesting some volatility or other difficulty. He combined these positions with more study, gaining a further undergraduate degree, as a member of St John's College, Oxford.

Only with his appointment in 1915 to the living of St Andrew's, Oddington, did he acquire a measure of stability, remaining Rector until his death in 1949. Even today, given the proximity of Oxford, the A34 and the M40, Oddington remains surprisingly tranquil and unspoilt. The church furnishings, many acquired during excursions to Belgium, still bear witness to his incumbency: candelabra, tabernacle, paintings, a Pietà, Stations of the Cross and statues, including one of St Andrew coloured by Scott himself. It is an unusual ensemble for rural Anglicanism. The exotic was what the villagers had to accustom themselves to—although some complained that they were displaced by visitors from the University who shared Scott's churchmanship. It is difficult to know what the farmers and labourers made of 'Harvest Festival' comprising Solemn Evensong and Benediction, Midnight Mass or subdeacons.[19] Scott presides over St Andrew's still. His life-size portrait, formerly in the Rectory, hangs in the church tower. The aspect is not the anticipated waspish aesthete. Instead, a youthful and sturdy figure is displayed; although in clerical dress and grasping a book, he appears ready to step out onto the College playing field.

The Yorkshireman, Fr Morton Howard, was another Papalist who added a second barrel to his surname. His friend for two decades, after Scott's death he wrote an account of Rectory life at Oddington. Scott, unlike Morton Howard, never married, but he had his own 'family' where every member was accorded a nickname. A long-term resident of the Rectory was Gustava Bonsack, 'Aunt B', 'the truest of friends'. A rheumatic German spinster, Scott's senior by some twenty years, she acted as benefactress to the Rector, enabling him to fill church and Rectory with beautiful things. (There were also 'Aunts' 'M' and 'F'.) 'Oddington was a second home to many an Oxford man', and various High Church undergraduates found themselves put to liturgical service at St Andrew's. Then there were 'distinguished friends from all over Europe and America'. Jones stayed at Oddington when undertaking research or attending meetings at Oxford. Morton Howard recalls a cheery home of informality and 'boisterous fun'. Scott was 'an accomplished musician and an artist of no mean ability'.

Morton Howard only hints at another side of Scott's character: 'He was altogether lovable, though often enough exasperating and provocative.' That was something of an understatement. Scott 'could never suffer fools gladly, and he had a bitter tongue and a vitriolic pen which he used without reserve, if he thought the occasion demanded it'. He had a wide circle of friends, but offended many.

The parish history suggests that Scott was appointed to Oddington to remove him from Oxford, where he had become 'a thorn in the side' of Bishop Gore. There may be more than a grain of truth to this. His first publication in 1923, the short book *Anglo-Catholicism and Re-union*, constituted a broadside against both the Anglican hierarchy's sentimental approach towards Reunion and Gore's Modernist theology which, Scott felt, jeopardised the possibility of rapprochement with either Rome or Orthodoxy. Drawing on the Church Fathers and the early Councils, Scott argued that agreement on 'doctrine must come first, and fellowship on the basis of that doctrine follows'. Debate on the validity of Anglican Orders was an irrelevant detail, Scott maintained, if the Church of England abandoned orthodox belief in the divinity of Christ. In his view, Gore's 'Kenotic theory', emphasizing the limits to the human knowledge of Christ, risked precisely that and owed more to modern German thought than to the early Church Councils to which Anglicanism supposedly subscribed.[20]

Scott's *magnum opus*, a work still consulted today, is *The Eastern Churches and the Papacy*.[21] It represents the thesis for his doctorate, which Oxford awarded in 1926 only 'after much demur and delay'. The reason for the hesitation of the University, still a bastion of Anglicanism in those days, is not hard to discover. Scott deploys his considerable learning to determine one syllogism: the Church of England accepts the first four ecumenical Councils of the Church; those Councils are based upon an acceptance of Roman primacy; therefore, assent to the papal primacy is Anglican doctrine. Like most Papalist writings, the book is strong on logic and historical research, while ignoring contemporary practical realities. In constructing his argument, Scott once more has Gore and his anti-Roman stance firmly within his sights.

The *Tablet* could barely contain its glee: 'No Catholic historian could have produced a clearer and more scholarly proof of the acceptance of the Papal Supremacy at Ephesus than Dr Scott.'[22] A Dominican likewise perceived the book's significance in demolishing Anglican claims that papal supremacy was a later Catholic accretion:

> Dr Scott sets out to prove not the validity of the Papal claims but that these claims were made consistently from the close of the first century and—this is the point—that they were accepted as a matter of course by the Churches of the East [...] he has marshalled the evidence in a way that has not previously been attempted.[23]

The Confraternity of Unity welcomed Scott's scholarship as a 'bomb' falling 'in the midst of the old fashioned theories of nationalist ecclesiasticism'.[24] Morton Howard acknowledged that it changed his perspective on everything. It had revealed to him:

> There is one Church. The Papacy is not something the Latin Church has added; it is something that the Easterns and the Anglicans have lost. And to my mind this opened the door to the Reunion movement, and we owe that to Dr Scott.[25]

Of course, for the vast majority of Anglicans, Scott was simply disloyal. The book was published by the Catholic house, Sheed & Ward, a crossing of confessional divides virtually unknown at the time.

Unlike some Papalists, however, Scott was not enamoured of all things Roman in the contemporary Church. He particularly deprecated Cardinal Bourne's attitude towards the Monks of Unity in Belgium. He was horrified when Dom Lambert Beauduin was compelled to leave the Benedictine community at Amay, the result, he believed, of pressure brought to bear by Westminster.[26] Scott visited Belgium on numerous occasions. He secured an interview with Cardinal Mercier in August 1925, and discussed with him the work of Reunion.[27] He visited Amay in November 1928. The monks were delighted by his book, and he was enchanted by all he found there—'a real inspiration and incentive to re-double one's efforts to bring together all those who love the Lord Jesus in sincerity'. He sought their advice: 'I hope to go on using my pen and if you can suggest any subject that I can usefully treat, I shall be most grateful. It is the cause which interests me most in life.'[28]

'Our Anglican friends'

A few more articles and monographs emerged, but no other definitive scholarly work. Scott spoke at various Papalist gatherings, including the Society for Reunion attended by D'Arcy. But he conceived a new project to advance the cause of Reunion. Already corresponding with Wattson at the Society of the Atonement, Scott made contact with the Confraternity of Unity shortly after its inception. Both Campbell and Pierce met with him when canvassing the likely level of support for the CU in England. Scott committed himself to the Confraternity in general, and Pierce in particular. For weeks on end Pierce was subjected, sometimes on a daily basis, to lengthy, well-nigh illegible, letters from Oddington. (Others endured a similar experience at different times.) Scott relentlessly urged Pierce and his sister to buy a property close by him. The plan was to found 'an Oratory for Reunion', 'a little Amay', at Oddington. Even Scott appreciated the opportunity for personal contact with Catholics and Orthodox would be limited. 'The work would be restricted chiefly to writing and studying.'[29] It is difficult to escape the conclusion that Scott was an obsessive compulsive, with a desire to control those satellites he drew into his orbit.

Pierce resisted the temptation to become Scott's satellite. He wisely declined the invitation to move to Oddington itself, but, with his sister, took leases of various Oxford properties in order to be close to Scott. From May to December 1929 the American acted as Scott's unpaid curate and secretary.[30] The end of this beautiful friendship, when it came, was both rapid and absolute. Scott manoeuvred to have his young protégé, John Hardwick, appointed to the neighbouring parish of Merton. The blow was doubly bitter, therefore, when the living actually went to Henry Major, a leading Anglican Modernist and the Principal of the theological college, Ripon Hall. Denying the doctrine of Original Sin, the Virgin birth, the physical Resurrection, miracles and the propitiatory nature of Christ's sacrifice on the Cross, Major was Scott's bête noire.

Pierce's 'crime' consisted of telling Jones of Scott's plan to disrupt Major's induction ceremony at Merton, and Jones in consequence counselling Scott firmly against what he believed would be a counter-productive action. Scott lost all sense of proportion, venting his anger on Pierce and Jones. In Pierce's case the break was permanent. Scott denounced him publicly from the pulpit as a 'disloyal churchman'. Morton Howard was also temporarily 'excommunicated'. Scott told his parishioners at St Andrew's that he 'probably would not be in this Church much longer; perhaps not in any Church'.[31] Those who knew Scott well recognised a pattern of behaviour: he was 'highly strung'; he had suffered 'a serious breakdown' some time earlier. In personal matters, Scott was unable 'to judge with that calm reasoning that he so marvellously displays in his great book'.[32]

Scott could not distinguish personal acrimony from academic or ecclesiological positions. 'Like the Red Queen in Alice, Dr Scott is in that state of mind that he just must deny something.'[33] The attack on Major (and the friends whom he felt had betrayed him) became all-consuming. He wrote to Campbell:

> To me the question of Major going to Merton is of far more consequence than this Movement—at the moment any how. The Incarnation, the Virgin Birth, the Resurrection, the Propitiatory Sacrifice, are *primary*, not the Papacy.[34]

He wanted nothing more to do, he said, with the CU or their vision of Catholic Reunion. He requested that the CU remove his name from his paper on 'The Centre of Unity', which was to have been distributed to every Anglican Bishop attending the 1930 Lambeth Conference.[35] In vain his friends protested his inconsistency: all his previous scholarship had been aimed at demonstrating that Modernism, which Major embodied, could only be defeated by union with Rome.[36] Scott was reconciled to Morton Howard, but then the two of them took umbrage when neither were invited to the CU meeting convened to consider the Confraternity's response to the Lambeth resolution on contraception.[37]

In the light of the pugnacious nature of his personal relationships, it is surprising to discover that, politically, Scott was a strict pacifist. He found the company of cats and dogs altogether easier than that of humans. The Rectory in Oddington was never without the pets to whom he was devoted. Having accidentally

'Our Anglican friends'

run over a dog in North Oxford, Scott never drove again. To the consternation of some and the bemusement of Morton Howard, he maintained animals too had immortal souls. Immortal souls or not, cats, dogs and aged horses had much to thank Dr Scott for; under the terms of his will, animal welfare charities inherited the bulk of his estate.[38]

Spencer Jones

Our next Papalist was also a published author, but with many more titles to his name. Of an altogether milder disposition than Dr Scott, we last encountered him preaching in St Matthew's, Westminster, and promoting the Society of St Thomas of Canterbury and the Church Unity Octave.

Jones was another Papalist who adjusted his name. Baptised 'Spencer John Jones', by the time of his death eighty-five years later, few were aware that 'Spencer Jones' was not his surname. He was born in 1857 in Croydon; four years later the family were resident in Marylebone. His father was a lawyer, the secretary of an insurance company. Jones was sent to Chatham House School in Ramsgate where he was captain of soccer and cricket. Having graduated from Worcester College, Oxford, Jones entered Wells Theological College in 1880. He had tremendous admiration for the High Church Principal, Dr Edgar Gibson, later to be Jones's superior again as Bishop of Gloucester. That respect was reciprocated; Gibson offered the newly-ordained the position of Vice-Principal of the College. Jones declined, preferring the pastoral ministry.[39]

There were curacies in Somerset, Hampshire and Battersea. During that time Jones married Elizabeth Coxwell, seven years his senior and a cousin by marriage of John Keble. Despite his advocacy of the benefits of clerical celibacy, their marriage was long and happy. In 1887 a College friend turned down the living of Batsford with Moreton-in-Marsh in Gloucestershire, forwarding Jones's name instead. He was to be in this parish of 1,500 souls for the remaining forty-five years of his active ministry. Jones was a faithful pastor. Unlike many of his fellow Papalists, he

Spencer Jones

exhibited a marked reluctance to leave his parish for any length of time. Moreton-in-Marsh is an attractive Cotswold town of honey-coloured stone, but Jones's heart would sink were he to return today. Of all the Papalists' churches, St David's retains least evidence of the tradition he introduced over half a century. It proudly professes itself a 'Bible-centred church'. There are no statues, no indication of Catholic devotions. The altar has been abandoned for a communion table. Only two stained-glass windows record the fact Jones was ever here. Batsford was the home of Lord Redesdale and the Mitford family. In 1905 Jones preached there in the presence of their guest, Edward VII—probably not on the subject of Catholic Reunion.

Jones first attracted attention outside of the parish, not because of his espousal of Reunion with Rome, but because of his pioneering work in the field of youth catechesis. The fact that most Englishmen regarded religion simply as a matter of taste and feeling disturbed him. 'Religion as a sentiment is the parent of confusion',[40] he wrote. Children had to be offered proper formation if they were to practise and understand their faith. Jones knew there was a better way of proceeding, having read the recent translation of Bishop Dupanloup's *Ministry of Catechising*, extolling the Sulpician method of catechesis. Its aim was to produce in the pupil a personal love of Christ. Shortly after arriving in Moreton-in-Marsh, Jones took himself off to Paris to witness the method for himself. He argued for systematic organisation, a planned curriculum, a trained body of clerical and lay catechists, formal instruction of the young in every parish each Sunday. Jones was asked to speak on this novel approach in towns and cities across the country, and then to publish on the subject.[41] The result was *The Clergy and the Catechism*, which ran to six editions in three years. He followed it up with two small volumes, one for use by catechists, the other by their pupils.

Even if they did not appreciate his underlying sacramental theology, the Anglican Establishment instinctively felt that the instruction of the young must be a good thing. In 1898 Jones was unanimously elected by his fellow clergy as one of the two Gloucester diocesan representatives to the Convocation of Canterbury. As such, he was present at St Paul's Cathedral for the Thanksgiving Service for Queen Victoria's eightieth birthday.

In his catechetical work Jones gratefully acknowledges his debt to his Roman Catholic sources. But, writing in 1895, he still concedes differences between the two Communions and places himself on the Anglican side of the divide. 'There are important lessons of form to be learnt from the Roman Catechisms, although, of course, the substance of their teaching does not everywhere coincide with our own.'[42] However, since the late 1880s Jones's thoughts had been turning towards the subject of Reunion, a matter he came to see 'as the chronic difficulty of the Anglican Church'.[43] A growing interest in the life of the early Tractarians proved a catalyst. But it was reading Newman's *Apologia* which 'converted him [...] it was the flame which lit the fire'.[44] Then came Lord Halifax's Bristol speech in 1898, and a clerical friend's suggestion the following year that papal claims needed to be judged solely against the Pope's 'position as the successor of St Peter'. 'This aspect of the great subject, though not new to me, occupied my mind throughout the following winter.'[45] The result was the 1900 Westminster sermon and, ultimately, *England and the Holy See*.

The force of Jones's argument lay partly with the unfailing courtesy with which he advanced it. But even more telling was the historical research upon which it was based. The opening up of various archives in the late nineteenth century permitted a comprehensive reassessment of the Protestant Reformation. Jones read the works of James Gairdner, based on these primary sources, which exploded the myth of the English Reformation as a popular movement. But Jones's books were the result of his own original research. Over many years, he made the sixteenth-century State Papers the subject of his personal investigation.[46] That research led to Jones's inescapable conclusions:

> An *Ecclesia Anglicana* not in conscious dependence upon the Holy See in spirituals is a phenomenon unknown to history before the reign of Henry VIII; [...] we know now, beyond any doubt, that the English people of that day were forced into a condition of separation from that See by an evil-minded monarch for purposes of his own.[47]

The very Protestant Bishop of Manchester accused Jones of attempting a Catholic Counter-Reformation within the Church of England. Jones cheerfully accepted the accusation and took it as the title of his book published around 1920 which constituted Catholic revisionist history in spades.

For the Anglican Establishment, the most alarming aspect of Jones's work was not so much his undermining of the historical basis of the Church of England, but rather the contemporary programme he advocated. He argued Keble, Pusey and Newman had begun something in 1833 which had to be brought to its natural conclusion. He declared himself unsatisfied:

> until the great Oxford Movement appears in its true light as a movement for a Catholic and therefore for a Counter-reformation, and for an enterprise of reunion, which must not rest until it has brought us back into full

communion with the Apostolic See from which Henry dared to separate us.[48]

Jones provided the Establishment with an uncomfortable critique on current developments in the field of Reunion. He acknowledged the achievements of the 1920 Lambeth Conference, but

> there was a hesitancy, a suggestion that Rome might 'remove obstacles' by denying or altering defined dogmas. This is of course ridiculous. Rome is prepared to concede points such as the use of a vernacular liturgy, or the marriage of clergy: but the faith delivered and defined is placed 'beyond the hazard of disputation'.

For Jones, there was simply no conceivable justification, in Scripture or elsewhere, 'for the co-existence of contradictory Communions within the Catholic Church'.[49] It was his life's work to ensure that this division was ended. To this end the Oxford Movement had to become a Roman Movement.

Jones was under no illusions as to the unpopularity of his stance within the Church of England. For the vast majority of Anglicans, it challenged the assumptions of a lifetime. It brought him into conflict with powerful Protestant and Modernist forces. For most Anglo-Catholics also, this was a cause too far, a position too extreme. In 1908 Jones's 'pro-Roman party in the Church of England' was denounced to Archbishop Davidson by, ironically, the notoriously unstable Arnold Matthew (at that point an Old Catholic Bishop):

> It encourages papalist pretensions and the Italian *libido dominationis*, promotes discontent and disloyalty within the Anglican Church and actually assists secessions to Rome. I have been told that certain individuals, who are acting as tools of the Jesuits and Dominicans, are financed by wealthy Roman Catholics so that their propaganda lacks nothing in the temporal order to make it a success.[50]

In the early 1920s Jones counselled a young Papalist: 'I am certain that no effective effort can be made in this enterprise of reunion without much "dirty" work. I mean being ready to be denounced as a traitor, etc., etc.'[51]

Most Catholics wished him well, but found Jones an enigma. Responding on Pius X's behalf to expressions of goodwill sent on the occasion of his Golden Jubilee of priesthood, Merry del Val relayed to Jones the Pope's prayer 'that God will grant you in His own time the gift of Faith necessary for communion with the Catholic Church'.[52] Vincent McNabb was one of the few Catholics who engaged with Jones and consistently wished him well: 'I think God is behind the activities in the English Church. The future is a sealed book. Yet there is a providential course in the Tractarian Movement.'[53] But even McNabb was puzzled as to why Jones did not take the apparently obvious next step. 'That he never felt the need of external communion with the See of Peter remains for me one of the mysteries of human life.'[54] Jones had already given his answer to this question: 'My purpose [...] is to permeate not to poison the body to which we belong; to leaven the entire lump not to persuade others to leave it.'[55] However much Catholics might urge the claims of personal salvation, Jones never wavered: Reunion must be corporate.

In the often prickly world of Papalism, Jones is a refreshingly attractive character. There was nothing difficult or devious about him. Whereas many Papalists were notoriously fractious and motivated by personal empire-building, Jones's only concern was the reunionist cause. He generously welcomed anyone prepared to share the labour. Despite their differing emphases, Jones was happy working with Lord Halifax and the English Church Union. He downplayed his own role in founding the Church Unity Octave so that Wattson might take the credit for it, thus ensuring Catholic support.[56] Jones had been promoting Reunion for more than a generation when the Confraternity of Unity was founded, but immediately threw in his lot with Campbell and Pierce on their arrival in England, consenting to act as the Confraternity's President. At their request, he recapitulated his teaching in *Catholic Reunion*, a copy of which was given to each of the 300 Anglican Bishops attending the 1930 Lambeth Conference.

The disadvantages of Jones's courtesy and kindness became manifest when that same Lambeth Conference sanctioned the use of contraception. Personally, Jones was clear. He viewed the

'Our Anglican friends'

Conference's resolution as 'the greatest blow in the sphere of morals ever struck against the Church of England; all this without a word of official protest; while society is left to sink back into sheer paganism'.[57] Yet one has to ask if Jones's public response was adequate. He counselled against attacking the Lambeth Conference and the Bishops directly, for fear of uniting the episcopacy against the protesters.[58] Lambeth's departure from the unanimous and unbroken moral teaching of the Church distressed and depressed many. Jones sought to comfort them by arguing that the Lambeth resolution had no authority and could safely be ignored:

> About Birth Control—of course it is shocking but I think it is likely to provoke protests perhaps on the part of the episcopal minority and from others—and, unless the rest of Catholic Christendom confirms it, which it never will, it has no Catholic authority and no claim on our conscience.[59]

Such an attitude seemed to justify Catholic criticism that the Papalist position, like all others within Anglicanism, was founded purely on private judgment, that there was no real understanding of the authority of the Church and the need for obedience to that authority. McNabb confronted his friend with a direct challenge: 'On what *Catholic principle* do you allow your souls to remain in communion with condemned heresy?'[60]

In the autumn of 1930 many Papalists suspected that they had arrived at a critical juncture. They continued to venerate Jones as their leader. Campbell extolled him: 'He is marvellous [. . .] so full of energy and zeal, as fresh as a young man.'[61] But Jones himself was indicating that his energies were coming to an end:

> I am prepared to help *in any way I can*—and in a position as subordinate as you like to make it. I am 73½ years of age, and too old to be very vigorous as a leader. But I should love to back up some younger men.[62]

The more astute Papalists were asking themselves where that future leadership was to be found—and were having great difficulty answering that question.

Assessing Jones, one senses a subtle difference from the other Papalists. Notwithstanding his praise of Mussolini and Franco, he was less political. There was a tangible holiness. Thus, his advice on preparation for preaching: 'If possible, a homily should be prepared from beginning to end on our knees, so that when it is produced it may be as if the children said, "I heard a voice from Heaven saying unto me".'[63] There was a note of caution for his fellow Papalists which others would have done well to heed: 'The danger of their movement was that they might fasten their attention on the outward and forget that everything must begin from within. Ceremonial must be the expression of the inward living heart.'[64] McNabb, his friend for forty years, paid him a singular compliment: 'He was a singularly humble and peace-loving soul. In discussion I never knew him lose his temper—nor the point under discussion.'[65]

Henry Fynes-Clinton

Various Anglo-Catholic clergy have been advanced as the model for the Rev. the Hon. Father Hugh Chantry-Pigg, 'the ancient bigot', in Rose Macaulay's novel *The Towers of Trebizond*. It may not have been Henry Joy Fynes-Clinton, Rector of St Magnus-the-Martyr by London Bridge, but he did provide Macaulay with the benchmark for extreme Anglicanism. Chantry-Pigg's own London church was 'several feet higher than St Mary's, Bourne Street and some inches above even St Magnus-the-Martyr'.[66] Fynes-Clinton amused Macaulay, who noted he possessed a collection of 'relics, and can liquefy blood!'[67]

In his case, the double-barrelled surname was inherited, rather than acquired. A distant cousin of the Dukes of Newcastle, Fynes-Clinton had the breeding and manners his fellow Papalists only aspired to. He was not indifferent to that genealogy, commissioning a stone effigy of his eleventh-century ancestor, Geoffrey de Clinton, for the new shrine church at Walsingham. All accusations of snobbery were deflected, however, by Fynes-Clinton's endearing habit of placing his own spectacles on the effigy just to emphasize the family resemblance.[68]

Fynes-Clinton was born in 1875 at Blandford Forum, Dorset, where his father was Rector. Pastorally minded, the father

'Our Anglican friends'

Henry Fynes-Clinton

possessed considerable gifts as an amateur scientist, engineer and artist. From a Low Church tradition, he gradually developed more Tractarian principles.[69] The son took that position and ran with it—fast and far.

After his schooldays at King's, Canterbury, Fynes-Clinton went up to Trinity College, Oxford. Academic studies do not seem to have detained him unduly; he graduated with a Third. The qualification was deemed adequate to act as a private tutor to the children of a Russian nobleman. Fynes-Clinton was to return to Russia after ordination. That experience was put to use as General Secretary of the Anglican and Eastern Churches Association. Archbishop Davidson appointed him to his Committee on Relations with the Eastern Orthodox Church. Having completed his studies at Ely Theological College, Fynes-Clinton was ordained in 1902 and served a series of lengthy curacies in Anglo-Catholic parishes in London and Brighton.

It is not entirely clear how Fynes-Clinton obtained his Papalist views. One anecdote has it that, discussing the possibility of

Reunion with the East, the Orthodox told him to sort out his own house first, i.e. to concentrate on Reunion in the Western Church.[70] While the East continued to exercise a fascination for Fynes-Clinton, he became increasingly preoccupied with the Latin Church. We have already detailed his involvement in the Catholic League and the Church Unity Octave Council. Fynes-Clinton was an organiser and officer of numerous Papalist institutions and committees. He was a co-founder of the Sodality of the Precious Blood, a group of celibate priests committed to using the Roman breviary in its entirety. Like Jones, he too welcomed the founders of the Confraternity of Unity when they arrived from the United States.

Fynes-Clinton was given free rein to implement his liturgical preferences when finally appointed to his own living, the City church of St Magnus-the-Martyr, in 1921. Immediately, he proceeded to transform the church to the appearance it bears today: a Wren preaching box filled with the accoutrements of Baroque Catholicism. The Book of Common Prayer was replaced by the English Missal interpreted by Fortescue and O'Connell. Otherwise kind and charming, Fynes-Clinton metamorphasized into a martinet on the sanctuary, barking at his altar boys: 'No well-trained butler would ever do that!' The changes to liturgy and furnishings did not go unchallenged. He financed the ensuing litigation from his own resources. Asked how he fared during this trying time, Fynes-Clinton replied categorically that he loved it![71] Part of him revelled in controversy and intrigue.

The Papalists knew how to put on a good show, both liturgically and socially, so it is sometimes difficult to judge how wealthy they actually were. Certainly, Fynes-Clinton was able to indulge in regular travel to Italy, France and Belgium. In 1926 he led his parish on pilgrimage to Rome, attending Pius XI's public audience. What the Vatican made of the Anglican pilgrims is not recorded. He forsook the Rectory in Finsbury Circus for his own furnished apartment in St Ermin's Hotel near St James's Park. It was not as if Fynes-Clinton lived a life of luxury; these were simply the trappings of his background. Personally, 'he lived very plainly and if necessary paid little heed to food though he enjoyed the social aspect of a good dinner out'.[72]

'Our Anglican friends'

Reading snatches of correspondence and lengthy tracts a century on, it is easy to parody the Papalists as obsessed with irrelevant ritual and obtuse theological points. We lose the sheer sense of fun — and the genuine zeal for souls which underlay it all. Another Papalist described Fynes-Clinton as 'Don Quixote in a biretta [...] constantly tilting at ecclesiastical windmills',[73] but acknowledged that there was more to the man than this. Invariably, people spoke of Fynes-Clinton's charm. It was more than a social veneer. He was a pastor, genuinely fascinated by people and intensely concerned for their spiritual welfare. Yes, he revelled in matters heraldic and genealogical, but he was absolutely without social prejudice, never speaking up or down to anyone. Fynes-Clinton was equally at ease conversing with a Jewish cabbie or a coster from Billingsgate Market as he was with a duchess or a dean.

Fynes-Clinton was not stupid, but no one ever claimed academic prowess on his behalf. His sermons inclined to dwell on Church politics rather than matters spiritual and theological. One of his altar servers professed himself 'shocked that Fr Fynes [...] actually read the *Daily Mail* rather than the *Times*!'[74] His published output amounted to half a pamphlet. He contented himself with living the Catholic life and the Papalist vision within the Church of England, rather than writing about it.

That does not mean that his clerical activity was limited to his own parish. He spoke on Reunion at Oxford. He wished to join every Papalist initiative, and, from the best possible motives, to control it. His own friends, however, conceded that Fynes-Clinton was not endowed with the gift of administration. In Jones's estimation, 'He is the dearest of men but at times very absent minded [...] Dear old F-C once made an appointment to preach at 3 [different] churches — London, Brighton and somewhere else on the same evening, *entre nous*'.[75] Canon Alan Rees formed the same opinion: 'his character inspires more respect for his personal integrity than confidence in his practical judgment. Personally, I have a great affection for Fynes-Clinton, but I should never trust him to give the right lead at the right moment.'[76]

Someone once said of Fynes-Clinton that he 'combined the mind of an Eastern with the religion of a Western'.[77] He enjoyed a love of intrigue and a penchant for complex schemes which never seemed to materialise. This characterised his response to the Lambeth resolution on contraception, 'the Moral Heresy':

> Fynes is conspiring with [the Jesuit] Woodlock, the idea being that [Woodlock] would move Westminster to issue a sort of general statement on the moral question from the Catholic point of view, if possible avoiding controversial points; so that, on its appearance, we can promptly produce a similar manifesto, 'welcoming and agreeing with' this weighty pronouncement. Fynes thinks this will be very impressive, if we can get it largely signed [...] Personally I think it doubtful that Bourne will resist the temptation to make capital out of the C of E, etc, as usual. Needless to say, this scheme is very much *sub rosa*, and nothing may come of it. (Very often nothing does, where dear Fr Fynes' schemes are concerned!)[78]

This was confirmation of Jones's assessment: 'Fynes is able and full of zeal and courage—but over-worked and apt to be absent-minded and so scarcely in a position to lead—I say this, of course, not in an unpleasant spirit, but his temperament is a fact.'[79]

His biographer is right to note one matter in which Fynes-Clinton differed from many of his fellow Papalists:

> He had a real love for the Church of England, which he saw as the ancient *Ecclesia Anglicana*, if not particularly for State Establishment Anglicanism per se. He loved Canterbury and its cathedral, he venerated King Charles the Martyr, whereas most Anglican Papalists sneered at the cult of a man who had not been canonised. He loved the City of London and all its ancient traditions.[80]

Even if unduly romantic and unrealistic, Fynes-Clinton was deeply attached to his own version of Anglicanism. Admitting the 'rebellious and uncanonical' actions of the sixteenth century, the only question was how the Church of England, as a body, could be brought 'back into union with the other Catholic churches'. Fynes-Clinton was adamant that this could only be on the basis of the Anglican acceptance of the teaching of the Council of Trent.[81]

How Fynes-Clinton stood practically in relation to the Roman Catholic Church, at least in its English incarnation, is not entirely

'Our Anglican friends'

clear. He attempted to summarise the position of the Catholic Church in England for the benefit of a French audience. Like other Papalists, he tended to ignore recusants and converts. Irish priests and Irish immigrants 'contribute to giving the impression the Catholic Church is a foreign institution'. Fynes-Clinton regretted the state of relations between Catholics and Anglicans existing in England: 'exclusive claims and proselytism on the one hand, and the inevitable counter-claims and extensive parish rights of the Anglican Church on the other hand, create a sometimes poisonous rivalry, a spirit of controversy and a serious obstacle to cooperation between us.'[82]

Those views and his subsequent record, therefore, make even more intriguing a report circulating in 1934:

> Did you know that Fynes-Clinton, six years ago I believe it was, took the preliminary steps to make his 'submission'? It was here in Rome. The faculties were actually obtained to receive him, and then he withdrew. I have this on excellent authority.[83]

Was there anything more to this than Vatican gossip and Pierce's desire to encourage other Papalist conversions? All we know for certain is that Fynes-Clinton was travelling in continental Europe in September 1928.

Robert Corbould

Robert Corbould was Fynes-Clinton's Papalist counterpart in London for much of the mid-twentieth century. Like Fynes-Clinton, he was perceived as wealthy and rather 'grand'. He collected Old Masters and travelled frequently, dying on holiday in Tuscany in 1957.

In Corbould's case the money came from West Country brewing. William Robert Corbould was born in Tiverton, Devon, in 1880, the grandson of a Bath brewer. His father was still active in the trade, and may not have approved of his son's ecclesiastical proclivities. At least it was not until his father's premature death that Corbould was able to pursue his vocation. The religion was

Robert Corbould

inherited from his mother's side of the family. It seems to have been his mother who taught him 'as a child to esteem [Lord Halifax] highly'. Having met Halifax as a teenager, Corbould 'fell at once under the charm of his personality'.[84]

Educated at Bristol Grammar School, Corbould shared with Archbishop Goodier the distinction of being our only Conversationalist who did not attend university. (Corbould was not even a graduate.) With money, however, came self-assurance. Unlike Goodier, Corbould felt entirely at home at the heart of the Establishment. He proceeded in 1902 to Lichfield Theological College, which 'was not particularly Anglo-Catholic in ethos'. Corbould's own brand of churchmanship survived 'the cold and Book of Common Prayer type of worship experienced there'.[85]

Following his ordination in 1905, Corbould never looked back. Beginning in a Tractarian parish in Bristol, he accompanied the

'Our Anglican friends'

vicar when he transferred to Basingstoke. He was soon back West, however, at the request of the vicar of St John's, Bathwick, where Corbould's mother and siblings were active parishioners. As senior curate, he was virtually running the parish given the vicar's ill health and lengthy absences. Corbould did not shrink from controversy and plain speaking, even from the pulpit, using 'violent language in speaking of heresy and heretics'. He was appreciated within the parish, but others were not so tolerant of this combative Anglo-Catholic. One outsider went on 'to say that the mentality of the Rev. W. R. Corbould seemed to throw them in the mediaeval period and was not all worthy of the truth and progress of the twentieth century'.[86] Corbould probably took that as a compliment. As secretary of the Bath branch of the English Church Union, he heard Jones tell his audience that 'they should cease treating [Rome] as if she were merely one among a number of communions, and on a plane of equality, and frankly recognise her position as unique, as that of the greatest as well as the oldest church in Christendom'.[87] Corbould wholeheartedly concurred. He was present at one of Pius X's audiences in Rome in 1907.

In 1919 he was appointed Rector of Carshalton in Surrey. All Saints occupies a quintessentially English setting with ponds and park, old pub, cottages and large houses. The church exterior is undistinguished, large with a low tower. There is no indication of the spectacular interior, the work of Bodley and Comper, with its gilded and painted high altar triptych, screen and rood, Lady Chapel and screen, and organ case. 'Corbould amused Comper. "His ecclesiastical tastes are rococo as well as his architectural ones," Comper wrote to John Betjeman in 1948, "he is perfectly satisfied so long as gold leaf is heaped on everywhere."'[88] Carshalton changed significantly during Corbould's long incumbency. A Surrey town of 14,000 on his arrival, the population quadrupled over the next four decades as London expanded relentlessly. Much of the work of the parish, with its three churches, was undertaken by curates.

The rambling Rectory, where Corbould was attended by his man servant, was very much a family home. His mother accompanied him to Carshalton; his brother, Captain Henry Corbould, was also later a resident. There too Corbould brought up his nephews, Paul and Peter, after their father died of the effects of being gassed in the First World War. A number of the family lie buried in the churchyard, Corbould himself beneath the gravestone designed by Comper. A chalice and bible are still discernible in relief, but the gravestone is so overgrown with moss that the inscription around the edge is difficult to decipher. On the path side, however, two words remain visible: 'Catholic Unity'.[89]

Corbould's promotion of Catholic Unity beyond the parochial level began in earnest in 1923. That summer he paid an extended visit to Belgium. He presumed to request, and was granted, an interview with Cardinal Mercier. The two men spent 1½ hours discussing the Reunion of Christendom. A suggestion of Corbould delighted a few, but caused apoplexy among the British Establishment and possibly even came close to derailing the Malines Conversations. Like Fynes-Clinton, Corbould was no scholar or theologian. He ventured that one *beau geste* on the part of Rome might achieve far more than endless discussions. Mercier asked what he had in mind. Corbould felt personal contact was the thing to 'remove many prejudices and create a spirit of goodwill'. He envisaged 'a distinguished Roman prelate' addressing a large body of Anglican clergy and others. Of course, 'no Roman prelate had such prestige in England as [Mercier himself] and that he could speak to the heart of the English people as could no other'. The two men got quite carried away with the possibility. Mercier said he was prepared to face down the likely reaction among English Catholics, if Halifax was willing to endure the unpopularity among Anglicans of hosting the Cardinal. Corbould replied, 'Lord Halifax has been so often called a Romaniser that I am quite sure that in so good a cause he would not mind being called so once more'.[90]

For Halifax, of course, such a visit by Cardinal Mercier 'would be the honour of my life, that nothing in the world with give me greater joy'.[91] He began speculating as to how it might be best achieved and executed: an invitation from the King, a speech to the Church Congress in Plymouth.[92] Archbishop Davidson could be relied upon to pour cold water on the proposal: only Anglicans

'Our Anglican friends'

should address the Church Congress, Foreign Office approval would be required.

> I cannot honestly say that I think the King would wish to step into the fray about the relation of Anglicanism to Romanism, and, if the visit were to have a religious rather than an ecclesiastical character or issue, he *would* be stepping into the fray. And what would Bourne and his friends have to say?[93]

Even the participants in the Malines Conversations were quick to disparage the scheme. Frere argued that Mercier in England would be seen as 'the ally of *recusants*, traducers and proselytisers. The Cardinal in Belgium is a hero, a patriot and a spiritual leader. For the present I think we do best to deal with him there.'[94] There were limits to Anglican tolerance. A flurry of correspondence, and the proposal was diplomatically shelved — to Corbould's immense regret.[95]

Corbould made use of the incident to maintain contact with Mercier and Halifax. He visited the Cardinal again the following August to tell him of another initiative. That spring he and another Anglican cleric, John Douglas, had helped found the undergraduate Society for Reunion at Oxford. Corbould was elected Warden to ensure continuity and assist with activities. The object of the Society was to consider 'the ideal of Reunited Christendom from the Anglican standpoint with regard to the Roman and Eastern Orthodox Churches'. As time went by the emphasis was less Eastern and increasingly Roman. Often meetings comprised no more than a handful of students gathering for informal discussion in their own rooms.[96] But they could attract greater numbers and well-known speakers. Corbould asked Mercier whether he might be prepared to send an expression of his good will to a meeting in November to be chaired by the Vice-Chancellor of the University and addressed by Gore and an Orthodox Archbishop.[97] Mercier willingly complied:

> It is very beautiful to see how, in the midst of the general upheaval in the political world, sincere souls seek to better understand and draw closer to each other. I know your devotion, your zeal for Christ; I entirely agree with them; from the

depths of my heart I pray the Holy Spirit accomplish in you and in the souls of the good and generous youth of Oxford His plans of wisdom and love.[98]

Mercier's message was read 'to the crowded gathering by the Vice-Chancellor—and was received with tremendous enthusiasm and applause'.[99]

Corbould himself addressed the Society on a number of occasions, reiterating the Papalist platform. There was little in the way of original thought. After listening to Corbould speak on 'The Next Step', one Oxford cleric 'complained that for the ordinary parish priest like himself there was little guidance in the paper. He supposed we must let the next step show itself and meanwhile cling to the Truth'.[100]

Another criticism levelled against Corbould was that he would 'touch nothing that he cannot dominate'. Certainly, he declined membership of the Confraternity of Unity managed by the Americans, but Rees's opinion that Corbould was 'nothing else than an ecclesiastical politician and an ignoramus'[101] is unfair.

The Papalists feared that the 1930 Lambeth Conference would present major challenges if the Bishops adopted Modernist theology or an approach to Reunion incompatible with Catholic claims. Faced by such threats, it was eminently sensible to attempt some rationalisation of the proliferation of Papalist societies (most comprising the same personnel) and ensure their cooperation. The suggestion seems first to have been mooted at a meeting of the Church Unity Octave Council held at Carshalton on 18 February 1930 and attended by a representative cross-section of Papalists, less the Confraternity Americans.[102] A few months later the Catholic League's *Messenger* reported the outcome:

> We are glad to announce that cooperation between the Societies working for Reunion with the Holy See is being secured by the formation of a joint Council representing CL, the Sodality of the Precious Blood, the Society of St Thomas of Canterbury, the Catholic Propaganda Society and the Confraternity of Unity, under the name of the Council for Promoting Catholic Unity.[103]

Not everyone was so glad.

'Our Anglican friends'

In November 1930, Campbell attended a CPCU meeting at St Magnus-the-Martyr chaired by Corbould. Despite the deepening crisis, no further meeting was planned for another six months. Campbell was not entirely sorry:

> For I don't altogether approve of that Council; it might so easily turn into another society and claim superior powers over the already existing organisation. I am afraid that I did not care for the famous Fr Corbould.[104]

It was not just the Americans. Fynes-Clinton also queried the wisdom of this development:

> [I] feel that we have enough societies and that it would be very confusing to have the CL, the Confraternity and a new one side by side with differences only in technical basis. They would have to form some very close means of cooperation or membership. I do not like to dampen them, but I think it would be very difficult.[105]

Others dismissed Corbould's chances of success: 'I don't think anything will come of his proposed new society.'[106] Corbould may not have consciously expressed it this way to himself, but one is bound to conclude that the CPCU was founded because he wanted his own society, just as Fynes-Clinton had the Catholic League and the Church Unity Octave Council.

It is difficult to be too harsh on Corbould. He was genial and cultured. Within his limitations, he laboured consistently over a lifetime for the cause dearest to his heart. Where that heart lay is apparent from the terms of his will:

> I commend my body to the earth and my soul to God. I die in the true faith of the One Holy Catholic and Apostolic Church. I submit my whole mind and will to her as an infallible and divine authority. If I have ever believed or taught anything contrary to the Catholic Faith I repudiate my error and I ask all men to believe that it was never my will but arose not from intention but from deficiency of knowledge. I have laboured for the amendment of the unhappy schism between England and the Holy See and if I die out of visible communion with the Holy Father it is not from any substantive difference of faith but from circumstances beyond my control. I most

sincerely ask pardon of all my sins through the saving merits of the Divine Redeemer Jesus Christ my Lord and God upon whose boundless mercy I rest all my hope of final salvation. I beg our Blessed Lady of whom I have ever endeavoured to be a devoted client, S Peter the Apostle, S Francis de Sales, S William, S Chad, S Robert and Blessed Pius X my patrons, my Guardian Angel and all the blessed saints to pray for my soul.'[107]

His Catholic nephew recalls asking: 'Uncle Robert, why aren't you a Catholic?' There was not a moment's hesitation: 'I *am* a Catholic. It is my mission to bring the Anglican Church to Rome.'[108]

Leslie Simmonds

Leslie Simmonds's involvement in these events is explicable entirely by the fact that he was Corbould's curate in Carshalton. As such, he was commandeered to act as secretary for various Papalist organisations such as the CUOC. Simmonds fell in with Corbould's wishes, but he was no cypher. He would not have taken the appointment in Carshalton if his own preferences had not lain in that direction.

Simmonds was the youngest of our participants. Born in 1901, he was the son of a pharmacist from Portland, Dorset. A scholar at Sidney Sussex College, Cambridge, he held the distinction of being a Wrangler (gaining a First Class degree in Mathematics). Simmonds remained in Cambridge to train for Anglican ministry at Westcott House, a theological college basing itself on scriptural scholarship and eschewing clerical partisanship in one direction or another. His first appointment made no such pretensions to neutrality. Simmonds taught for two years at Ardingly College in Sussex, a Woodard Foundation firmly in the Anglo-Catholic tradition. From there he went to Carshalton in 1926, serving as Corbould's curate for ten years.

Simmonds delivered papers to the Society for Reunion and others, and wrote pamphlets for the Papalists. These were mainly historical. They followed the party line, but with none of the exuberance apparent in the other Papalists. After Carshalton, he moved to a curacy at All Saints, Margaret Street, in central

'Our Anglican friends'

Leslie Simmonds

London. It was another bastion of Anglo-Catholicism, but Simmonds's intellectual apostolate developed in a different direction. He published a series of lectures given in the parish as *What Think ye of Christ?* Simmonds aimed to unite the devotional and intellectual aspects of faith. He set out the Church's faith regarding the nature of Christ in a non-adversarial fashion, systematically expounding orthodox doctrine. He touched on the question of Christ's human knowledge—the issue which had first propelled Scott into the limelight in his dispute with Gore—in a much gentler fashion: 'The solution of the problem is to be found not in the putting away of omniscience but in its restraint. Beyond that we cannot go nor do we need to do so.'[109]

A more substantial work followed in the successive year, an attempt to give a rational account of the faith in the light of 'modern researches in every branch of science and learning'.[110] In many ways it is a very modern book. Simmonds tackled evolution head-on:

> Now there is, on the face of it, nothing in this theory at all contrary to religious conceptions [...] [Evolution is] not an argument against the existence of God, but rather the evidence of an immense Mind and Energy pervading the whole of creation. Darwin himself said the understanding revolts against the proposition that the universe had evolved by 'blind chance'.[111]

Christianity had no problem in accepting that the human being comprised a unity of soul, created directly and from nothing by God, and physical body, which was the subject of evolution. Simmonds also demonstrated how the Church had been part of God's design from all ages:

> The idea of individualist Christians, that is of followers of Christ apart from the body of believers, thinking out their own creed and making their own rules of worship, is one which was never even visualised in the primitive days of Christianity, and which, in fact, never entered the human mind for fifteen centuries after the Resurrection.[112]

Simmonds has nothing to say, however, on where that Church is to be found today and avoids all confessional controversies. Interestingly, he cites D'Arcy, but no Papalist.

Presumably, Simmonds had satisfied himself as to any qualms of conscience he may have had regarding the Church of England. He seems to have decided that the differences between Anglicanism and Catholicism were of less import than addressing the scepticism prevalent in the world. Although he directed his energies elsewhere, temperamentally he seems to have been closest to Jones, exercising a ministry which was simultaneously pastoral, devotional and intellectual, avoiding harsh polemics where possible. In September 1932, Simmonds gave a paper to priests:

> There is increasing danger, as the policy of numbers becomes increasingly attractive to its leaders, that Anglo-Catholicism will become a mere ritualistic modernism, an empty shell of Catholic ceremonial without the Catholic Faith behind it. And what does ceremonial matter if it is not the outward and visible symbol of a living faith?[113]

Exactly the same message delivered by Jones a generation earlier.

Simmonds obtained his own parish, St Alban the Martyr, Teddington, 'the cathedral of the Thames valley', in 1941. Seventeen years later he moved to Gloucester Cathedral, where he remained until his sudden death in 1966, acting as sacristan and precentor. His obituary is a record of a vanished world of Anglicanism:

> Not only had he a true and sweet tenor voice, but his character had a flavour of Barchester. Trollope would have loved to chronicle his enthusiasm for church music, growing roses and watching county cricket. He taught mathematics in our King's School [...] where he was regarded with respect and affection; and we miss in The College the warmth of his friendship, salted as it was with a sly sense of humour.[114]

William Monahan

In many respects William Beattie Monahan was the most unusual of the Anglican participants: Irish (at least on his father's side) and a convert to Anglicanism. He was born in 1867 in Co. Donegal, the eldest son of a well-known Methodist minister. After studying at Trinity College, Dublin, Monahan became a Methodist minister himself, crossing over to England to serve in Cheltenham, Wisbech and Birmingham. A sermon preached by Charles Gore in Birmingham had a dramatic impact. Subsequent meetings with the Anglican theologian convinced Monahan of the need for the sacramental system and catholicity in Church life.

In 1894 Monahan announced his resignation from Methodist ministry to take orders in the Church of England, giving as his reasons doubts as to the ecclesiastical status of Methodism and opposition to the itinerancy principle, whereby ministers were frequently rotated between chapels.[115] Two of his brothers followed him into the Anglican Communion, one ending his days as the Bishop of Monmouth. Their father cut them off completely. A fourth brother remained a Methodist minister, serving in India.

After curacies in Birmingham and Coventry, Monahan arrived, with his wife and eldest daughter, at his own living of St Swithun's, Worcester, in 1902. (Old St Martin's was added as a chapel of ease

William Monahan

three years later.) He was not content with some Low Church counterpart to Methodism. Photographs show the young Anglican cleric confidently attired in cassock and biretta. Although Gore was responsible for his entry into the Church of England, Monahan maintained a critical attitude towards his mentor from the outset, believing 'that Gore was inclined to allow his freedom to pass into licence'.[116] The reservations were reciprocated. Inducting Monahan to St Swithun's, Gore, by now Bishop of Worcester, warned his parishioners:

> The Rector had made the solemn declaration of adhesion to the doctrines of the Church of England, and the solemn promise that he would use the services prescribed in the Book of Common Prayer, and these only, except so far as lawful

'Our Anglican friends'

authority allowed. 'I hope you took note of that', continued the Bishop [...] '[the parishioners] have a perfect right and duty', added his Lordship with emphasis, 'to claim that nothing shall be taught except what can be taught out of the Holy Scripture [...] then you have a right and a duty to claim that they shall use the services of the Prayer Book and those only [...]'[117]

Monahan chose to ignore the episcopal admonition in its entirety.

Immediately, he threw himself into the activities of the Worcester branch of the English Church Union, and he began a long and gradual campaign to adapt his parish to Catholic ceremonial and teaching. When the Bishop refused permission for the Blessed Sacrament to be reserved in the church, Monahan simply established a chapel for the purpose in the churchyard, bringing the Blessed Sacrament into the church and placing it on the high altar for safety reasons during the First World War. With his brother, Monahan compiled the *St Swithun's Prayer Book*, a compendium on Catholic devotions and sacraments. The Anglican hierarchy was not amused. Successive Bishops refused to visit to confer Confirmation. The Rector does not seem to have been unduly concerned.

Monahan was a man of many parts: a prize golfer, a poet and, later in life, an accomplished watercolourist. He also wrote prolifically. There were a series of tracts under the pseudonym, 'The Voice from Worcester', the titles clearly indicating their ecclesiastical stance, e.g. *Rome the Goal of the Oxford Movement, Benediction in the Church of England* and *Canterbury and York: Two Provinces of Rome*. Monahan compiled a number of commentaries on the *Summa Theologica*, and published *St Thomas Aquinas on the Sacraments*.

His position was perfectly Papalist. The Church of England was a valid part of the Universal Church but 'suffering from a functional disability, which only union with Rome can remedy'. Monahan had no time for liberalism or moderate Anglo-Catholicism: 'We see the Modernists with the trappings of Catholicism denying that Jesus is God.' The Oxford Movement was providential; its role was to help Anglicans understand the ultimate destination to which they were called: 'Rome will be the only harbour from the tidal wave of the anti-Christian teaching, and from the onslaught of Communism, and of militant atheism, and from the worldwide power of the Anti-Christ.'[118]

Yet simultaneously, Monahan deprecated individual submissions to Rome and held out for corporate Reunion. He welcomed the work of the Roman clergy in their midst and conceded that Anglicans would have to look increasingly to the Roman hierarchy for guidance on moral issues. But he then issued the most solemn of warnings:

> *To leave the Church of England would be the abandonment of a trust* laid on them by Almighty God, the dereliction of a duty to the Church of their birth, and a desertion of those priests from whom they have learned the way of salvation, to whom they owe their love of the Catholic Church and from whose lives they have learned their devotion to the sacraments.[119]

Monahan passed over in silence his own 'abandonment' of the Methodism of his birth. More positively, he argued for the validity of Anglican sacraments and a specifically Anglican spirituality with a significant contribution to make to the life of the wider Catholic Church.

Monahan remained in Worcester until his death in 1948. His vision was essentially parochial. It was for the priest to introduce and develop the Catholic life in his parish, which he did consistently over almost half a century. This bottom up movement would, he hoped, eventually lead to Anglican Bishops understanding themselves as the centre of Catholic authority in their dioceses and regularising their position in the eyes of Rome and the East.[120] In many ways Monahan was isolated from Papalist life elsewhere in the country, known to a wider audience only through his pamphlets. The Confraternity of Unity were delighted, therefore, when he agreed to attend and deliver a paper to their meeting in Oxford in September 1930 to determine 'how we stand in the light of the Lambeth pronouncements'.[121]

'Our Anglican friends'

Notes

1. Goodier to Marchant, 17 March 1931, OUL, Marchant, 299/174.
2. Butler to Marchant, 28 November 1927, OUL, Marchant, 299/13.
3. Ramsay to Marchant, 11 April 1928, OUL, Marchant, 315/66; 18 April 1928, OUL, Marchant, 315/69.
4. J. G. Morton Howard to Pierce, 4 December 1929, PHA/Rea/CU1/209.
5. Marchant to Lang, 12 November 1929, LPL, Lang Papers, 97/208.
6. Marchant to Pierce, 26 December 1929, PHA/Rea/CU1/216.
7. Marchant to Lang, 14 May 1931, LPL, Lang Papers, 107/22-4.
8. A. Hughes, *The Rivers of the Flood: A Personal Account of the Catholic Revival in England in the Twentieth Century* (London: Faith Press, 1961), p. 148.
9. 'Paulinus', 'Why don't they go over?', *The Pilot*, 59 (July 1938), pp. 1-8.
10. D. Hole, *'Anglican Papalists'* (London: Society for Promoting Catholic Unity, 1942), pp. 27-8.
11. See Mascall, 'The Ultra-Catholic', p. xix.
12. J. de B. de la Saudée, *Anglicans et catholiques: Le Problème de l'union anglo-romaine (1833-1933)* (Paris: Libraire Plon, 1948), p. 208.
13. H. St John, OP, 'Pietas Anglicana', in *Essays in Christian Unity, 1928-1954* (London: Blackfriars Publications, 1955), p. 39 (originally published in *Blackfriars*, March 1937).
14. T. Whitton, *The Necessity for Catholic Reunion* (London: Williams & Norgate, 1933), p. 49.
15. B. and M. Pawley, *Rome and Canterbury through Four Centuries: A Study of the Relations between the Church of Rome and the Anglican Churches 1530-1981* (London: Mowbrays, 1981), p. x.
16. Yelton, *Anglo-Papalism*.
17. G. Curtiss, *Paul Couturier and Unity in Christ* (London: SCM Press, 1964), p. 163.
18. *London Gazette* (22 Nov. 1940), p. 6729.
19. S. H. Scott to Pierce, 19 October 1928, PHA/Rea/CU1/82; Scott, *Islip Rural Deanery Magazine* (Nov. 1924).
20. S. H. Scott, *Anglo-Catholicism and Re-union* (London: Robert Scott, 1923), pp. 7, 10, 16, 31.
21. S. H. Scott, *The Eastern Churches and the Papacy* (London: Sheed & Ward, 1928).
22. *Tablet* (4 June 1927), p. 26.
23. H. Pope, OP, Review of *The Eastern Churches and the Papacy*, *Blackfriars*, 9/104 (Nov. 1928), p. 697.

24 *Bulletin*, 5 (Epiphany 1929), p. 3.

25 Morton Howard, 'Sidney Herbert Drane-Scott', *The Pilot*, 3/1 (March 1949), p. 19.

26 Scott to Pierce, 14 March 1929, PHA/Rea/CU1/99.

27 Scott to Jones, 21 August 1925, PHA/Rea/CU1/63a.

28 Scott to de Lilienfeld, 1 December 1928, Chevetogne/de Lilienfeld.

29 Scott to Pierce, 31 October 1928, PHA/Rea/CU1/84.

30 Pierce to Morton Howard, 13 February 1930 (copy), PHA/Rea/CU2/248.

31 Pierce to Scott, 8 March 1930 (copy), PHA/Rea/CU2/268; Pierce to A. Acheson, 7 February 1930 (copy), PHA/Rea/CU2/240; Morton Howard to Pierce, 12 February 1930, PHA/Rea/CU2/246.

32 Morton Howard to Pierce, 30 October 1929, PHA/Rea/CU1/186; 14 February 1930, PHA/Rea/CU2/251; 4 December 1929, PHA/Rea/CU1/209.

33 Campbell to Morton Howard, 31 March 1930 (copy), PHA/Rea/CU2/292.

34 Scott to Campbell, 30 January 1930, PHA/Rea/CU1/233.

35 Pierce to Marchant, 23 October 1929, PHA/Rea/CU1/181; Scott to Campbell, 30 January 1930, PHA/Rea/CU1/233.

36 Morton Howard to Pierce, 12 February 1930, PHA/Rea/CU2/246.

37 Morton Howard to Campbell, 23 September 1930, PHA/Rea/CU2/500.

38 Morton Howard, 'Sidney Herbert Drane-Scott', pp. 16–19; Scott, Will, 20 November 1943.

39 M. Villain, 'Preface', in S. J. Jones, *L'Église d'Angleterre et le Saint-Siège: Propos pour la réunion* (Grenoble: B. Artaud, 1940).

40 S. J. Jones, *The Clergy and the Catechism* (London: Skeffington and Son, 1895), p. 11.

41 *Ibid.*, pp. 2–3.

42 *Ibid.*, p. 56.

43 Jones, *England and the Holy See*, p. vi.

44 Villain, 'Preface', p. ix.

45 S. J. Jones, 'Steps to Reunion', Part I, *Reunion*, 1/1 (March 1934), p. 14.

46 Jones, *The Counter-Reformation in the Church of England*, pp. 49 n. 117.

47 *Ibid.*, p. 11.

48 *Ibid.*, p. 116.

49 Jones, Address, 'Rome and Reunion', 4 June 1928, PHA, OUSR, Minute Book, vol. I, pp. 154, 153.

50 A. Matthew to Davidson, 1 October 1908, LPL, Davidson Papers, 332/329–30.

51 Jones to S. M. Harris, 24 July 1922, PHA, Harris Papers.

52 R. Cardinal Merry del Val to Jones, 8 January 1909, PHA/Rea/CU1/53.

53 McNabb to Jones, 11 August 1903, PHA/Rea/CU1/31.

54 McNabb, Memorandum, 17 March 1943 (copy), Douai Abbey, Dominican Archives.

55 S. J. Jones, 'Catholic Reunion: Question and Answer', *Bulletin*, 11 (Michaelmas 1930), p. 4.

56 Campbell to Pierce, 26 November 1930, BCA, Pierce Bequest, CU Founding and Letters.

57 Jones, 'Foreword', in Whitton, *The Necessity for Catholic Reunion*, p. 14.

58 Campbell to Pierce, 21 November 1930, BCA, Pierce Bequest, CU Founding and Letters.

59 Jones to Pierce, 23 August 1930, PHA/Rea/CU2/437.

60 McNabb, Review of *Catholic Reunion*, *Blackfriars*, 11/126 (Sept. 1930), p. 579.

61 Campbell to Pierce, 26 November 1930, BCA, Pierce Bequest, CU Founding and Letters.

62 Jones to Pierce, 8 September 1930, PHA/Rea/CU2/466.

63 Jones, *The Clergy and the Catechism*, p. 97.

64 Jones, Address to the Leamington branch of the English Church Union, *Leamington Spa Courier*, 13 October 1911, p. 4.

65 McNabb, Memorandum, 17 March 1943 (copy), Douai Abbey, Dominican Archives.

66 R. Macaulay, *The Towers of Trebizond* (London: Collins, 1956), p. 18.

67 Macaulay to H. Johnson, 18 July 1951 cited Macaulay, *Letters to a Friend, 1950–1952* (London: Collins, 1961), p. 155.

68 B. Lunn and J. Haselock, *Henry Joy Fynes-Clinton* (London: The Church Literature Association, 1983), p. 4.

69 I. R. Young, Draft article on Fynes-Clinton, undated, LPL, Young Papers, 4288/63–6.

70 Interview with B. Lunn, 6 March 2014.

71 *Ibid.*

72 Young, Draft article on Fynes-Clinton, undated, LPL, Young Papers, 4288/70.

73 C. Stephenson, *Walsingham Way*, 2nd edn (Norwich: Canterbury Press, 2008), p. 135.

74 W. R. F. Browning at http://www.achs.org.uk/newsletter.html (accessed on 29 November 2013).

75 Jones to Wattson, 25 May 1934, GARC, Wattson 821-2-16.

76 A. H. Rees to J. H. Clements-Ansell, 21 August 1936 (copy), PHA/Rea/CU3.

77 Lunn and Haselock, *Henry Joy Fynes-Clinton*, p. 5.

78 Joblin to Pierce, 7 October 1930, PHA/Rea/CU2/529.

79 Jones to Pierce, 8 September 1930, PHA/Rea/CU2/466.

80 A. T. J. Salter, *The Anglican Papalist: A Personal Portrait of Henry Joy Fynes-Clinton* (London: The Anglo-Catholic History Society, 2012), p. 57.

81 H. J. Fynes-Clinton, Address, 'The Tridentine Creed', PHA, OUSR, Minute Book, vol. I, p. 164.

82 H. J. Fynes-Clinton, 'The Current Position of Anglicanism', *Revue apologétique*, 64/616 (Jan. 1937), pp. 67, 68.

83 Pierce to Harris, 28 February 1934, PHA, Harris Papers.

84 W. R. Corbould, Sermon on the centenary of Halifax's birth, *The Pilot*, 70 (June 1939), pp. 4–7.

85 M. Yelton, *Alfred Hope Patten and the Shrine of Our Lady of Walsingham* (Norwich: Canterbury Press, 2006), p. 30.

86 *Bath Chronicle and Weekly Gazette* (25 Nov. 1911), p. 2.

87 *Bath Chronicle and Weekly Gazette* (2 Dec. 1909), p. 6.

88 A. Symondson, SJ, and S. A. Bucknall, *Sir Ninian Comper: An Introduction to His Life and Work with Complete Gazeteer* (Reading: Spire Books, 2006), p. 184.

89 The full inscription, as requested by Corbould, reads: 'First President of the Society for Promoting Catholic Unity'.

90 Corbould to Halifax, undated (August 1923) (copy), BIY, Halifax, Malines Papers, A4/271/1.

91 Halifax to Portal, 24 August 1923 (copy), BIY, Halifax, Malines Papers, A4/271/1.

92 Halifax to Portal, 24 August 1923 (copy), BIY, Halifax, Malines Papers, A4/271/1.

93 Davidson to Halifax, 28 August 1923, BIY, Halifax, Malines Papers, A4/271/1.

94 Frere to Halifax, 28 August 1923, BIY, Halifax, Malines Papers, A4/271/1.

95 Corbould to Mercier, 7 November 1923, AAM 6/465.

96 PHA, OUSR, Minute Book, vol. I, pp. 2, 4.

97 Corbould to Mercier, 22 November 1924, AAM 14/659.

98 Mercier to Corbould, 24 November 1924 (copy), AAM 15/660.

99 Corbould to Mercier, 8 January 1925, AAM 16/661.

100 PHA, OUSR, Minute Book, 19 November 1928, vol. I, pp. 163–4.

101 Rees to Clements-Ansell, 21 August 1936 (copy), PHA/Rea/CU3.

102 Joblin to Pierce, 19 February 1930, PHA/Rea/CU2/255.

103 *Messenger*, 66 (April–June 1930).

[104] Campbell to Pierce, 21 November 1930, BCA, Pierce Bequest, CU Founding and Letters.
[105] Fynes-Clinton to Campbell, 26 February 1931, PHA/Rea/CU3.
[106] Joblin to Campbell, 6 March 1931, PHA/Rea/CU3.
[107] Corbould, Will, 27 July 1952.
[108] E. Corbould, OSB, Interview, Ampleforth, 17 February 2014.
[109] L. F. Simmonds, *What Think ye of Christ?* (London: The Centenary Press, 1938), p. 81.
[110] L. F. Simmonds, *The Framework of Faith* (London: Longman, Green & Co., 1939), p. xi.
[111] *Ibid.*, p. 23.
[112] *Ibid.*, p. 227.
[113] L. F. Simmonds, 'Modernism and Reunion', cited *Bulletin*, 17 (Chair of Peter 1933), p. 22.
[114] Dean S. Evans in Friends of Gloucester Cathedral, *Annual Report* (1967), p. 6.
[115] *Gloucester Citizen* (15 Jan. 1894).
[116] W. B. Monahan, Memoirs, vol. II, PHA, Monahan Papers.
[117] *Worcestershire Chronicle* (7 Feb. 1903), p. 6.
[118] W. B. Monahan ('The Voice from Worcester'), *Rome the Goal of the Oxford Movement* (undated, c. 1933).
[119] W. B. Monahan ('The Voice from Worcester'), *Loyalty to the Church of England* (undated).
[120] W. B. Monahan, *What is Catholic Authority? And how can we use it in the Church of England* (1928).
[121] Pierce to Joblin, 2 September 1930, PHA/Rea/CU2/458 (copy).

✠ 5 ✠

The Thackeray Hotel

'The Preliminary Meeting'

In the autumn of 1930 both Sir James Marchant and the Papalists were looking for someone to talk to. In the three years since Marchant's initial approach to Archbishop Davidson, he had consistently failed to secure Anglican participation in, or approval for, his proposed conversations.

The Papalists were shocked and confused in the aftermath of 'the Moral Heresy' of the Lambeth Conference. Speaking for those in the Church of England who shared his views, Pierce wrote: 'Unless our Catholics do something really effective regarding this birth control business, we are fatally compromised and our position made impossible.'[1] Everyone agreed that united and decisive action was required. But what form should it take? With fond memories of his moribund Society of St Thomas of Canterbury, Jones suggested 'inviting RC leaders to read well-conceived and serious papers'. He wondered whether the CU might care to organise such a programme in Oxford.[2]

In October 1930, Marchant informed Archbishop Goodier of a new attempt to give impetus to conversations on the subject of Reunion, and sought his cooperation. Goodier assured him:

> I thoroughly sympathise and agree with all you are doing; and I need not say that I will gladly help in whatever poor way I may be able. But do not expect too much of one. I am notoriously not clever at answering difficulties.

The Archbishop was not particularly helpful or specific as to the identity of possible Anglican participants: 'You do not want men from either side merely because they are well known, but because they are very much in earnest.'[3]

In fact, these were precisely the type of Anglicans who eventually emerged: men not 'well known', but 'very much in earnest'. They were men whom the Catholics expressed a desire to meet on the basis of the books they had written and the Catholics had read. That suggestion is unlikely to have come from Goodier. He admitted to his lack of contacts outside the enclosed world of English Catholicism. Far more likely the suggestion originated with Butler and D'Arcy. Butler had long been accustomed to mixing with Anglicans in consequence of his scholarly activities and time at Cambridge. His book of essays, *Religions of Authority and the Religion of the Spirit*, published that summer, took issue with the same liberal Anglo-Catholics whom our Papalists opposed. D'Arcy, through his presence in Oxford and particularly his attendance at the Society for Reunion, had met most of these Papalists.

Scott was the Papalist whose work the Catholics were most familiar with. His *Eastern Churches and the Papacy*, published in 1928, had been widely and favourably reviewed in the Catholic Press. Scott had spoken on the subject to a mixed audience at the final meeting of the Society of St Thomas of Canterbury the preceding summer. He regularly attended meetings of the Oxford Society for Reunion. Marchant contacted Scott concerning his proposed conversations some time towards the end of 1930, and received a favourable response. Interestingly, some Anglicans viewed Scott as one of the main instigators of the Conversations. The CU viewed this development as Scott's latest salvo in his ongoing campaign against Pierce. Having been briefed by Jones, Campbell believed that the Conversations had been 'engineered by [Scott] and Sir James Marchant [...] Evidently this is SHS's counterblast to CU.'[4]

Butler and D'Arcy also knew of Jones. His classic Papalist text, *England and the Holy See*, had been updated just that year as *Catholic Reunion*, reviewed by McNabb in *Blackfriars* in September 1930. Jones cited Jarrett in this later work, and makes passing reference to Butler's recently published history of the First Vatican Council. Jones had founded the Society of St Thomas of Canterbury with the very intention of bringing together Catholic and Anglican scholars. D'Arcy would have encountered him in Oxford at the

The Thackeray Hotel

Society for Reunion. Marchant implies that the Catholics asked to meet Jones in addition to Scott. The initial approach came through Scott in a confidential letter sent at the very end of 1930. It was an invitation to a preliminary meeting on 6 January 1931 at the Thackeray Hotel. Jones declined.

With arrangements for the Conversations already at an advanced stage, Marchant made one final attempt to secure official Anglican recognition and approval for his endeavour. He understood that Archbishop Lang had been unwilling to commit himself prior to the Lambeth Conference. Very well, the Conference was over, would the Archbishop now be willing to make contact with Cardinal Bourne? If Lang was not prepared to do that, would he at least allow Marchant to tell the participants that the Conversations had his blessing? To encourage him, Marchant informed the Archbishop that Goodier, Butler and D'Arcy were attending with the Cardinal's blessing.[5]

Marchant received no response. While Lang was desperate to avoid any form of commitment, this was not a calculated snub. Having suffered a blood clot through the heart, the Archbishop struggled with serious health problems and was away from his duties for the first four months of 1931. We know his thoughts, however, from his correspondence with Temple at York. The two Archbishops agreed that, as spiritual head of the worldwide Anglican Communion, Lang could not be treated simply as the counterpart of the Archbishop of Westminster. Given 'the Pope's avowed attitude' expressed in *Mortalium Animos*, they felt any involvement by Lambeth inappropriate. Temple advised:

> you should confine yourself to expressions of friendly interest in any discussions which may be privately arranged. Certainly I see no reason to hinder them, and a good deal of reason why they should happen *provided* that you are not implicated, and that they have no official status at all.[6]

The relapse in Lang's health meant that the Conversations began without even these 'expressions of friendly interest', but Marchant felt that he could delay no longer.

As Sir James Marchant's professional and social profile increased, he moved from New Barnet to the Georgian elegance of Bloomsbury's Bedford Square. He and Lady Marchant did not remain there long; in the late 1920s they settled in Bournemouth. However, Sir James retained a central London base in rooms at the Thackeray Hotel, directly opposite the British Museum. American tourists of the time waxed lyrical in praise of the 'quaint and comfortable' hotel. In fact, it was barely forty years old. It boasted modern facilities and a respectable family reputation, but others found this Temperance establishment modest and austere. The building is still there today at 57 Great Russell Street. Brick with stone facings, it has the appearance of a mansion block in an affluent London neighbourhood. It is now a student hostel, Helen Graham House. But eighty years ago over a six-month period, it hosted a curious gathering of clerics meeting for highly confidential discussions.

We only know of the meeting on 6 January through Jones, who was not present, and William Hough, the 71-year-old suffragan Bishop of Woolwich. How he came to be there, we are not certain; he was unclear himself. This was the closest Marchant came to catching an Anglican bishop. This preliminary meeting sought to identify other Anglican participants. Marchant, Hough and Scott were present, and, it would seem, Goodier and D'Arcy. Marchant no doubt mentioned his most recent attempt to gain recognition for the Conversations from Archbishop Lang. The two Jesuits counselled caution: 'Don't insist on making these groups *formal* or asking for them to be recognised, or you'll wreck them.'[7]

While most apologetic and praying 'for God's blessing on your venture', Hough excused himself the following day from any further involvement. He protested that he was ill equipped 'to enter into a discussion with skilled Roman theologians'. This was really not his scene at all: 'I am an old-fashioned High Churchman, who follows the teaching of Bishop Gore, and I have no Roman tendency.' Hough was not quite the moderate he professed to be—he had preached at a CUO Mass at St Magnus-the-Martyr— but admitting discipleship of Bishop Gore would have aroused Scott's immutable wrath. Hough was wise to withdraw.

What made Bishop Hough feel 'rather out of place there [were] the names considered'. Hough helpfully gives the names of those

Anglicans under consideration, men who 'represent a point of view which is not my own': Jones, Fynes-Clinton, Baverstock and Corbould.[8] Alban Baverstock (1871–1950) was another Papalist and a former Master of the priestly Society of the Holy Cross. After three decades as Rector of the Dorset village of Hinton Martel, he had recently taken up the position of Priest-Director of the Holy Family Homes near Reigate. Jones mentions the hope that Baverstock would be present at a meeting the following month, but there is no evidence of his actually attending any of the Conversations.[9]

Fynes-Clinton had no literary output associated with his name. He owes his involvement to Scott's recommendation. The two men had travelled together to Belgium in November 1928 to visit the Monks of Unity.[10] Scott discovered in Fynes-Clinton a similarly unyielding spirit. He had invited Scott to address the Catholic League priests 'on the menace of Modernism'. The meeting resolved to form a committee to draft an open letter protesting against Bishop Headlam's invitation to Henry Major to speak at the Church Congress. That anti-Modernist committee comprised Scott, Fynes-Clinton and Jones.[11] Fynes-Clinton and Corbould came as a package, and Simmonds followed in Corbould's retinue. Monahan, too, would have been known to Scott through his pamphlets and appearances at Oxford.

As late as 29 December 1930, Marchant was expecting three Catholic participants. The addition of a fourth, Jarrett, at a late stage might simply reflect a desire to give the Catholics a greater parity of numbers when faced by six Anglicans.

'Talks over tea'

Having declined Scott's invitation to the preliminary meeting, Jones received a second letter, this time from Marchant. He was flattered by the attention. Perhaps he could make it up to London after all. It might even prove convenient given Sir James's suggested date fell within the Church Unity Octave when Jones was due to return to preach at St Matthew's, Westminster. If he was not too tired after the effort, Jones agreed to attend the meeting at the Thackeray Hotel at 2.30 pm on Wednesday, 21 January.

Jones went along in a bit of a muddle as to his expectations. His thoughts were still firmly bound to Papalist societies past and present. These Conversations with Catholics might lead to 'the revival and perhaps reconstruction of the Society of S. Thomas of Canterbury'. He hoped Scott would not 'deter Sir James from joining the Confraternity of Unity if he begins to look in that direction'.[12]

If Jones was confused as to the objective of the Conversations, he was not alone. For Cardinal Bourne, they were simply 'conversations of explanation',[13] which it was so much more appropriate should occur at home than in Belgium. The Anglicans maintained that this was their desire too: 'to attain to that clarity on both sides by which we may come to understand each other plainly and without any ambiguity'. Yet clearly there were far more ambitious goals, some stated, others not. The Anglicans stated their desire 'to end the external schism'.[14] The Catholics only mentioned the word 'conversion' amongst themselves,[15] but the Papalists assumed that such would be the calculation of their Roman counterparts. The real complication was the lack of transparency on the part of Marchant, who chaired the Conversations. No doubt thinking to increase the likelihood of success, he told the Anglicans the only purpose was to give mutual explanations and 'to ease the situation between the Catholic Roman Church' and others.[16] Meanwhile Marchant enticed Cardinal Bourne with the prospect of the Papalists being received into the Church as the forerunners of a much more numerous group of Anglicans.[17] Such incompatible stances adopted by the 'impartial' chairman did not bode well for the future.

The prestige of the Catholic Church in the eyes of the Anglican participants had risen enormously immediately prior to the first Conversation. The preceding autumn Fynes-Clinton had devised a plan, considered fanciful by others. He envisaged Cardinal Bourne making a statement of orthodox moral teaching, to which sympathetic Anglicans would subscribe. Bourne did strongly condemn Lambeth's approval of contraception. But his statements were eclipsed by the Encyclical Letter on marriage, *Casti Connubii*, published just days earlier. In a wide-ranging defence and promotion of the institution of marriage, Pius XI singled out

The Thackeray Hotel

for censure the Anglican Bishops who had departed 'from the uninterrupted Christian tradition' in the erroneous belief they could 'declare another doctrine'. The Pope wished no one to be in any doubt: the deliberate frustration of the generation of new life was 'an offence against the law of God' constituting 'grave sin'.[18] The Papalists could be assured that they had found that doctrinal certainty which they were seeking.

There were eleven who met on 21 January: Goodier, Butler, D'Arcy and Jarrett for the Catholics; Scott, Jones, Fynes-Clinton, Corbould, Monahan and Simmonds for the Anglicans. They were hosted by Marchant in his private room at the Thackeray. Simmonds took notes.

The American members of the Confraternity found themselves conflicted in their response to these London Conversations. On the one hand the talks represented by far the most practical achievement to date of all that they strove for: actual contact with senior, authorised Catholics to discuss their respective positions with a view to advancing the cause of Reunion. On the other, they were disinclined to believe that anything substantive could be attained in proceedings to which they were not a party. Both Pierce in Rome and Campbell in Oxford were desperate to discover what was taking place at the Thackeray Hotel.

The participants had learnt one lesson from Malines: the cause of Reunion was not helped by publicity. There were those on both sides who would do all in their power to prevent and wreck such contact. As Jones recorded, the need for confidentiality was impressed upon everyone from the outset:

> It may be best not to talk about it generally, as we all are very anxious the Press should not get hold of it to 'mess about' with it. Not that there is any want of straight forwardness or any mystery—but the Press might *make* it such.[19]

The success with which this injunction was observed is apparent from the fact that, eighty years on, the Conversations are still largely unknown. Only Marchant, in an effort to exaggerate his own significance, was unable to resist the temptation to reveal the meetings. And even he seems to have restricted his confidences to Cardinal Bourne, who was never given to gossip, and Archbishop Lang, who wished the whole matter simply to disappear. The Conversations are known, therefore, only from surviving papers circulated between the participants themselves and fleeting references elsewhere.

Campbell professed to wish the endeavour well, but proceeded to belittle its chances of success. He could 'not see how four or five Anglicans and four or five RCs comparing secretly notes together can amount to much, especially as very few Anglicans would back what their self-established protagonists say!' While the unrepresentative nature of the Anglican participants was undoubtedly true, it was the unrepresentative nature of Campbell's own position. He chose to ignore the significance of the fact that the Catholics were there on the authority and with the blessing of the head of the Catholic Church in England and Wales. The Anglicans were concerned that the Conversations might be derailed by one of their own number. Jones continued to be alarmed at Scott's temperament: 'he so lacks charity and is so belligerent, he [Jones] fears all good will be negatived'.[20] But Halifax's instinct in travelling to Malines in the preceding decade had been sound; personal contact of itself was crucial in the initial attempt to overcome ignorance and prejudice. Jones required less convincing than most. He wrote of the meeting of 21 January: 'The R.C.s were very charming and kind.'[21] The sentiment appears to have been reciprocated all round.

'The Four Documents'[22]

We have no detailed record of what was said on 21 January. Owing to Marchant's ill health and Goodier's commitments elsewhere, the group as a whole did not meet again until 26 March. We can, however, surmise the conclusions of the first Conversation. There was sufficient goodwill and interest for the meetings to continue. We know also, from subsequent events, the format agreed for future proceedings. Again, Malines served as a precedent. It was accepted that the Anglicans should write various papers detailing their position which would be considered, and responded to, by

The Thackeray Hotel

the Catholics. Given their Oxbridge education, most participants were entirely comfortable with this rather academic way of proceeding—with the important exception of Goodier.

In the intervening two months, Marchant engaged in a certain amount of shuttle diplomacy. He met D'Arcy and Jarrett on 4 February; later in the month he was arranging to dine with Butler.[23] No doubt there were similar private appointments with the Anglicans. Sir James was determined to do everything within his power to promote the success of the Conversations.

The Anglicans committed to producing two papers. These arrived with Goodier on 5 March in preparation for the second conversation originally scheduled for 9 March, but postponed to 26 March. Goodier's correspondence with Marchant reveals that he was not anticipating a prolonged series of scholarly discussions:

> I can only go on praying, and I do, that the happy ending may come soon, and that, as I know you wish, others may see more clearly what they already see dimly. When the two documents come I will study them with all the sympathy I can command. It will bring us nearer to the crisis, for I feel that a crisis must come; but when it does come, please God we shall see, all of us, eye to eye. That will indeed be a consummation worth all our prayers.[24]

The Archbishop was hoping for some rapid and dramatic conclusion to the Conversations.

He was to be disappointed. Goodier was puzzled by the two papers delivered to his Chelsea Rectory. He had been expecting an outline of theological differences or personal difficulties. Instead, he received two historical monographs. He would have been less surprised had he been acquainted with Scott's and Jones's published works. Goodier had the two documents copied to his Catholic colleagues. They can be found among Abbot Butler's papers at Downside. There is no attribution in the papers themselves, but the content and the references in Goodier's correspondence make it clear that one is by Scott and the other by Jones.

Jones's paper is entitled 'The Position'. It is a restatement of Papalist belief along the lines of his Oxford addresses and his recently published *Catholic Reunion*. Its entire contention is that the Church of England is fundamentally Catholic and Papalist. It required only education and effort to convince the majority of Anglicans of this. With the true nature of the Church of England recognised, she would be liberated from the taint of Protestantism, Modernism and State control.

Jones offered no detailed explanation as to how this was to be achieved in practice. Instead, he provided a 400-year history lesson in support of his contention that 'the English Church, *as such*, is pledged to a position of union, not disunion, in relation to the Holy See'. Drawing on his own research, Jones convincingly maintained 'that England was *forced* away from the Holy See on *political* not religious grounds. The Reformation in England was unconstitutional throughout.' More controversial was his proposition that the post-Reformation 'Church of England never formally repudiated the Papacy'. Article 37 of the Church of England's Thirty-Nine Articles declares: 'The Bishop of Rome hath no jurisdiction in this Realm of England.' It is likely to have come as an unwelcome shock to the drafters of the Articles and to contemporary Anglicans that only the Pope's temporal power was restricted; his spiritual authority in England remained unimpeded.

From the Reformation to the current day, Jones claimed there had existed among Anglicans a 'Roman' or 'Petrine' school and this alone constituted 'the true continuation and representative of the Church of England'. As examples, he cited the seventeenth-century Bishop Montagu of Chichester and Archbishop Bramhall of Armagh. The Oxford Movement was simply the heir to a continuous current within Anglicanism, flourishing as the times became more propitious. Having claimed a historical and 'constitutional' basis for Anglican Papalism, Jones concluded somewhat weakly: our movement's 'method is to report conclusions from time to time to *our* authorities. (As it is, they are constantly acting on misinformation as well as on prejudice.)'[25]

Functioning, as he was to do throughout, as spokesman of the Catholic group, Goodier shared with Marchant and Butler his reservations about Jones's paper. In his search for a historical justification for Papalism, Goodier felt Jones was clutching at straws. How could such men, claiming to accept papal primacy and jurisdiction, remain in a Church which, the vast majority of its adherents believed, was founded on the explicit rejection of such assertions? 'It is an impossible position anywhere else but here in England.' Goodier conceded that, purely as a 'historical statement, and that from their point of view', Jones's paper was 'very interesting'. But he did not see how it advanced the cause of Reunion in their own day. For a Catholic, it simply proved 'that the old faith died hard; the old tradition could not be killed, and those who had to kill it, were not happy in their consciences. They tried to compromise, to convince themselves, and these declarations are the result.'

Had he stopped there, Goodier's critique would have been convincing. Historically and logically, the Papalist case was flawed. Unfortunately, Goodier proceeded to posit a false dichotomy between history and truth, implicitly acknowledging history might, after all, support Jones:

> In all study of history, which is human, there comes a point when the searcher for God and the living truths must lay it aside; for the truth does not depend on history. History must confirm the truth, it cannot prove it. The truth was there before history, and is here today while history is only in the making.

The Archbishop would have been far wiser to recognise the existence of historical truths and, where these appeared to favour the Papalists, to place them in the wider context. Writing to Butler, the Lancastrian's self-doubt resurfaced: 'My remarks don't count for much. I shall be most tremendously pleased if you can give me some impressions of your own so that we can act together.'[26]

Butler saw much more clearly the Papalist objective. They wanted to be told by the Catholics: 'You are right in your position; carry on as you are doing, spreading Catholic ideas for all you are worth.' That simply was not possible. The Catholics had to state explicitly that the Anglican Communion was 'certainly in schism' and 'its bishops and the great bulk of its members, committed to heresies of many kinds'. However, the question of conversion 'and submitting to the Catholic Church and Pope, is a matter of personal call and individual conscience: till one feels the definite doubt and the clear call of conscience, one may abide in good faith and carry on the propaganda'.

Butler was more sanguine than Goodier. Catholics had been praying and working for the conversion of England for years. Yet, to Butler's mind, that prospect seemed as distant as ever. 'From the human and natural point of view, the [Papalists] are doing a Catholicising work that we can't do; they are in fact touching wide and ever wider circles that none others reach, or can reach; they are certainly preaching and successfully spreading Catholic ideas, beliefs, practices.' The Abbot mused: Were these Conversations 'God's way of preparing for something? [...] Are these men preparing the way for some such consummation? Are they being used by God as instruments for His work?' If that were a possibility, then all the Catholics need do now were to state clearly the Catholic position that the Church of England was schismatical and heretical. 'And leave the thing in God's hands.'[27]

The postponement of the March Conversation allowed the second paper to be typed and circulated among the Catholic participants. Entitled 'Schism *in* the Church', Scott drew on his field of expertise, the Eastern Church during the First Millennium. The Papalists fiercely rejected any suggestion of heresy. The Catholics conceded that, as individuals, they might be doctrinally orthodox. Scott held, therefore, that the question at issue was rather one of schism. Not being in visible communion with the Apostolic See, were they separated from the Church?

Arguing that their position was analogous to that of the Eastern Orthodox, Scott maintained that the Anglicans might be in schism *in* the Church, but not in schism *from* the Church. Citing the research of the Catholic, Louis Duchesne, Scott demonstrated in the period of 'the Undivided Church', the Eastern Church had been out of communion with Rome for 217 of 506 years, and had been led by heretical patriarchs for 19 years of that time. Yet most Eastern priests and laity remained 'true, loyal to, believing and practising the Catholic Faith [...] [even when] governed by bishops [...] who contradicted and denied that Faith'. Even if ruled by 'hireling shepherds' the sheep could remain 'faithful'.[28] Was it meaningful to employ the term 'schism' in the classic sense in such circumstances? Scott left the Catholics to apply the implications to Anglicans in their own day and their own country.

Goodier instinctively felt that the Anglican situation was fundamentally different from that of the Eastern Orthodox. Even if the Papalists were personally orthodox, how could they justify maintaining 'active communion' with those in the Church of England espousing heretical positions? Goodier was feeling his way to composing his own paper in response to Jones and Scott. Increasingly, he came to appreciate what was at stake: 'The question is not one of history; it is dogmatic, that is, what exactly is the unity of the Church, and on what principle does it rest.'[29]

Before the second conversation, Scott produced another paper, 'On Schism within the Church', which Goodier forwarded to Butler on 19 March. Quoting St Thomas Aquinas, Scott held that schism must always be intentional. He quoted the Church of England's canons and liturgy to demonstrate that she considered herself a part of the Universal Church and condemned the sin of schism. He dealt at length with the position of the Celtic Church. Claiming the support of the nineteenth-century Catholic historian, John Lingard, Scott argued that it was possible to be 'outside Catholic communion', while remaining 'a true Catholic Church' possessing 'a true hierarchy and valid sacraments'. The Celtic Church 'was a true part of the Church, and yet it was in schism. Therefore schism is possible within the Church'. Scott gave the further example of 'the threefold schism within the Western Church' prior to the Council of Constance.[30] (It is difficult to see that the Western Schism holds water as a valid comparison. Presumably, all factions sincerely believed that they were in communion with the successor of Peter; there was no intention to separate from the Apostolic See and, therefore, they remained Catholic. Could that really be said of sixteenth-century Anglicans who separated, or consented to remain in separation, from Rome?)

Speaking on 26 March, Goodier makes reference to *four* documents received from the Anglicans. The fourth appears to be the anonymous paper in the Downside Archives headed 'A Summary of the History of Attempts at and Proposals for Reunion from 1538 to 1833'. It elaborates Jones's first paper, just as Scott expanded his own first paper. The author states his intention at the outset:

> to show from historical evidence that the 'Roman School' in the Church of England is not, as is generally imagined, a growth of modern times or even merely an offshoot of the Tractarian Movement. Our claim is that there have always been men of our views within the Anglican Communion, who have regarded the state-created division between Canterbury and Rome as a disaster, and have striven with all their power to heal that breach.

The paper gives an extended account of tentative negotiations between England and Rome under the Stuarts and subsequently, as alluded to by Jones in his first paper, but adds nothing further of substance to the discussions.[31]

Who was the author of this fourth paper? Sending it on to his Catholic colleagues on 17 March, Goodier believes it to be written by Jones.[32] However, given the content largely coincides with that of his pamphlet published the following year and of a talk he gave in Oxford around the same time,[33] it is not unreasonable to postulate Simmonds's authorship, no doubt advised and assisted by Jones. The conjecture is corroborated by Pierce, who heard that Simmonds had contributed an especially valuable paper to 'the Secret Conversations'.[34]

'On the war path'

It was assumed by all concerned that the Catholic response to the Anglican papers would be delivered by Archbishop Goodier when the group reconvened on 26 March. Probably this was because Goodier, acting as an auxiliary bishop in Westminster, was the one authorised by Cardinal Bourne to conduct the Conversations and report back to him. (D'Arcy and Jarrett were occupied by significant duties elsewhere.) It was not the happiest of choices.

Goodier drafted his response ten days before the second conversation. He explained his method to Marchant: 'My experience shows me it is often better when I prepare the material very carefully beforehand and am allowed to speak to it, rather than to read it.' Goodier had felt for some time that the Catholics and Anglicans would discover 'on some quite fundamental points we had quite different definitions'. Having read the Anglican papers, he concluded that differing understandings of the concept of *unity* constituted the principal difficulty. The Archbishop proposed addressing this. If some convergence could be achieved here, then, he believed, it would be easier to arrive at a shared understanding of *authority*.[35]

Butler had urged the need for clarity in their dealings with the Anglican Conversationalists. Whatever his other failings, Goodier had not betrayed his Northern roots. Forthrightness was his forte. Back in Marchant's room at the Thackeray Hotel, the Archbishop began by expressing his surprise at the historical nature of the four Anglican documents: 'I will confess, beforehand, that I expected something more dogmatic.' Nevertheless, Goodier said, he would take as his starting point the historical assertions which had been made. He would ask what the implications were, whether the historical statements were proved and, even if proved, whether they supported the claims made by the Anglicans.

Goodier noted the Papalists had adduced 'evidence of what we may call a Roman stream flowing through the Church of England from the days of Henry VIII'. He then asked the perfectly reasonable question: 'Can this stream in any sense be made to count for the Church of England itself?' And the Archbishop answered his own question: 'Whatever authority, representing that Church, we may choose to invoke, we are compelled to say that it has declared itself, not merely anti-Roman, but heretical.' How could the Church of England claim to remain Catholic in the fundamentals when, not just the State, but also their ecclesiastical authorities and laity, had desecrated Catholic churches and martyred Catholic priests, simply for their fidelity to the Mass? He did not deny an element within the Church of England might be merely schismatic rather than actually heretical. But, if this were the case, he maintained that they had fatally compromised themselves by communion and cooperation with the heretical element. And that, in the eyes of the Catholic Church, constituted apostasy.

Goodier directly challenged Scott's assertion that the Anglicans were supported by St Thomas Aquinas in his teaching that schism had to be intentional. The Thomist definition, the Archbishop argued, cleared the Celtic Church and the adherents of mediaeval anti-popes of the charge of formal schism because at all times they really believed 'they were acting as loyal Catholics'. Only in such circumstances was it legitimate to speak of 'schism inside the Church'.

It was insufficient to make appeal 'to the undivided Church', the Archbishop argued, to justify schism from the See of Peter. Virtually every schismatic and heretic of the past had sought to vindicate the act of separation by claiming: 'The Church says one thing; I say another, and I appeal to the Universal Church as my support.' Used in this sense, *the Universal Church* was not an ecclesiastical reality, but rather 'a voiceless chimera'. On this basis, Goodier concluded, all Anglicans were in schism *from* the Church because there was 'a conscious acceptance of that which is wrong'. It was futile to argue that they remained within the Church of England to promote a future good, namely the catholicising of their own Communion and Reunion with Rome. Moral theology condemns the proposition that the end justifies the means, that evil might be tolerated that good might come of it.

So far, so good. As he had advised Marchant he would, Goodier then proceeded to expound his belief that Catholics and Anglicans understood different things by the concept of *unity*. The Archbishop had correctly stated that simply appealing to 'the undivided Church' was an insufficient guarantee that one was fully united to the Body of Christ as actually constituted on earth. But then Goodier undermined his own argument by stating that for Catholics 'unity is essentially an interior matter [. . .] It is a consciousness, a life, a oneness, which we know, even as the body is conscious of itself, and lives and knows itself, and cannot express itself in any other way to a member that is not of it.' One understands what Goodier means: there must be an intentionality to unity. It is not, as he goes on to say, simply a mechanical matter. Yet, he lays himself open to attack by minimising the significance of the external bonds of unity, by dismissing 'merely historical argument'.

The Thackeray Hotel

There is the wonderful irony of a Jesuit Archbishop telling his Anglican audience: 'they seem to make more of the Pope than even we do'. Goodier attempts to explain. Communion with the Pope is the consequence, rather than the cause, of unity. He fears that the Anglicans hold an organisational, rather than an organic, concept of unity. For unity to exist, there must be doctrinal agreement, spiritual communion. It causes Goodier to minimise the importance of the papacy as the centre of unity. There is no mention of the unity brought about through the sacraments. Perhaps one is expecting him to hold a fully developed system of 'degrees of communion' within the Church a generation and more before the Second Vatican Council.

Goodier concludes by an appeal to the individual conscience. Again, there is no hint of irony that a Catholic Archbishop is urging this on Anglicans above an appeal to authority. At the moment of death, Goodier states, judgment will be a matter solely between Christ and the individual soul. The Archbishop then presumes to tell the Papalists what Christ would say to them were He present at the Thackeray Hotel that Thursday afternoon in 1931: 'Become one first with Me, and then you will find yourselves one with each other. Become one first with Me in my body, in my Church, and then, all other things will follow.'[36]

What of the response? What had been intended as a series of discussions between four Catholic and six Anglican participants risked degenerating into a duel between Goodier and Scott. Goodier had been offended, and probably worsted, by the Anglican critique of his paper. Reflecting on his own contribution, the Archbishop noted that it was given 'in the greatest simplicity, spontaneously and without even thinking it out'.[37] However, what he described as 'manoeuvring' and 'mere fencing' on the part of the Anglicans, they would have viewed rather as a search for academic rigour.[38] Here Goodier's lack of experience of the parrying of the Oxbridge Senior Common Room was most telling and most damaging.

It was not just the Anglicans who were critical of Goodier. Butler was far too charitable to voice any misgivings, but his two younger colleagues had no such inhibitions. Jarrett and D'Arcy were clearly dissatisfied with the Archbishop's exposition of the Catholic Faith:

> They complained that I was inclined to be too easy with our friends; they were surprised that I took some things lying down; it was only when I spoke out plainly about the idea of the Church that they were reassured.[39]

His fellow Jesuits noted that Goodier had little time for speculative theology. He would spare no effort if he believed he could be of practical assistance to another. Yet the moment he felt the other was interested only in debate for its own sake, then Goodier sought to disengage.[40] At this point Goodier offered to change the venue and format: to the Jesuit house of studies at Heythrop in Oxfordshire where he would deliver a spiritual retreat to the Anglicans. There would be no discussion, only private conversations with individuals; there was to be no word of controversy.[41] It would have played to Goodier's strengths: making Christ real to others, and allowing them to deduce the implications of that. No one took the Archbishop up on his invitation.

The next conversation was arranged for 2.30 pm on Monday, 11 May. Everyone except Jarrett was able to attend. Other Anglican documents were circulated in the interim, including one apparently entitled 'Newly created succession'. No copy of this has survived. It is difficult to reconstruct the contents from Goodier's subjective comments. The Archbishop summarised its objective as 'a patching together of broken pieces in the hope of making a new whole, an entirely human contrivance with not a trace of life in it'.[42] Elsewhere he described it as 'a bond of union brought from outside to both communities [...] seeking life by means of an outside galvanic battery'.[43] The imagery is intriguing. It suggests the type of exotic scheme devised by Marchant and Orchard to create a new ecclesial body at the Weigh House Chapel. Or are we catching a glimpse of Scott's former theory 'that Reunion, when it does come, will come via the Orthodox'? Doubting that there would ever be a direct meeting of minds between Rome and Canterbury, Scott had speculated that the solution to the conundrum of disunity would come through Eastern prelates

The Thackeray Hotel

regularising Anglican Orders.[44] Whatever lay at the heart of this paper, it was presumably deemed impractical as nothing further is heard of it.

The main item on the agenda on 11 May was a lengthy Anglican paper responding to Goodier's earlier submission. If the Archbishop had been stung by verbal criticism of his position on 26 March, he was to be more distressed by the offensive launched on 11 May, retreating subsequently into two days of reflection and prayer. His experience led him to believe 'all further discussion for the present is useless'.

The Anglicans had met more than once between the March and May Conversations 'to draw up a re-statement of their position in the light of what [Goodier] said'.[45] But the principal authorship and the delivery was Scott's. Goodier's sense of hurt resulted partially from his own lack of self-confidence and lack of familiarity with the secular academic world. But, as Jones had feared earlier, Scott cannot escape culpability. Whether he was conscious of it or not, Scott's tone was perceived as neither 'frank' nor 'charitable'. From the Archbishop's perspective—and it was one shared by many who encountered Scott—the Rector of Oddington was engaging in controversy for its own sake. 'He was on the war-path from the beginning to the end, and he gave me the impression that he was anxious to score off any weak point in my somewhat spontaneous statement, rather than that he desired to agree with me on anything.'[46] Scott did not begin well, characterising Goodier's paper as 'his personal reaction', as if it did not represent the position of the Catholic Church or the other Catholic participants. Scott acknowledged that what he was about to say might be perceived as 'captiousness', but he felt able to presume upon the charity of those present at 'these private and friendly personal conversations'.

That did not mean that Scott was entirely wrong. He ruthlessly exposed flaws in Goodier's argument. Why had the Papalists concentrated on the historical, rather than the dogmatic, aspect? Precisely because the Archbishop himself at an early stage in the Conversations had requested evidence of a 'Roman School' within the Church of England prior to the Oxford Movement.

> It was clearly a primary matter to show the Roman Catholic theologians that the Anglican Conversationalists were not mere voices crying in the wilderness, religious eccentrics with no past, no present support, and no future, but representative of a continuous school of thought which has found expression in all generations since the unhappy division between the English Church and Rome.

Scott did not claim that the Papalists were a majority, or even a substantial minority, within the Anglican Communion, but he did contend that they embodied 'the *true* Anglican position'. He presumed that their historical papers had achieved their purpose given Goodier in March had accepted the continuous existence of such a school of thought in the Church of England which he had been unwilling to concede previously.

Beyond the narrow point in issue, Scott gave a spirited Catholic defence of the importance of history, enlisting St Thomas and Abbot Vonier of Buckfast Abbey as witnesses to his case:

> Can we afford then to make so little of the merely historical argument? Our Blessed Lord Himself is a historic Person, that is, He revealed God to men in the plane of history and the supreme Act of Redemption of the world is a historic as well as a mystical reality.

Goodier would have been mortified as he was implicitly included among those whom Scott rounded upon for endangering the Faith by 'over-spiritualising' it. Catholicism was incarnational or it was nothing. 'Can the mystical view be separated from the historical, or indeed exist without the foundation of the historical in any point of faith?'

Scott challenged Goodier. How was the Church of England heretical? Having spent years railing against Anglican Modernists, Scott was not about to allow them to be made the official spokesmen of his Communion. 'Individuals may be heretical, but of what heresy is the Church of England guilty?' (He conveniently forgot that just months earlier his colleagues were bewailing 'the Moral Heresy' of the 1930 Lambeth Conference.) For official Anglican teaching, one should turn to the Book of Common Prayer and that, Scott maintained, was doctrinally orthodox. He cited Daniel Murray, the Catholic Archbishop of Dublin, who a century earlier had written: 'Were the Church of England true to the principles laid down in their Prayer Book, the doctrinal differences, which appear considerable but are not, would soon be removed.' (Scott glossed over the fact that about the same time the living voice of Anglicanism, the bishops, had censured Newman for claiming the Thirty-Nine Articles were susceptible of a Catholic interpretation.) Questionably, Scott alleged that the English Martyrs had suffered, albeit unjustly, for political rather than doctrinal reasons. (We do not know whether the Catholics present challenged his claim.) Scott chose to ignore Goodier's reference to Reformation iconoclasm representing an attack on the Mass.

Scott dealt no more gently with Goodier's statement that, even if not personally heterodox, Anglicans had effectively apostatised by remaining in communion with heretics. Such a position, Scott maintained, was frankly Donatist rather than Catholic, the appeal to a Church of the pure which did not exist. Would Goodier have had St Athanasius abandon the Church of Egypt given the Arian stance of his brother bishops? Scott's rhetoric was forceful, but did it withstand rigorous analysis? Was the situation of the post-Reformation Church of England really analogous to those defending Christological orthodoxy in the fourth century? Athanasius knew that he and those who believed as he did were alone upholders of the true Faith. Whereas from the sixteenth century onwards there was one body, the Church of Rome, which claimed this exclusive position whom Anglicans defined themselves against. Christian Tradition was clear where the *sensus fidelium* was to be found in the fourth century. Scott needed to demonstrate more convincingly where was it to be found in England after the Reformation.

He accepted Goodier's proposition that to be in schism, an individual has to be conscious that he is outside the unity of the Church and acquiesces to that situation. On that basis, Scott argued, the Anglicans were not schismatics. 'We are conscious that we are within the Church, and we assert with reason that the Anglican Church as a whole has never departed either in will or in deed from the Church Catholic.' Was this self-certification adequate? Scott claimed the Church of England did not differ essentially from the early Celtic Church or the contemporary Orthodox. That assertion needed to be tested.

Scott alleged that Goodier oversimplified the Papalist position. The Archbishop had condemned them for perpetuating an evil (remaining in communion with heretics) that good might come of it (eventual Reunion). 'Were it so simple as this we should all be glad to come into the Roman obedience today. But we are the victims of very complex circumstances.' The Papalists believed 'in the validity of our orders and our canonical commission to exercise them'. They baptised validly, they absolved from sin validly. 'We believe that day by day we offer to the Father the one Sacrifice in sacramental mystery for the world's Redemption, and feed our people with the Body of Christ.' Goodier had cited one principle of Catholic moral theology. Scott cited another: faced by two unavoidable evils, the lesser evil was to be chosen. Scott conceded that being out of visible communion with the Apostolic See was an evil, but denying his priesthood and sacramental ministry, when he knew these to be valid, constituted a greater evil. Regardless of the Papalists' grounds for belief in the validity of Anglican sacraments, their sincerity certainly diminished their moral culpability.

Scott welcomed Goodier's declaration that Catholics viewed unity as essentially an interior matter to be understood primarily in terms of a living organism. That, Scott maintained, brought them in line with the Orthodox and Anglicans, whereas it was feared that Catholics supposed unity to be primarily a juridical issue. Scott denied, therefore, any difference between Catholic and Anglican concepts of unity. 'We have that same consciousness of unity with the Church as that to which he bears witness, a consciousness of unity of life and of faith.' It was this primacy which they accorded to spiritual unity which made the Papalists so anxious to attain 'the ideal of external unity', an ideal which Scott was concerned Goodier discounted.

This led to the novel position of the Anglican Papalists claiming to be more Catholic than the Jesuit Archbishop. Yes, they did believe that unity derived from the papacy. If, as Goodier claimed, the Catholic belief were the reverse of this, then that relegated the papacy to *de iure ecclesiastico*, not *de iure divino*, a human rather than a divine institution. Of course, ultimately, the unity of the Church derives from Christ Himself. Yet the Papalists held 'that Our Lord made St Peter the centre of unity, because without him and his successors unity could not be preserved'. The Pope was only one member of the Church, his relations to the episcopacy had still to be defined. Nevertheless, the Pope was the head of the Church on earth, its 'controlling force'. As head, the Pope's role was to 'make the rest orderly and useful, and keep all the members in harmony of action one with another'. Goodier's earlier comments allowed the Anglican to lecture him on the Catholic understanding of the Petrine Office.

Vatican II, three decades later, would appear to support Scott on this issue, its dogmatic constitution on the Church declaring the Pope to be the 'lasting and visible source and foundation of the unity both of faith and of communion'.[47] Yet one has to ask how meaningful this question as to the priority of the Pope or unity really was. Both were ordered to the other, both were intrinsically connected in the mind and economy of God.

Finally, Scott recalled the Archbishop's invitation issued to each of them on behalf of Christ Himself to be one with Him. They were, Scott assured him, 'already one with Our Lord by the links of Faith and Sacrament'. Yet here he revealed divergence from the Catholic position. The Church, he maintained, was only *'potentially* Catholic, universal, one and holy'. The Papalists were doing their part to realise this, but the 'outward and visible unity under the one Shepherd of all who hold the faith of Christ' would only follow in God's time.[48] Catholics, by contrast, while acknowledging the sinfulness of her members, held that the Church herself, because she was Christ's, was already one and holy. Here was a differing view of unity our Conversationalists had yet to explore.

For all its faults and polemical nature, Scott's paper was a *tour de force*. Those present left the Thackeray Hotel that afternoon with much to ponder. We know what Goodier thought. Still smarting from the rebuffs received, he criticised Scott's paper as 'pompous' and largely concerned with semantics. The Archbishop acknowledged that his own 'looser writing in some places' had rendered him vulnerable, but it had resulted in the Anglicans overplaying their hand and revealing their true position:

> They want to offer terms upon which they will come in, and one of those terms, though they may not put it down, certainly will be that they should not alter any one of their beliefs. In other words, they must remain Protestant while they become Roman Catholics, just as at present they are Protestants while they call themselves Roman Catholics.

That being so, the Archbishop proposed writing to Sir James Marchant to tell him that, while 'much good has come from our Conversations, the situation is still too immature for us to consider it worthwhile going on with them for the present'.[49]

Goodier was surprised to discover himself in a minority of one among his Catholic colleagues. Butler, D'Arcy and Jarrett all wished to continue the discussions; therefore, the Archbishop agreed to proceed with the next Conversation arranged for 18 June. Goodier hoped for a little more intellectual support from the others, suggesting the four meet in advance to coordinate their response. Bede Jarrett had indicated the line he wished to adopt: to press the Anglicans relentlessly on the source of their authority. 'If the Prayer Book or the Articles are to be taken as a definite statement, on what authority does that rest? Then, each time they bring up anything, he would evidently wish to keep urging, By what authority—by what authority, until, at last, they would be forced to say there was none whatsoever.'

Martin D'Arcy favoured a different approach. 'He is inclined to separate Dr Scott from the others.'[50] On receiving Scott's initial papers back in March, Goodier had already identified him as the most impressive of the Anglicans: he 'is both the most earnest and the most difficult nut to crack'.[51] While Goodier now determined that Scott was immoveable, the consummate convert-hunter, D'Arcy, viewed him as a personal challenge. Pierce, who had also suffered Scott's irascibility, concurred with Goodier: 'Unless perhaps he fell heir to a fortune, and so could be independent, Scott would never, under any circumstances, become a RC: he could never submit to any phase of the discipline.'[52] Time was to prove the Archbishop and the American correct.

The Two Hierarchies

In early May, Marchant unexpectedly received a reply to his letter written four months earlier to the Archbishop of Canterbury, whose health now allowed him to resume his duties. There is no indication that Lang was aware that discussions were actually taking place. He ruled that the attitude of the Catholic Church rendered his involvement in, or blessing of, these Conversations impossible. Nevertheless,

> there is nothing to prevent private informal conversations taking place between members of these Churches and I could have no possible objection to such informal conversations, and while I should be glad to know of them I should not be prepared to give them any kind of official recognition though I should be much interested to hear of any results that might take place.

Lang confirmed that this represented the joint approach of the two Anglican Archbishops.[53]

Marchant's response was unusually coy, fearing that Canterbury and York might object to Papalists purporting to represent the Anglican Communion in talks with Catholics. Thus, he referred only to 'some tentative contacts' and gave only the briefest sketch of what had occurred since the beginning of the year: 'a few fireside, informal talks over tea, envisaging *the* problems'. Marchant gladly identified the Catholic participants and referred to Cardinal Bourne's approval, but made no mention whatever of the Anglicans involved. Rather he chose to envelope the proceedings in mystery: 'Our talks are under the seal, may I put it, of the Confessional, and the fact that they are taking place is entirely unknown save to Your Grace and Cardinal Bourne, and those who take part in them.' He hoped to persuade Lang to take some greater role in the future by treating him as his confidant now: 'I expect it is indiscreet for me to write about these matters—I am not doing so to the Cardinal or to any member of the group. But I should feel happier if Your Grace were, unofficially and privately, as fully informed as the Cardinal.'[54]

Lang's subsequent reply characterised his attitude throughout: formal courtesy combined with studied disinterest.

> I thank you for telling me about these very informal conversations between Anglicans and Roman Catholics. As I explained to you, I do not feel justified at the present stage in taking any official cognisance of them but I am glad to know that these conversations are desired and are taking place and I shall be very glad to know from you at a later stage about their results.[55]

There is no reason to doubt Lang's sincerity. In his exchanges with Lambeth, Temple spoke the same language. It was rather otherwise in his private correspondence:

> I think that people who are drawn to Rome are mostly people who would not be very valuable to the Church of England [...] Some day, no doubt, in the very remote future, the question of union with Rome will become practical. At present I regard it as almost infinitely remote, and do not believe that we gain greatly by retaining in our body those who are capable of being much attracted to the other.[56]

And it is this mentality one suspects is more typical of the Anglican Establishment. Disregarding the statements of the 1920 Lambeth Conference, Reunion with Rome was not plausible. The Church of England was better off without those Papalists who clamoured for it.

What of the Catholic hierarchy? Cardinal Bourne probably did not rate the chances of success of the Conversations significantly higher than Lang did. He was too cautious and wise to be taken in by Marchant's prophesies of an imminent seismic shift in the ecclesiastical landscape. He was pleased that the discussions were being conducted by Englishmen on English soil. That alone ought to secure a greater degree of realism than prevailed at Malines. But Bourne was too sensitive to the workings of the Holy Spirit to close down any possibilities. Within limits, he was prepared

The Thackeray Hotel

to give his sanction to persons and projects. If they were of God, they would flourish; if not, then he need not be too concerned.

The Papalists were to discover that Bourne and Rome were pragmatic. Principles were not negotiable, but numbers mattered. If one was simply talking about six Anglican Conversationalists, then the whole affair would remain an academic exercise unless or until they chose to convert as individuals. However, if they represented something greater, then all manner of disciplinary concessions might become possible. Goodier met Bourne frequently, and no doubt took the opportunity to update him regularly on the progress of the talks. In early April 1931 Goodier showed the Cardinal three documents provided by the Anglicans through the medium of Marchant. One listed more than 300 clergy who supported the Papalist position. (Ever the pessimist, Goodier feared that such a large number would be a disincentive to individual conversions.) The Cardinal considered the documents 'very carefully. He is much impressed by the long list of Supporters, though, of course, most of them are unknown to either him or me.'[57] Who knew what lay around the corner?

What did Bourne make of these exotic Papalists, so far removed from his own experience of Catholicism? Insular Catholics simply could not comprehend such a strange phenomenon. Claiming to accept fully Catholic doctrine within the Anglican Communion, many English Catholics felt that the Papalists had to be either fools or knaves. The intellectual credentials of men like Jones and Scott gave ample proof that they were not the former. The Cardinal came to understand that they were not the latter either. Although his personal exposure to the Papalists was limited, we know that he gave considerable thought to the matter—and arrived at novel solution.

Pierce had the opportunity to discuss the subject with Bourne in the summer of 1934. This was the Cardinal's opinion of the Papalists:

> All my life those friends of yours have been a great difficulty to me. It's been almost impossible to believe in their good faith, accepting, as they profess, to believe 90% or 99% of the Faith, and then not acting on it and submitting to the authority they claim to recognise. But in these my last days a new thought

has come to me: that perhaps in these puzzling cases, of these good men, who go on for years, perhaps even to their death, without *acting* on their professions, we see a very special instance of God's gentleness and love. For, in addition to mere intellectual convictions, His grace, in the end, is necessary for conversion; and from some of these He may withhold that final grace because, if they received it, and conscience gave the command to submit, they might, many of them, be called upon for sacrifices too great for human nature to face; would fail to take the great step, and *then* they really *would* be in bad faith and in great danger.[58]

Disregarding the theology of it, such a statement certainly indicates Bourne's desire to be generous and sympathetic.

The Memorandum

Acting as secretary to the group, Simmonds presumably took minutes of the London Conversations. Sadly, these do not survive. Possibly they were among the papers Corbould ordered to be burnt after his death.[59] Other than references in correspondence from some of the participants, we have to rely, therefore, on the (incomplete) papers delivered to piece together what actually transpired at the Conversations. Given the strong personalities and powerful intellects present, it is unlikely that they sat silently by, listening to the papers without comment. Goodier thanked Butler for his contributions: 'You have done more than, probably, you think; for I never failed to learn something every time you spoke at the meetings.'[60] We know others shared the Archbishop's appreciation of the Abbot's interventions.

Goodier was less appreciative of the Anglican tendency in the discussions to back each other up all the time.[61] This unanimity, however, was more apparent than real. Some of the Anglican Conversationalists were increasingly alarmed that if the proceedings continued in their current vein as a personal confrontation between Scott and Goodier, at some point in the near future the Archbishop would lose patience and call a halt to them. Very little would have been achieved for the cause of Reunion. The

Anglicans met with Marchant on 9 April and other occasions as well. Ostensibly, this was to formulate a response to Goodier's paper of 26 March. In fact, something of a power struggle seems to have occurred, with those who favoured a less polemical approach prevailing to a large degree. Scott got to deliver his riposte to Goodier on 11 May, but something else emerged as well.

The Archbishop's information is clearly derived from Marchant:

> I am told that, after their discussions, what they want to put on paper is not any answer to what we have said, but a plain statement of what they would like to have from the Church, supposing they came in.[62]

This is the origin of *the* Memorandum, which was to dominate proceedings for the rest of the year. Fynes-Clinton and Corbould were not theologians. They were practical parish priests. For decades they had been organising prayer, liturgies and meetings to promote Reunion; they wanted actual proposals to advance that cause. They did not see this being realised in the asperities traded between Scott and Goodier. The very fact that the Memorandum was written, its content and tone, reflected the fact that the pendulum had swung in their favour. The Memorandum's historical statements and line of reasoning suggest that Jones also favoured this approach and was involved in its drafting. Characteristically, however, Marchant claimed the credit for this 'important document which I thought it worthwhile to encourage them to compose, expressing their Faith, and their hopes'.[63]

The six-page Memorandum was read at the meeting on 18 June, attended by all except D'Arcy. Goodier had written off any prospect of success in advance: 'I understand that they are going to put before us certain proposals, and I have a feeling that they will be proposals which we cannot accept.'[64]

The Papalists were anxious in the Memorandum to avoid the perennial charge of disloyalty. Knowing they had no specific mandate to engage in these discussions, they claimed that, in doing so, they were 'attempting at once to respond to an injunction laid upon us by our own authorities at Lambeth'. They were referring, as they did frequently, to the 1908 and 1920 Lambeth

Conferences, which had affirmed Anglican willingness to discuss conditions of Reunion at any time should Rome wish to do so. The Papalists acknowledged that the work for Reunion had ultimately to involve all Christians, but that it was right to focus on Rome 'because the Church of England has her home and centre within Western Christendom'. Again, they sought to protect themselves by quoting the Lambeth Conferences' insistence that any scheme of Reunion ignoring 'the great Latin Church of the West' would be incomplete.

Jones's influence is discernible in the initial assurance that the Papalists sought to avoid past mistakes by not demanding from Rome 'changes and concessions' which it was impossible for her to grant. Rather they appealed only for certain disciplinary changes which they felt were not unreasonable. To avert accusations of impertinence, they pledged themselves at the outset to a recognition of 'the authority of the Church of Rome'. They proceeded to spell out in detail what this entailed. They believed in the infallibility of the Church and her Creeds, they accepted all doctrinal definitions whether made by General Councils or by the Pope speaking *ex cathedra*. In consequence, doctrinally, they maintained, 'there cannot be any difference between us and the Holy Roman Church'.

There followed a rehearsal of the Papalist interpretation of the events of the Reformation. The rupture from Rome was forced unconstitutionally upon the Church of England by the secular power. Therefore, she had 'not forfeited her inherent share in the life of the Universal Church'. A verbatim repetition of Scott's paper of 11 May reaffirmed the Papalists' belief in the validity of their orders. Holding this to be true, they could not deny the sacramental life of the Church of England, even for the sake of ending a damaging schism. From their perspective, that schism could only be ended 'by a corporate union and not by individual secessions'. The Papalist mission was to strive unceasingly 'to create throughout our communion a desire for that true unity which can only be found with the Papacy at its centre'.

The Papalists claimed the support of 400 Anglican clergy and 'a constantly increasing percentage' of the laity. Giving no evidence for such a bold assertion, they also contended that the 'partially informed and inarticulate' majority within the Church of England would immediately support Reunion with Rome should they be requested to do so *by authority*. Next we hear echoes of Corbould's proposal to Cardinal Mercier in the preceding decade: 'It is only necessary for contact to be made, for Rome to make some definite advance, and these inarticulate voices would become a chorus for unity.'

The Memorandum recognised the English people's 'very real sentimental feeling for the Church of England', even when they failed 'to conform to her teaching and practice'. 'She is their mother [...] they will allow no one else to take her place.' Until the Church of England was in communion with Rome, most Englishmen would continue to view the Pope as an alien power. While separated from the Holy See the Church of England lacked efficacy in the work of the care of souls. The division of Christians hindered Christ's mission in our land. 'We and our Roman Catholic brethren strive side by side but divided to convert our people and we each have only a minimum of success because we each suffer from disadvantages. It is only by our union that these disadvantages can be done away.'

The Papalists state that they are making 'practical suggestions as to terms of union' at the request of their 'Roman Catholic friends'. Their proposals were not new; most had been advanced in the Malines Conversations. But lessons had been learned. It was understood that Bourne had objected strongly to Beauduin's paper, 'The Anglican Church united not absorbed', in large measure owing to the Belgian's high-handed proposal that the existing English Catholic hierarchy simply be swept away upon the attainment of Reunion. The Papalists trod carefully. They explicitly stated their assumption that the existing English Catholic hierarchy 'would retain its positions, dignities and privileges unimpaired or enhanced. We accept this as axiomatic.'

To soften the anticipated resistance, the Papalists made it clear that many of the disciplinary concessions sought were not for their own benefit, but for Anglicans of more tender conscience where papal claims were concerned. Such concessions were necessary to gain Anglican agreement to Reunion, but need only be of a temporary nature.

Another sweeping assertion was then made. The English were pre-eminently a practical people, not much given to theories and concepts. Accepting that, it was a massive leap to allege 'that dogmatic agreement may be more easily arrived at than is generally supposed'. At a practical level, anti-Catholicism was still deeply engrained in the national psyche in the early twentieth century. Memories of the fires of Smithfield, the Spanish Armada and the Gunpowder Plot were intentionally revived each year on 5 November with some potency. The Papalists were on much safer ground in stating: 'Ignorance in England concerning the Roman Church is colossal.'

Scott had an academic interest in the early Eastern Church. Fynes-Clinton and Corbould shared a much more practical interest in the contemporary Eastern Church, promoting links between the Church of England and Orthodoxy, hosting various Eastern prelates. The plight of the Russian Church following the 1917 Revolution, the acquisition of new British imperial interests in the eastern Mediterranean and the Near East meant Orthodoxy acquired a reality among the English for almost the first time. Personal contact had helped create a new 'atmosphere of harmony'. If the English perceived Rome as utterly unbending, they were likely to take offence and turn to the Orthodox 'in the attempt to form what is called a non-papal Catholicism'. The Papalists deplored such a possibility, but 'the harsh language' employed against Anglicans 'by some Roman Catholic newspapers and even in some pulpits' served only to alienate the English against Rome and the possibility of Reunion. The Papalists pleaded with their Catholic brethren not 'to humiliate the Anglican Communion'. So much more might be achieved if only Rome were prepared to make a generous and dramatic gesture. It was to this end that the Papalists felt emboldened to suggest various concessions which might be made.

Having dwelt at length on the background, the Papalists stated their desired concessions with a surprising brevity. There was no originality. Lord Halifax's publication the preceding year of

The Thackeray Hotel

the documents of the Malines Conversations rendered their task very much easier. The terms of the 1931 Memorandum derive almost entirely from two documents contained in Halifax's book: a short memorandum drawn up by Robinson, Frere and Halifax in preparation for the Second Conversation in March 1923, and Beauduin's paper, 'The Anglican Church united not absorbed', read by Mercier in May 1925.[65] All three documents make the sweeping assumption that dogmatic agreement will be easily attained, and then proceed to the consequent practicalities.

It is worth examining each proposal in turn:

1. The Archbishop of Canterbury should be created 'Patriarch of such Anglican churches throughout the world as should desire to enter into the union'. The Papalists do not elaborate in any way. The 1923 Memorandum had made passing reference to this possibility. Beauduin expanded upon it and the implications, arguing that the Archbishop of Canterbury had enjoyed patriarchal status prior to the Reformation and this should be revived following Reunion. After only the Pope himself, he might take precedence over all others, including Cardinals, in the Latin Church.

2. For the time being at least the Anglican Church should 'be governed by her own canon laws'. Beauduin had noted that the Uniate churches of the East already had their own canon law distinct from the Latin code. The same concession might be granted to the Anglicans. The 1931 Memorandum allowed for the possibility of appeals to the Holy See.

3. The Anglicans should be allowed 'to appoint their own bishops'. For Beauduin, this right would reside with the Archbishop of Canterbury by virtue of his patriarchal status.

4. Personally, most Papalists were more than happy with Latin and the Roman Missal and breviary. However, they felt it expedient that those coming into union with the Holy See should be offered a distinctively Anglican liturgy, 'an English rite', the Book of Common Prayer revised only to ensure its unambiguous concordance with Catholic doctrine. Here they differed from Beauduin. Betraying his involvement in the Liturgical Movement, Beauduin suggested the Anglican Church use a version of the Roman rite shorn of more recent accretions, reflecting more clearly

'the beautiful classical Roman liturgy' — an Anglican *Novus Ordo*. The Papalists, who personally revelled in Baroque accretions, returned to the 1923 proposal of 'the use of the vernacular and the English rite' for those who preferred that sort of thing.

5. Use of the Authorised Version of the Bible would be permitted 'until such time as a revised edition of it can be agreed upon'. This constitutes the only novel term in the 1931 Memorandum, reflecting perhaps Fynes-Clinton's known weakness for the cadences of the traditional language of the Anglican liturgy.

6. The Pope would 'regularise the orders of the Archbishop of Canterbury', who, in turn, would regularise the orders of all other clergy. This was based on suggestions of both the Lambeth *Appeal* and the 1923 Memorandum. The Papalists carefully repeated that such an action would not involve Anglican clergy denying the validity of their present orders.

7. Existing Anglican bishops and priests should be allowed to remain in office including married clergy. Citing the example of the East, Beauduin did not see the necessity for imposing clerical celibacy on England. The 1923 Memorandum had sought the same concession. Where Mercier and Portal had been flexible on other issues, they thought celibacy so engrained in the Western tradition that a permanent dispensation for England would not be tolerated. There was no precedent for married bishops. Mercier was prepared to concede only the possibility of existing married clergy continuing to exercise their ministry. Those ordained after Reunion would have to embrace celibacy.[66] The Papalists had taken note of Mercier's advice. Addressing the Oxford Society for Reunion in 1928, Scott had warned, 'The marriage of the clergy might have to be given up'.[67] So the 1931 Memorandum allowed only for the future ministry of those clergy 'who should already be married'.

8. Finally, there should be the option of Communion under both kinds, the possibility of offering the chalice to the laity, as recommended by the 1923 Memorandum.

Having set out their conditions with almost indecent haste, as though embarrassed by their role as supplicants, the Papalists found it easier to dwell at length on the advantages which would accrue from Reunion. They emphasized England's position as a world power. If restored to the Catholic Faith how much good might be achieved, they urged. 'England would be the greatest defender of the Papacy and her people the Church's greatest strength.' The English were not given to anti-clericalism. They would prove a bulwark to the Church against the menaces of Communism and extreme nationalism threatening so much of Europe. And it was not just practical and political support from which the Papacy might benefit. There were genuine and distinct 'spiritual riches' which Anglicans would bring to the Universal Church. Increasing numbers of male and female religious in the Anglican Communion were zealously living the evangelical counsels of poverty, chastity and obedience. There was an impressive tradition of devotion among those Anglican laity whose lives were sustained by prayer and the sacraments.

The Papalists concluded with practical suggestions as to how union might best be achieved. In promoting more harmonious relations, there was no substitute for personal contact. The 'English people are not likely to desire union with people whom they do not know and with hierarchs whom they have never seen'. Catholics and Anglicans alike should commit themselves to 'making public statements conducive to a growing spirit of harmony and friendship'. In the same desire to move away from bitter polemics, the Papalists wondered whether Catholics might produce pamphlets for their own people explaining 'the best side of the Anglican Church' and the benefits attaching to Reunion. (As we shall see, the style and the suggestions are Corbould's.) All this was with the intention that Catholics and Anglicans 'know and understand one another better, that they may enjoy that union of heart which must inevitably result in final outward communion and complete unity'.[68]

'Up against a stone wall'?

The Memorandum having been presented, two typed copies having been sent to Goodier at his request, no one seemed to know quite how to proceed next. For most of the participants, it felt that a natural terminus had been reached. The day after the final Conversation, Marchant wrote to Goodier on behalf of the Anglicans. There was a vague suggestion that the Archbishop might wish to consult elsewhere in the light of the Memorandum. Otherwise, the Anglicans were effusive in their thanks for these 'friendly contacts' which had proved 'of inestimable value' to them, but there was a real sense that this was a parting of the ways.[69]

Conscious of the Papalists' unrepresentative nature, Marchant proposed similar conversations between the Catholics and 'Anglicans of other schools'. (Curiously, he suggests that Goodier had agreed to meet such Anglicans in the autumn. They would be 'more influential' than the Papalists, 'in some respects better scholars, but not so free from old prejudices'.[70] There is no evidence that such contact ever took place.) Even Butler was sceptical of such a suggestion. He disputed the Papalists' claim at the final Conversation 'that if only contact be established, doctrine will in time settle itself'. Ultimately, there had to be full acceptance of the Catholic doctrinal position, including the Councils of Trent and Vatican I. That proved the sticking point at Malines 'and will do the same over here'. This might not prove an insurmountable obstacle for the Papalists, but for most Anglican theologians and 'pretty well all the Bishops, it would be about hopeless'. Although of a more optimistic disposition than Goodier, Butler queried whether anything further could be achieved. Nevertheless, he assured Marchant, he would never close the door to the possibility of Reunion: 'Of course I'll go to any meetings arranged.'[71]

The Thackeray Hotel Conversations ended, Marchant indulged in pure fantasy in writing his report to Cardinal Bourne. His initial goal at least was within the realms of possibility: that the Roman School to whom the Catholics had been talking 'could in time be detached' from the Anglican Communion. There were good reasons why this might not happen, but deep-rooted concerns about Anglican Modernism had unsettled many Papalists and made them wonder whether they had a long-term home in the Church of England. They might, Marchant speculated, 'become the forerunner of a wide and continuous movement towards communion with the Holy See'. Such a hope was illusory. One of the reasons the Papalists gave for staying put was that their departure would make the Church of England a more Protestant and Modernist body. That was surely a more accurate analysis.

Marchant made one pertinent point. What exactly did the Papalists mean by 'corporate reunion'? Publicly, they insisted that Reunion had to involve the Church of England in its entirety, conceding that the prospect of this was not imminent. But, given the other Papalist *sine qua non*, that unity could only ever be on the basis of full dogmatic agreement, how exactly did they envisage the Protestant and Modernist branches of Anglicanism ever embracing Reunion with Rome? It seemed that there would have to be flexibility on one or other of these two conditions, if Reunion were ever to be a reality.

Sir James proceeded to dictate to the head of the Catholic Church in England and Wales how he should act and what the consequences might be. 'In a year or so' it might become 'practical politics' to receive the Papalists and their congregations. 'If such a movement were once begun it would gather in momentum.' Of course, the Cardinal would wish to consider appointing one or two of the Papalists as Catholic bishops. One wonders whom Marchant had in mind. Scott would certainly have enlivened the proceedings of the Catholic hierarchy.

Then it was back to the daydreaming. Marchant painted a picture of a 'landslide' movement 'on a large scale' into the Catholic Church. He imagined the resistance this would encounter from the Anglican 'Bishops and the Government and Throne'. The Church of England would be irrevocably split. Marchant paused for a moment to admit: 'Of course, we were looking a generation or two ahead.' But 'an insubstantial dream' was always more alluring to Marchant than the cold light of day. So he congratulated Bourne: 'What a glorious thing it would be if, during your reign as Archbishop of Westminster, such a movement began as should in the long end bring England again to the feet of the Holy Father!'[72]

No one ever accused Archbishop Goodier of being a fantasist. He foresaw the Catholic Church having to pronounce definitively against at least some of the concessions sought by the Memorandum. In fact, he hoped that the Papalists would approve of the likely negative response given it was the immutable nature of the Church which so appealed to them.[73] Goodier was courteous. He promised his future assistance in any form Marchant felt helpful. But he was also clear: 'The Memorandum [...] bumps one up against a stone wall, and I see no way through.' But he forwarded the Memorandum to the Cardinal, 'who has promised to study it; and probably he in turn will submit it, just as it is, to the Holy Father himself, that he may see exactly what its authors think and feel'.[74] And there matters were left over the summer of 1931.

One is conscious of being a spectator to proceedings at a considerable remove from external events. No reference is made in the Conversations or correspondence to the tumultuous events of a world struggling with the consequences of the Great Depression. Following a run on the pound, Ramsay MacDonald resigned as Labour Prime Minister on 24 August and formed a National Government. The following month witnessed the extraordinary phenomena of the Royal Navy mutiny at Invergordon in protest at the Government's austerity measures, and Britain's abandonment of the Gold Standard. Nevertheless, the National Government won a landslide victory in the General Election on 27 October.

The same week Marchant supplied Goodier with a slightly revised copy of the Memorandum incorporating amendments suggested by the Archbishop so that it might be in a form suitable for presentation to the Pope. Most changes were relatively minor, clarifying matters here and there. The most significant amendment was to the opening paragraphs 'to make it clearer that our friends whilst speaking for themselves represent a growing body of opinion in the Anglican Church, but of course unofficially'.[75] Cardinal Bourne was directly involved at this point; he was sufficiently astute to appreciate that Rome might be interested in pursuing this further—provided a substantial number of Anglican clergy supported the proposals.

Bourne asked Goodier to prepare a statement for the benefit of those who would read the Memorandum in Rome. This he did, giving some background as to the identity of the Papalists, tracing the history of the Conversations and recording his own impressions of them. Goodier chose not to consult with

The Thackeray Hotel

Butler before fulfilling his task—'as all seemed to me quite clear'. Instead, he seems to have spoken with his fellow Jesuit, Francis Woodlock, who had plotted with Cardinal Merry del Val to derail the Malines Conversations. It reinforced the Archbishop's natural tendency to fatalism where relations with the Anglicans were concerned. Woodlock maintained that 'Anglicanism is to be met not by sympathy, which is only exploited, but by clear and emphatic definition of the differences between us'. The Papalists had argued, anticipating the Second Vatican Council, that baptism already placed them within the Catholic Church; they had only to address the need for full obedience to the Pope. Goodier agreed with Woodlock: 'there is need of a further definition from Rome, which shall make it quite clear that baptism alone does not put one in the Body of Christ'.

The Archbishop worked himself up into a state of indignation. 'The more I have thought about the outcome of these conversations, the more I am disappointed, not to say annoyed.' In his statement he emphasized 'the determination of our friends to be considered a schism of the Catholic Church, and no more, and only an accidental one at that'. He noted that the Papalists had never once mentioned 'conversion' to the Catholic Church. He felt that all they wanted 'was recognition by Rome, on the ground that they were already just as Catholic as ourselves'. While Butler would have agreed with many of these criticisms, his approach would have been more rounded. Goodier made no reference to the Papalists' real sorrow over the tragedy of division nor their insistence on the need for doctrinal agreement. He gave them no credit for their very genuine desire for unity.

As a token of their gratitude for the privilege of being allowed to participate in the Conversations, the Anglicans invited the Catholics to lunch. Goodier replied that commitments prevented him from accepting, but he saw no reason why Butler, Jarrett and D'Arcy should not attend.[76]

Cardinal Bourne left for Rome on 6 December. Marchant wrote just prior to his departure, assuring him once more that the Memorandum which he carried represented the views of 'several hundred' Anglican clergy. What was it they sought?

> Simply to know that the Holy Father prayed for them and had listened with a Father's heart to their faltering plea [...] If on your return you bear a little message and blessing you will have a welcome of which you will be ever thankful.

The Cardinal could count on constant prayer being offered for 'the sympathetic reception' of the Memorandum in Rome.[77]

Bourne was received by Pius XI in audience on 9 December. We do not know what the Cardinal told the Pope about the Papalists or their Memorandum. Obviously, he was sufficiently committed to have presented it to the Holy Father in the first place; the thought seems to have been his. There is no doubting his own desire for Reunion, on a proper basis, nor his willingness to make any personal sacrifice necessary to advance that end. But Bourne could be frustratingly detached on occasion. He would not prevent others taking initiatives, but often did precious little himself to further them. Did he simply present the Memorandum to the Pope, and await developments from Rome? Possibly.

The Cardinal left Rome on 27 December. He discussed his audience with Goodier, but neither felt it necessary to contact the Anglicans. Their suspense must have been unbearable. Finally, on 19 February 1932, Corbould could contain himself no longer. He came up from Carshalton to visit the Archbishop, spending 1½ hours with him in Chelsea. Goodier could hardly have been surprised: 'He was very anxious to know what the Holy Father had said about the Memorandum.' Goodier was reluctant to disclose anything:

> Being compelled to speak, I told him that he had received it sympathetically, but that he did not see what more he could say or do than he had already said and done. I told him this in such a way as to safeguard the Holy Father.

Quite why the Pope needed safeguarding is unclear. The Archbishop was anxious that he had handled matters as the Cardinal would have wished. However, Corbould left 'evidently more than satisfied'.[78]

The following week Corbould wrote requesting a resumption of the Conversations. But the Archbishop had been appalled by the recent Anglican agreement for intercommunion with the 'Old Catholics', most of whom had separated from Rome in consequence of the First Vatican Council, which the Anglican Papalists claimed to accept. For Goodier, this represented a conscious decision on the part of the Church of England 'to accept its heresy in preference to the truth'.[79] The Archbishop saw no point in meeting again. He reiterated his belief that 'we had got, for the present, as far as our conversations are likely to lead us'.[80] They had, it appeared, reached an insurmountable impasse.

Notes

[1] Pierce to Joblin, 2 September 1930 (copy), PHA/Rea/CU2/458.

[2] Jones to Pierce, 8 September 1930, PHA/Rea/CU2/466.

[3] Goodier to Marchant, 17 October 1930, OUL, Marchant, 299/167.

[4] Campbell to Pierce, 8 February 1931, BCA, Pierce Bequest, CU Founding and Letters.

[5] Marchant to Lang, 29 December 1930, LPL, Lang Papers, 107/18–19.

[6] Temple to Lang, 6 January 1931, LPL, Lang Papers, 107/20.

[7] Jones to Pierce, 14 January 1931, PHA/Rea/CU3.

[8] W. Hough to Marchant, 7 January 1931, OUL, Marchant, 300/40.

[9] R. J. Farmer, *Father Alban Baverstock SSC: An Exploration of His Life* (London: The Catholic League, 1997); Jones to Campbell, 2 February 1931, PHA/Rea/CU3.

[10] Scott to Pierce, 1 December 1928, PHA/Rea/CU1/85.

[11] *Messenger*, 60 (Oct.–Dec. 1928).

[12] Jones to Campbell, 2 February 1931, PHA/Rea/CU3; Jones to Pierce, 14 January 1931, PHA/Rea/CU3.

[13] Marchant to Lang, 12 November 1929, LPL, Lang Papers, 97/208.

[14] Anon. Anglican paper, undated, annotated '18 June', paper referred to in Goodier's letter of 13 May 1931, DAA, Butler, P/7.

[15] Goodier to Bourne, 28 October 1931, AAW, Bo. I/107.

[16] Marchant to Lang, 22 December 1928, LPL, Lang Papers, 97/214.

[17] Marchant to Bourne, 1 July 1931, AAW, Bo. I/107.

[18] Pope Pius XI, *Casti Connubii* (1930), n.56.

[19] Jones to Campbell, 2 February 1931, PHA/Rea/CU3.

[20] Campbell to Pierce, 8 February 1931, BCA, Pierce Bequest, CU Founding and Letters.

21 Jones to Campbell, 2 February 1931, PHA/Rea/CU3.
22 Goodier, Paper delivered 26 March 1931, LPL, Fynes-Clinton Papers, 4297/29.
23 D'Arcy, Appointments Diary, 4 February 1931, ABSI; Butler to Marchant, 26 February 1931, OUL, Marchant, 299/29.
24 Goodier to Marchant, 27 February 1931, OUL, Marchant Papers, 299/169.
25 Jones, 'The Position', DAA, Butler Papers, P/7.
26 Goodier to Marchant, 5 March 1931, OUL, Marchant Papers, 299/170; Goodier to Butler, 5 March 1931, DAA, Butler Papers, P/7.
27 Butler to Goodier, 6 March 1931 (copy), DAA, Butler Papers, P/7.
28 Scott, 'Schism in the Church', document forwarded under Goodier's letter of 7 March 1931, DAA, Butler Papers, P/7.
29 Goodier to Marchant, 15 March 1931, OUL, Marchant Papers, 299/172.
30 Scott, 'On Schism within the Church', DAA, Butler Papers, P/7.
31 [Simmonds?], 'A Summary of the History of Attempts at and Proposals for Reunion from 1538 to 1833', DAA, Butler Papers, P/7.
32 Goodier to Marchant, 17 March 1930, OUL, Marchant Papers, 299/174.
33 Simmonds, *What do English Divines Say?* (London: Council for Promoting Catholic Unity, 1932); Simmonds, 'Reunion Movement before 1833', 14 November 1932, PHA, OUSR, Minute Book, vol. I, p. 263.
34 Pierce to Joblin, 2 October 1931, PHA/Rea/CU3/205b. Pierce's information appears to have come from Scott via Campbell.
35 Goodier to Marchant, 17 March 1930, OUL, Marchant Papers, 299/173–4.
36 Goodier, Paper delivered 26 March 1931, LPL, Fynes-Clinton Papers, 4297/29–33.
37 Goodier to Marchant, 31 March 1931, OUL, Marchant Papers, 299/175.
38 Goodier to Marchant, 31 March 1931, OUL, Marchant Papers, 299/175.
39 Goodier to Butler, 22 June 1932, DAA, Butler Papers, P/7.
40 H. Keane, SJ, 'Archbishop Goodier: A Memoir', in A. Goodier, SJ, *St Ignatius Loyola and Prayer: As Seen in the Book of Spiritual Exercises* (London: Burns Oates & Washbourne, 1940), p. 2.
41 Goodier to Marchant, 4 May 1931, OUL, Marchant Papers, 299/178.
42 *Ibid.*
43 Goodier to Marchant, 17 April 1931, OUL, Marchant, 299/177.
44 Scott, *Anglo-Catholicism and Re-union*, p. 46.
45 Goodier to Butler, 7 May 1931, DAA, Butler Papers, P/7.
46 Goodier to Butler, 13 May 1931, DAA, Butler Papers, P/7.
47 Vatican II, *Lumen Gentium* (1964), 18.

48 Anonymous Anglican paper, undated, mistakenly annotated '18 June', DAA, Butler Papers, P/7.

49 Goodier to Butler, 13 May 1931, DAA, Butler Papers, P/7.

50 Goodier to Butler, 18 May 1931, DAA, Butler Papers, P/7.

51 Goodier to Butler, 19 March 1931, DAA, Butler Papers, P/7.

52 Pierce to Harris, 31 May 1933 (copy), BCA, Pierce Bequest, Correspondence 1930–3/212.

53 Lang to Marchant, 2 May 1931 (copy), LPL, Lang Papers, 107/21.

54 Marchant to Lang, 14 May 1931, LPL, Lang Papers, 107/22–4.

55 Lang to Marchant, 2 June 1931 (copy), LPL, Lang Papers, 107/25.

56 Temple to unnamed parish priest, 1933, cited F. A. Iremonger, *William Temple, Archbishop of Canterbury: His Life and Letters* (London: Oxford University Press, 1948), p. 419.

57 Goodier to Marchant, 31 March 1931, OUL, Marchant Papers, 299/175; Goodier to Butler, 7 May 1931, DAA, Butler Papers, P/7; Goodier to Marchant, 17 April 1931, OUL, Marchant Papers, 299/177.

58 Pierce to Jack, 29 March 1951, PHA/Rea/CU4.

59 Corbould, *Will*, 27 July 1952.

60 Goodier to Butler, 27 October 1931, DAA, Butler, P/7.

61 Goodier to Butler, 26 May 1932, DAA, Butler, P/7.

62 Goodier to Butler, 7 May 1931, DAA, Butler Papers, P/7.

63 Marchant to Bourne, 1 July 1931, AAW, Bo. I/107.

64 Goodier to Marchant, 14 June 1931, OUL, Marchant Papers, 299/180.

65 C. L. Halifax, *The Conversations at Malines 1921–1925: Original Documents* (London: Philip Allan & Co., 1930), pp. 79–82, 240–61.

66 Barlow, *The Malines Conversations*, p. 100.

67 Scott, Address, 12 March 1928, OUSR, Minute Book, vol. I, p. 142, PHA.

68 Memorandum (revised), DAA, Butler Papers, P/7.

69 Marchant to Goodier, 19 June 1931, AAW, Bo. I/107.

70 Marchant to Bourne, 1 July 1931, AAW, Bo. I/107.

71 Butler to Marchant, 24 June 1931, OUL, Marchant Papers, 299/32.

72 Marchant to Bourne, 1 July 1931, AAW, Bo. I/107.

73 Goodier to Marchant, 22 June 1931, OUL, Marchant Papers, 299/181.

74 Goodier to Marchant, 24 June 1931, OUL, Marchant Papers, 299/182.

75 Marchant to Goodier, 24 October 1931, AAW, Bo. I/107.

76 Goodier to Butler, 27 October 1931, DAA, Butler Papers, P/7; Goodier to Bourne, 28 October 1931, AAW, Bo. I/107.

77 Marchant to Bourne, 28 November 1931, AAW, Bo./ALN.

78 Goodier to Bourne, 21 February 1932, AAW, Bourne/ALN.
79 Goodier to Marchant, 2 February 1932, OUL, Marchant Papers, 299/193–4.
80 Goodier to Marchant, 25 February 1932, OUL, Marchant Papers, 299/195.

✧ 6 ✧

Cadogan Gardens[1]

'A controversy with Sir James'[2]

The mere existence of the Thackeray Hotel Conversations has been known to Church historians for a generation. John Dick came across references to them in the Westminster and Lambeth Archives while researching his book, *The Malines Conversations Revisited*. He mistakes Marchant for a Catholic, while Bernard Barlow has Archbishop Lang approving and Cardinal Bourne attending the talks. Both authors maintain that the Conversations took place from June to October 1931, that they ended with no substantive result and that 'our knowledge of these discussions is scant'.[3] Reading the correspondence of Goodier and Marchant, of Bourne and Lang, filled in and corrected some of the details, but seemed to confirm the general outline suggested by Dick and Barlow. It came as a surprise, therefore, to discover that the Conversations did not end in 1931.

When Corbould visited Cadogan Gardens on 19 February 1932, it was not just with the intention of discovering the Pope's reaction to the Memorandum. There was discontent within the ranks of the non-Catholics. Aged just thirty, Leslie Simmonds was the youngest of the Thackeray Hotel Conversationalists. He might have attended simply as Corbould's curate, entrusted with the task of taking minutes, yet his assessment of the underlying motivation of the other participants was remarkably perceptive. By 1932, Simmonds had arrived at the conclusion that Sir James Marchant was deeply untrustworthy. He was not alone in that view.

Marchant's support for the cause of Reunion was undoubtedly sincere. As was his admiration for Dr Orchard. Like many others, he found Orchard intellectually impressive and spiritually inspiring. Marchant saw their futures inextricably linked as Orchard searched for sacramental certainty for his ministry. Together they ranged over the options, Marchant probably the less concerned of the two that those options were logically contradictory: validation by the Anglicans and Orthodox, a gradual drift towards Rome, 'an episcopal ministry for the Free Churches'. At one point Sir James seemed to have his sights set on a mitre as 'Orchard's colleague at the Weigh House',[4] In October 1931, he was making enquiries of Bishop Bell of Chichester, Davidson's former Chaplain, as to whether the Archbishop of Canterbury might license Orchard to preach in Anglican pulpits without the need to subscribe to the Thirty-Nine Articles. The very same week Marchant was helping the Anglican Papalists finalise their Memorandum setting out terms for Reunion with Rome.

For Orchard, the crisis came towards the end of 1931. He ruled out the Church of England on the grounds of Modernism, the State connection and the doubtful validity of its orders. Marchant arranged for Goodier to visit Orchard in his rooms at the Thackeray Hotel on 3 December. The Nonconformist was experiencing an 'anti-Roman "horror"', the residual English fear of papal tyranny and intellectual slavery. On the other hand, he knew increasingly what had to be done. 'His mind is not finally made up, but in his bones he feels it will be Rome.' Goodier's own self-doubt and lack of polemical zeal were exactly suited to these circumstances. Orchard's dilemma elicited the Archbishop's compassion: 'I understand every bit of the agony through which he is going, and I empathise with all my heart.'[5]

Orchard wrote his letter of resignation to the Weigh House Chapel on 5 January, but continued in ministry there until Easter. His plan was then to travel to Rome with the intention of converting to Catholicism. Staying in Bournemouth as Marchant's guest, Sir James acted as Orchard's intermediary with Bourne, who arranged accommodation for him in Rome and an introduction to Mgr Charles Duchemin, the Rector of the Beda College, the English seminary in Rome for converts and late vocations. Orchard was to be received into the Catholic Church on 2 June and was later ordained a priest of the Westminster Diocese. His

Cadogan Gardens

ministry as a Catholic attracted far less publicity than those heady days in Mayfair in the 1920s.

Orchard's conversion became Marchant's dilemma. What was he himself to do? His predicament became particularly acute as the Government's austerity measures resulted in the winding up of the National Council of Public Morals. Aged 64, Marchant was without a job or a salary. He enjoyed 'only the most slender private means and a small Civil List pension of £75'.[6] Initially, he seems to have considered the Papalists his route to securing the future. Simmonds also made his way to Bournemouth in January. There he was painted 'a glowing picture of our reception into the Roman Church compared with the fact that in the C of E we should get nothing and our departure would be welcomed'. Simmonds was probably correct in 'feeling on account of this that there was more behind our meetings than we knew — that in fact, the Romans had been led to anticipate that we would form a Uniate — with Dr Orchard'.[7] The Papalists were not about to be bounced into union with Rome simply to help Sir James out of a personal quandary.

At the same time Marchant was getting nowhere with Goodier in his attempt to reopen the Conversations. The Archbishop believed a display of Catholic disinterest the only means of proving to the Anglicans that Rome was not 'anxious to receive them on their own terms'. He too had the measure of Marchant. Goodier felt Sir James 'has in his mind some sort of dramatic debacle which will make history as did the Oxford Movement'. The Archbishop sought to disillusion Marchant, explaining to him both by letter and in person that conversion must be individual; groups would not be contemplated. Writing to Bourne, Goodier reflected that if Marchant 'ever offers his submission, I fancy he will get the shock of his life when he finds he will have to go under instruction, and will not be received the next day with acclamation!'[8] By early March 1932, even Sir James had to accept that the Conversations between Anglicans and Catholics which he had spent years attempting to engineer were going no further — at least not under his chairmanship.

Why did Marchant never become a Catholic? Cardinal Bourne later wrote him the most sympathetic letter:

> I know and appreciate deeply the difficulties of your position and I understand your good faith. At the same time in the eyes of the world at large that position, as you will readily recognise yourself, is anomalous and perplexing. You are on the very threshold and still hesitate to enter [...] May God guide you and bring you safely in His own time to the harbour of rest.[9]

It was not to be. Status and salary were a consideration. Perhaps the Nonconformist beliefs and mind-set were too entrenched, although Orchard maintained, 'I do not think you have a single conviction to keep you back'. Like the Papalists, Marchant pleaded that he could better serve the cause of Reunion by remaining where he was. Orchard dismissed this argument as 'inadequate'. He felt that the true reason lay elsewhere: 'it is simply a personal and domestic difficulty that keeps you back'. We know very little of Eleanor Marchant, save that the couple married in South Shields in 1895. But she appears to have been a formidable lady. Sir James feared his conversion to Catholicism 'would break up [their] home'.[10]

One has to admire Marchant's resilience. The dreams of a decade dashed, he immediately picked himself up to explore another avenue. Writing to the Archbishop of Canterbury, he presented his misfortunes as an opportunity: 'This sets me free to realise a desire to help the Church of England.'[11] Disregarding his actions and statements of recent weeks and months, Marchant failed to notice the incongruity as he now denigrated 'the *awful* attitude' of the English Catholics.[12] He offered himself for ordination in the Church of England.[13] The Anglicans were suspicious and hesitant. Bell cautioned Lang: 'He has done his very best to discourage Orchard from any scheme of affiliation with the Church of England [...] I cannot help a sense of his playing off one person against another.' Marchant was not proud. He settled instead for Anglican support for an increased Government pension.

Given this lack of consistency and transparency, it is not surprising that the Papalists raised their own doubts about Marchant when Corbould visited Goodier:

These Anglican gentlemen want to get rid of him altogether, saying he is unsafe; that while he is affecting to be the friend of everyone he is really trying to found a sort of church of his own. What appears to have finished them is an offer he seems to have made to them to join him, holding out the bait of at least one bishopric.[14]

Marchant had never really understood the Papalists. Whatever their misgivings about the Church of England, the last thing they wanted was a supporting role in some new denomination created by a Nonconformist fantasist.

But their grievance with Marchant did not end there. Some time in January or early February 1932, Corbould, Scott and Simmonds had a final meeting with Marchant at the Thackeray Hotel. He told them that their Memorandum 'which was sent to Rome had been shown to the Archbishop of Canterbury who disapproved of it'. Sir James alleged that it had been given to Archbishop Lang by Cardinal Bourne. Corbould went to Chelsea partly to establish the truth of this allegation. Goodier assured the Papalists that this was not the case. He shared their suspicion that Marchant himself was the guilty party.[15] The Papalists claimed that they did not object to Lang seeing all their papers, but to see the Memorandum alone 'would give him a false impression as to what was going on'. They deeply resented Marchant's breach of confidence. Simmonds spoke for the others when he stated: 'I could not agree to continuing further with Sir James present.'[16]

Finally, Goodier and the Papalists had arrived at common ground—a shared determination to be shot of Marchant. Corbould felt this might be sufficient to kick-start the Conversations. The Papalists assured the Archbishop that they were 'anxious to push out Sir James Marchant, and to hold the conversations without him'. They offered to meet at some new venue on 21 March. If Goodier were not free, they asked whether they might still continue with Butler, Jarrett and D'Arcy. In fact, we know that this was their preferred option. Simmonds confided to Jones his hope that they 'might have the chance to begin afresh with Abbot Butler, because I am sure we shall do nothing with Goodier, charming and saintly as he is. We must I am sure deal with the OSB and not with the SJ.' If the Archbishop was reluctant to meet the Papalists at this stage, he was no more willing to transfer responsibility for the conversations to Butler or anyone else. This was a duty the Cardinal had entrusted to him. Marchant also wrote to Goodier one last time seeking a date for another meeting — before concluding definitively in March 1932 that courting the Anglican Establishment offered him a better prospect.[17]

The Archbishop adamantly rejected the various overtures made to him: 'I feel that there is little more to be gained by the conversations at present, and that so long as we work for corporate reunion only we shall merely go round and round.'[18] This time Butler, Jarrett and D'Arcy agreed that 'the "conversations" lead nowhere, and therefore may cease'.[19]

Corbould and Fynes-Clinton were nothing if not persistent. They contacted Goodier again in May 1932, asking to resume the Conversations and to meet with him in Chelsea. The Archbishop felt that he had gained a tactical victory: 'I think our coolness has done them no harm.'[20]

It was the recurring squabble with Marchant which brought the Papalists back to Goodier. Sir James had contacted Simmonds, as secretary to the Conversationalists, requesting him to hand over all the documents in his possession. One wonders how Marchant intended to use these, given his contact with both the Papalists and the Catholics was at an end. Quite correctly, Simmonds refused. He felt unable to release the material 'without the consent of all the Conversationalists. I have the only complete set, and if it goes to him, we have no record of what took place.' Marchant had not anticipated such an act of non-compliance from the young clergyman, and aired his displeasure: 'He was astounded! deeply pained!! etc.!!! and threatened an awful fate if I persisted.' Simmonds stuck to his guns, and handed the papers over to Corbould.

The Papalists were gentlemen, but they were also resolute. They explained to Marchant that their hesitation was a result of the Memorandum having been disclosed to the Archbishop of Canterbury. In their opinion, this constituted a clear breach of confidence, it having been 'understood that [the documents] are private and confidential, not to be used in any way or shown to anyone outside the meetings without the author's consent'. They pointed out, with perfect propriety, that ownership was vested in them on the basis both of authorship and the fact that they had paid for the manuscripts to be typed. They did not dispute Marchant's right, as convener of the Conversations, to have a complete set of the documents. They would happily have copies made, if he wished, at his expense. Marchant disputed this, particularly the question of ownership of the documents.[21]

So when Corbould and Fynes-Clinton arrived in Chelsea, the Archbishop was surprised that they 'had only come about a quarrel that had arisen between them and Sir James Marchant, which they wanted me to settle for them'. We do not know Goodier's solution, but it appears to have satisfied all parties. If he had been uncertain before, the Archbishop was left in no doubt now that there had been an irretrievable breakdown in relations between the Papalists and Marchant. 'They no longer trust him, and he no longer trusts them; a queer situation for men working for "reunion" with us!'[22]

'My tiny room'

The parish of St Mary's, Chelsea, has its origins in the chapel built by a French émigré priest for the Catholics at the Chelsea Hospital and the Chelsea and Knightsbridge Barracks. The current church, opened by Cardinal Manning in 1879, and the adjoining rectory, were designed by J. F. Bentley. Benefactors had purchased a substantial site which Manning briefly considered as a possible site for his new cathedral and seminary. Bentley, of course, subsequently built Westminster Cathedral elsewhere, but the centrality of the location meant that for almost a century St Mary's Rectory was invariably occupied by one of the auxiliary bishops of Westminster. Assisting Cardinal Bourne in the Diocese, Goodier took up residence in the autumn of 1930.

Corbould and Fynes-Clinton asked to meet in his room there at 3 pm on 31 May 1932. It is not altogether clear why Goodier relented and agreed to their request. He still felt, somewhat unfairly, that they were approaching Reunion from the wrong perspective: 'They want union first and unity of faith afterwards.' The Archbishop obviously felt more comfortable in the company of Corbould and Fynes-Clinton, who made no pretence to be more than parish priests, than Scott and Jones, who had serious academic and theological credentials. He hoped that, with only two Anglicans attending this time, 'we ought to get more to the point and keep there'. Goodier and the Anglicans wanted Butler to join them, but he was otherwise engaged.[23]

That meeting was primarily concerned with the Papalists' dispute with Marchant. But the three of them agreed to resume their earlier Conversations at St Mary's Rectory at 3 pm on 27 June. The Archbishop protested that his 'tiny room' was scarcely large enough to host the company. In fact, it was a spacious and well-appointed first floor study, and the Papalists insisted that 'they preferred it to anywhere else'. Corbould and Fynes-Clinton were to attend with two other, unidentified Anglicans. This time Butler was able to join them, but Goodier ruled out the involvement of Jarrett and D'Arcy, still smarting from their earlier criticism of his conduct of the Catholic case.

Writing to the Anglicans, the Archbishop summarised the Catholic position:

1. That we Catholics cannot look upon the Church of England as anything but an heretical Church, and not merely schismatical as they would have us believe;

2. That there can be no question of corporate reunion as such, but that each individual case will have to be taken on its own merits.

He claimed that the Papalists seemed willing to accept the second point. (This seems unlikely in view of what they had said and were to say.) The Anglicans would prepare a paper for the next meeting putting their case as to why the first contention was wrong. Goodier expected this to be the usual restatement of historical arguments. If so, he would look to Butler 'to put them right; they respect your historical mind tremendously'. The Archbishop intended to concentrate on 'the recent carryings-on with the Old Catholics'. If the Papalists claimed that the Church of England was not heretical, how could they justify intercommunion with a body which, in his opinion, clearly was?[24]

Goodier and Butler rehearsed the Catholic case in correspondence in advance of the meeting. For Goodier the critical issue was the question as to whether the Church of England was a heretical body, or simply schismatic. In England, at least, it would have been difficult to find a Catholic who did not hold the Church of England to be heretical. Whereas, of course, the Papalists maintained that the Anglican Communion was simply in schism, and that not of its own making and understood only in a limited sense of schism *in* the Church rather than *from* the Church. Such language can jar on twenty-first century ears, accustomed to a far gentler vocabulary concerning the status of non-Catholic Christians. Why the obsession in the 1930s with determining this contentious point? After all, the Malines Conversations had not dwelt on the matter—which, of course, in the eyes of our English Catholic participants was precisely where they had erred and ultimately failed. At least the Papalists understood the importance of the point, as evidenced by Scott's papers the previous year.

Goodier appreciated that it all hinged on the Anglican desire for Corporate Reunion as opposed to individual conversions. The Papalists could not have it both ways. They could not argue that Reunion could only be corporate, while asking the Catholics to rely on their *personal* orthodoxy. The Archbishop was correct: 'It does not seem to me, at present, a question of individual belief, but of the larger question of the Anglican Church itself. If it is, as they would like to maintain, only schismatical, then all would be easy.' If the Church of England held, in its entirety, the faith of the Universal Church, but were simply out of communion with the See of Peter, then, with the right will, rectifying that situation ought to be relatively simple. Two orthodox churches would be entering communion with each other with no need for fundamental change on either part. But Rome would never enter into communion with a heretical body. Barring wholesale doctrinal change, the conversion of individuals (or groups of individuals) was the only means of entry into the Catholic Church. Knowing this to be critical, the Papalists clung, therefore, to their conviction that, while individual Anglicans might be heretical, corporately the Church of England had always maintained the orthodox faith.

The difficulty was in finding an authoritative statement of Anglican teaching.

Butler felt the weight of the potential consequences of these talks weighing upon him. He shrank from driving the Anglicans further than the Holy Spirit led them. Goodier agreed but was equally afraid of 'leaving them under the impression that we have doubts of the heretical, not merely schismatical, position of the Church of England'. He recalled that Newman and Manning had taught 'that up to a point the Anglican movement should have our support'. But Newman had thought the time would probably come when that support could no longer be given. With the Church of England seeking reunion with Lutherans, Old Catholics and 'Calvinist Nonconformists', the Archbishop felt that moment may well have arrived.[25]

'Already so much in common'

The Papalists came to Chelsea on the afternoon of 27 June with a good deal to prove. As in the preceding spring, Goodier and Butler were not given the paper they were expecting. The delivery and—so the tone and content would suggest—the authorship was Corbould's. Gone were the aggressive polemics of Scott and the detailed historical evidence of Jones. This was an appeal to the heart.

Goodier had asked the Papalists to demonstrate that the Church of England was not heretical. Corbould believed that the Archbishop was asking the impossible: to vindicate the Anglican position to his satisfaction. Corbould placed one matter beyond doubt at the outset: 'We have no other thought in mind than Corporate Union.' The Papalists had understood that the Pope was prepared to contemplate this given his official recognition of the Malines Conversations. It seemed that the English Catholics would never agree any position 'justified which involves external separation even for a time from the communion of the Holy See'.

Corbould asked the Catholics to accept another approach. Arguing whether or not the Church of England was heretical 'leads only to a deadlock and can only involve a return to the old controversies between our communions which we understood were to be excluded from these conversations'. If they were serious about unity, could the Catholics not admit a gradualist strategy? Were the Anglicans to make all the sacrifices?

> We have often emphasized in these conversations that we recognise that no union can be effected except by true dogmatic agreement—but will not our Roman Catholic friends help us as a body to attain stage by stage to this ultimate end?

He reassured the Catholics that he was not asking them to make doctrinal concessions nor to avoid the issues. But did the Catholics really wish the Papalists to leave the Church of England immediately if the consequence were to 'hand that great communion over to a debased and unchristian Protestantism?'

What, then, did Corbould ask? He admitted that there was tremendous ignorance of Catholicism in the Anglican Communion. There was a desperate need for information and explanations, a practical drawing together. And here he appealed to Goodier and Butler's pride and compassion. 'You who are animated by so much charity and possessed of such learning can do much to help' achieve this.

There was a crying need to move beyond the futility of the old arguments. What stood in the way of unity? It had been thought that *Apostolicae Curae*'s declaration against the validity of Anglican Orders had created an insuperable barrier to Reunion. But a path forward had been found: the 1920 Lambeth Conference had resolved that, other matters being agreed, the Anglican Bishops were 'willing for the sake of unity to submit to such regularisation of their status as the Holy Father may think fit'. Here Corbould could not resist parading his personal connections. He mentioned how Cardinal Mercier had confided in him that, when Mercier had told Cardinal Gasparri of this 1920 Lambeth Resolution, Gasparri had been reduced to tears, saying 'that it was one of the most beautiful acts of humility of which he had ever heard'.

For a man so conservative in matters of religion and politics, Corbould proceeded to advocate a very modern approach to the question of Reunion. He urged 'that inherited prejudices and animosities should be dropped and that we should proceed by a more excellent way'. Yes, there were matters which divided the two Communions, but, regarding the essentials, 'there is already a large measure of agreement in theory'. Would the Catholics not work with the Papalists in helping to consolidate and build on this?

Corbould did then turn to history, but not, like Jones and Scott, to marshal facts with which to confront and confound an opponent. Rather, it was an admission of weakness and human frailty, a plea for empathy and assistance. The Papalists had 'nothing but the utmost reverence and admiration' for those English Catholics after the Reformation who had lost life and livelihood as the price of their loyalty to Rome. But the Church of England was descended from those, the great majority, 'who bent before the storm'. Corbould conceded that their behaviour was not heroic, 'but it was natural and human'. Most of those original Anglicans did not explicitly deny defined Catholic doctrine. They were confused and timid in a time of flux. Probably they fully expected England to be reconciled with Rome within their lifetime. It was not easy to die for the Pope when 'the prestige of the Holy See was at its lowest ebb' and the importance of the office of the papacy as the centre of Catholic unity was obscured by the abuses and scandals of the office-holders.

The Papalists' very presence at these Conversations was the consequence of their profound wish to heal that schism. But they could not simply ignore 400 years of history. Could the Catholics attempt to understand how the Papalists found themselves in their current, admittedly imperfect, situation? 'That we Anglicans return where you would have us be depends so much upon you and the charity and wisdom with which you deal with the present situation.'

Corbould was not prepared to take all the blame. He confronted the English Catholics with some uncomfortable truths. They would have known that such allegations were commonplace in the aftermath of *Apostolicae Curae* and Malines:

Cadogan Gardens

It is always being said: 'The English Roman Catholics will do nothing towards healing the schism: they will do nothing to meet you: you must seek for the sympathy and understanding only on the Continent', and many of our friends in your own communion on the Continent say the same. Is this really so? We who have taken part in these conversations hope and believe that it is not. We desire supremely that the rapprochement which we hope in the first instance to effect shall be through the authorities of your great communion in England. Do you tell us that the door is shut?[26]

Corbould concluded with a final entreaty for cooperation in the great cause of corporate unity.

The tenor of the entire paper had been unashamedly emotional, but was Corbould not entitled to make recourse to the greatest commandment of all, the commandment to love? The Catholics no doubt would retort that the claims of conscience and truth could not be ignored, that there could be no unity without a secure foundation. How were the claims of charity and truth to be reconciled?

What, in fact, did the Catholics say? We do not know. Butler almost certainly would have been prepared to admit the strength of Corbould's heartfelt plea, without conceding that it necessarily took them any further in resolving the underlying issues. Goodier may have remained impervious to such an approach, reasoning that the appeal to sentiment only demonstrated again the weakness of the Papalist case. All we know is that six weeks later, his health beginning to fail him, the Archbishop left London for good, retiring to the Benedictine Sisters at St Scholastica's Abbey, Teignmouth in Devon. For all practical purposes it seemed that contact between the Catholics and Anglicans was at an end.

Notes

[1] In the 1930s the address of the church of St Mary's, Chelsea was given as Cadogan Gardens. Today it is known as St Mary's, Cadogan Street. The rectory joins the church, but the entrance is in Draycott Terrace.

[2] Simmonds to Jones, 12 May 1932, PHA/Rea/CU3.

3 Dick, *The Malines Conversations Revisited*, p. 189; Barlow, *The Malines Conversations*, p. 209.

4 Marchant to Lang, 28 February 1932, LPL, Lang Papers, 112/161.

5 Marchant to Bell, 30 January 1932, LPL, Bell Papers, 211/20; Goodier to Marchant, 30 November 1931, OUL, Marchant Papers, 299/186; Goodier to Marchant, 14 December 1931, OUL, Marchant Papers, 299/187; Marchant to Bell, 4 December 1931, LPL Bell Papers, 211/13.

6 Lang to Bell, 19 March 1932, LPL, Bell Papers, 211/27.

7 Simmonds to Jones, 12 May 1932, PHA/Rea/CU3.

8 Goodier to Bourne, 14 February 1932, AAW, Bo./ALN.

9 Bourne to Marchant, 9 March 1933, OUL, Marchant Papers, 314/235.

10 Orchard to Marchant, 2 September 1932, OUL, Marchant Papers, 301/42.

11 Marchant to Lang, 28 February 1932, LPL, Lang Papers, 112/161.

12 Marchant to Bell, 13 March 1932, LPL, Bell Papers, 211/25.

13 Lang Memorandum, Interview with Marchant, 12 March 1932, LPL, Lang Papers, 112/170.

14 Goodier to Bourne, 21 February 1932, AAW, Bo./ALN.

15 There is no record of the Memorandum in Lang's papers at the Lambeth Palace Library, but it is entirely plausible that Marchant showed the Archbishop a copy, given their contact at this time.

16 Simmonds to Jones, 12 May 1932, PHA/Rea/CU3; Goodier to Bourne, 21 February 1932, AAW, Bo./ALN.

17 Goodier to Butler, 11 March 1932, DAA, Butler Papers, P/7; Simmonds to Jones, 12 May 1932, PHA/Rea/CU3.

18 Goodier to Marchant, 29 February 1932, OUL, Marchant Papers, 299/196.

19 Goodier to Bourne, 19 April 1932, AAW, Bo./ALN.

20 Goodier to Butler, 26 May 1932, DAA, Butler Papers, P/7.

21 Simmonds to Jones, 12 May 1932, PHA/Rea/CU3.

22 Goodier to Butler, June 1932, DAA, Butler Papers, P/7.

23 Goodier to Butler, 26 May 1932, DAA, Butler Papers, P/7.

24 Goodier to Butler, June 1932, DAA, Butler Papers, P/7; Goodier to Butler, 21 June 1932, DAA, Butler Papers, P/7.

25 Goodier to Butler, 22 June 1932, DAA, Butler Papers, P/7.

26 'Paper read by the Rev. W. Robert Corbould at St Mary's, Cadogan Gardens, 27 June 1932', LPL, Fynes-Clinton Papers, 4297/24–5. A summary of this paper was published by the French Jesuit, Jacques de Bivort de la Saudée, in his 1948 book *Anglicans et catholiques*, pp. 196–8, although sixteen years on he still felt it prudent to withhold the author's identity.

✢ 7 ✢

St Ermin's Hotel

'A larger circle'

Corbould had admitted to a 'great ignorance' of the Catholic Church on the part of Anglicans generally, and alluded to the need for 'conciliation and explanation'. He and Fynes-Clinton felt that they had hit upon the means of addressing these issues. What was required, they believed, was 'a series of conferences to which larger numbers of the clergy of both communions will be invited'.[1] Throwing open the Conversations would benefit many others. It might also minimise the risk of their being brought to an end at the whim of one or two individuals. Again, the influence of Jones can be discerned: his desire to resurrect the Society of St Thomas of Canterbury, reducing the distance between Catholics and Anglicans through mutual explanation and personal contact.

The proposal was communicated simultaneously to both the Anglican and Catholic hierarchies on 27 July 1932. Having been told that their Memorandum of the preceding year had been shown to Archbishop Lang without their permission, Corbould and Fynes-Clinton determined that *they* should keep Lambeth fully informed as to what was afoot. And so they wrote, what Lang already knew, that for the last 18 months 'a group of Anglican clergy has been holding a series of conversations of a private and purely informal character with certain distinguished clergy of the Roman Catholic Communion'. They offered, should he wish, to produce the names of the Anglicans involved and copies of the papers delivered. Without giving reasons, they recounted their decision to part company from Marchant. Corbould and Fynes-Clinton gave as the Conversations' objective 'mutual explanations and the cultivation of very happy personal relations'. They painted a positive picture of the experience. Now they wished larger numbers to be involved in these proposed conferences. There was no request for any official sanction or blessing, obviating the possibility of a veto. They were simply writing to give the Archbishop 'some cognisance of what has been done'.[2]

It suited both Lang and the Papalists to keep relations at arm's length. The reply they received came from the Archbishop's Chaplain, Alec Sargent. He restricted himself to vague expressions of benevolence and complete detachment. The Archbishop heard of the Conversations with 'much interest'. He was 'interested' to learn that they would continue on a wider basis. 'He trusts that through such friendly and entirely unofficial conversations mutual explanations may be offered which may tend to the removal of misunderstandings and the creation of a spiritual Christian fellowship.'[3] He ignored the offer of further information.

What Goodier thought of the new proposal was, fortunately, immaterial. He dutifully took the matter to the Cardinal for his instructions. For all his caution, Bourne had no intention of being the one who 'shut the door' on the attempt to further Reunion. He had taken note of Corbould's express desire to effect rapprochement through the authorities of the Catholic Church *in England*. He recommended Goodier to accept the invitation, although he did not see the need to invite other Catholics. The Anglicans had initiated the overture, it was for their benefit. Goodier, however, wanted Jarrett and D'Arcy to attend if large numbers of Anglicans were to be present. The Cardinal's only other stipulation was that the matter should be kept out of the papers, a view shared by the Papalists.[4]

'The Ideal of the Church'

Corbould took the initiative regarding the format and organisation of the conference, the subject of which was to be 'The Ideal of the Church'. The conference was to be chaired by an Anglican. Perhaps Jones was chosen as the doyen of the Papalists and given his experience of the Society of St Thomas of Canterbury. Corbould wisely forestalled objections by making the Catholics solely responsible for the prayers and blessing. There were to be six papers of fifteen minutes each, three from Anglicans and three from Catholics. Goodier complained that this created 'a sense of equality'. He could not possibly be expected to restrict himself to so short a period. The Archbishop grew increasingly anxious as the conference approached, returning to the Cardinal. Bourne urged discretion, but was happy for the meeting to proceed. Attempting to reassure himself, Goodier restated his position to Butler:

> I will try to let them see that we are there, not to argue, nor to come to an agreement, but simply to state the facts. I have always tried to let them see that, however sympathetic I have tried also to be.

He asked the Abbot if he would be prepared to cast an eye over his paper in advance of the meeting.[5]

Meanwhile the Papalists sent invitations to sympathetic Anglican clergy. A circular was sent in early October, one version signed by Jones, Fynes-Clinton and Corbould, another by Baverstock, Corbould, Fynes-Clinton, Jones, Scott and Simmonds. No doubt these went to members of different Papalist societies, the former perhaps to the Catholic League and the CU, the latter to the Society of the Holy Cross and the CPCU.

Both versions sought to give a veneer of official sanction by citing the 1908 Lambeth Conference 'that there can be no fulfilment of the Divine purpose in any scheme of reunion which does not ultimately include the great Latin Church of the West'. It was 'in the spirit' of the Lambeth Conferences, therefore, the authors claimed, that they had met with 'distinguished and learned' Catholic clerics over the preceding eighteen months for 'purely informal conversations' to discuss 'matters at issue between our two communions'. The authors wished 'a larger circle' of Anglicans to benefit from their 'mutual explanations and discussions'. Unity could only be achieved were an atmosphere of 'consideration and goodwill' to be built up between the two parties. For this reason, they were issuing an invitation 'to the first of a series of conferences which we hope to hold'.

Goodier's condition was respected: 'There will not be a debate: our object is explanation and understanding of one another and not controversy.' The Papalists imposed only one condition of their own: that those who attended accepted that there could be no union save on the basis of full dogmatic agreement.[6]

The conference started at 11 am on Tuesday, 25 October 1932 at St Ermin's Hotel, followed by lunch at 1.15 pm. The venue was Fynes-Clinton's home. He had lived in a serviced apartment here since abandoning the parish house in Finsbury Square, commuting daily to St Magnus-the-Martyr in the City. Situated just minutes from Westminster Abbey, Westminster Cathedral and the Houses of Parliament, the Hotel provided the perfect backdrop for the final scene of our Conversations. Built as mansion blocks in 1889 on the site of the fifteenth-century chapel of St Ermin, it was transformed into a hotel in 1899. The interior was reworked by the Victorian theatre designer, J. P. Briggs, his opulent plasterwork and craftsmanship creating an atmosphere of fashionable flamboyance. In its history the Hotel has been no stranger to mystery and intrigue. Churchill founded the Special Operations Executive here during the Second World War, with MI6 operating just two floors above. Guy Burgess was to betray State secrets to Soviet agents in the bar in the 1950s. Today the Hotel continues to welcome guests and diners in the heart of Westminster.

The conference was attended by 120 Anglicans. (In addition to the Conversationalists themselves, it is probably safe to assume that the signatories to the Centenary Manifesto which appeared that month were all invited to the conference.) The most remarkable fact of the entire proceedings may be that so many clergy attended, and not a word was breathed to the Press. One of those attending felt this was an opportunity missed. The very fact of such a joint conference being published would, he felt, have been of far more value than anything actually said there. 'I am sure that if the meeting had been advertised, or the mere fact that it was held published, many all over the country would have been heartened. And we want this new blood brought into the Movement, to push on the talkers.' He could not understand why Cardinal Bourne had imposed a condition of secrecy. What had the Catholics to fear?[7]

Goodier, Butler and D'Arcy presented papers for the Catholics. The Archbishop had his way. His paper was substantially longer then the quarter of an hour originally allotted. It was also far more tightly and effectively argued than that he had given the previous March, which suggests that D'Arcy and Jarrett, as well as Butler, were consulted in its preparation. By refusing to take questions, Goodier avoided the risk of being intellectually savaged subsequently. He had learnt one lesson from Corbould in June: the need to win hearts and minds, as well as the argument. And so he began by acknowledging that he and his Anglican audience shared much in common: 'We have a common desire that all believers in Jesus Christ our Lord, the true Son of the true God, should be one, even as He and the Father are one.' This shared ambition for Christian unity was not, he stated, 'a mere Utopian dream'. Such language constituted a significant softening of his previous approach.

Nevertheless, there was a caveat. However much they shared the same objective, the Archbishop felt there was 'a fundamental difference of outlook' between Catholics and the Anglican Papalists. It was less a matter 'of theological definitions as of philosophical first principles'. Both Catholics and these particular Anglicans might claim to believe the same truths, but they were built on very 'different foundations'. The Papalists professed to believe Catholic dogma in its entirety, but on the basis of personal choice and preference. 'To them truth is more subjective, more a matter of personal judgment, and personal interpretation, than it is to us; to them it is something that comes rather from within a man himself than from without.' Goodier ventured that Anglican Papalism believed 'in authority so far as it is interpreted and approved by its own personal judgment'. Whereas Catholicism 'believes on authority first, and its personal judgment confirms it'. This represented a significant change of tack on his part. The new emphasis on authority rather than individual conscience implies Jarrett's hand in the formulation of the argument. We know that, this time, Jarrett approved Goodier's paper: 'Simple, clear, sympathetic in tone and temper, it sets out our concept of authority in the Catholic

Church [...] Here is controversy *in excelsis*. Archbishop Goodier is in the tradition of St Francis de Sales.'[8]

Goodier returned to what he presumed all present held in common:

1. Belief in God;
2. An expectation of God's self-revelation to humanity;
3. The necessity of God making Himself known if, in this fallen world, man was to live as God wished;
4. That this revelation took place in Jesus Christ, the Second Person of the Trinity, Who became incarnate, was true God and true man, Who died and rose again from the dead. While on earth Jesus revealed to men what 'He had learnt from His Father, what His Father had given Him to make known; a knowledge of God, His Father and our Father, and a rule of life in accordance with that knowledge, which of himself man could never have attained.' All this they shared and made them Christians.

Beyond that, however, Goodier felt their agreement ended. It was one thing to believe in 'the Christian religion', quite another to believe in 'the Christian Church'. Some Christians even denied that Christ had founded a Church. While others acknowledged that He had founded a Church, they maintained either that it was entirely spiritual or, to the extent it had any existence on earth, its form was a purely human construct. Yet others professed some belief in the vague authority of all bishops as successors of the Apostles, but only if they spoke with one united voice and without recognising any form of primacy among their number. For many the structures and constitution of the Church were solely a matter of social and historical conditioning easily adaptable to time and place. Struggling with the status of non-Catholic Christians, Goodier implicitly criticised those who held that belief in Jesus and baptism were sufficient for membership of the Church.

Goodier contrasted this with the Catholic understanding of the Church which he shared with 300 million others:

1. The Church Jesus spoke of was 'a definite religious society'. He founded the Church 'to be the recipient of His doctrine; by its means that doctrine was to be preserved and propagated'.
2. Jesus bestowed on the College of the Apostles the privilege

of infallibility, it would be preserved from error in teaching on matters of faith and morals.

3. Jesus also gave to the Apostolic College 'full legislative, judicial and coercive' authority to rule the Church.

4. This privilege and authority was not personal to the Apostles only, but was intended to be enjoyed for all time by their successors, 'the duly elected and lawfully consecrated college of the bishops of the Church'.

5. The Archbishop noted that he was taking his case a stage further by introducing the person of Peter, whom Jesus had chosen from among the Apostles to teach and rule the universal Church. When Peter spoke in this capacity, 'his voice was the voice of Christ Himself. He was in the full sense the Vicar of Christ upon earth.' Catholics believed that this primacy was not for Peter alone but, by divine right, for his successors, the Popes.

6. In this way, and only in this way, God had ensured that the Church 'stood out in the past against all efforts to destroy her, as a visible, united society'. For this reason Catholics were confident that the Church would never fail and that she would last until the end of time essentially the same as she was today and had been since the beginning.

7. The Archbishop concluded this section of his paper by defining the Church of Jesus Christ as 'a complete society, an independent society, depending on no human or temporal power, confined to no one place or time or generation or circumstance'. Thus defined, the Church of Christ is and always has been seen 'in the Church of Rome, and in no other'.

How could one locate the Church of Christ today? Goodier employed a familiar formula. To determine whether a body was indeed the Church of Christ, it must demonstrate the four 'marks', or characteristics, of the Church set out in the fourth-century Nicene Creed: it had to be *one, holy, catholic* and *apostolic*.

Unity must be something more than simply spiritual, Goodier argued, otherwise the Church would not exist other than in some vague form in the hearts and minds of believers. Unity must be external and visible, 'one for all the world to see'. Internally, there must be unity of faith; externally, there must be unity under one government. No one disputed that the Church of Rome possessed this unity of doctrine, liturgy and discipline. Indeed, 'by many she is censured for this unbreaking unity; she is called intolerant, uncompromising, exclusive'. In many ways this had been the principal unanswered question of the Thackeray Hotel Conversations: was the unity of the Church real or simply something potential to be attained, hopefully, in the future? Finally, Goodier seems to have established the Catholic case that the unity of the Church is a reality and exists in the Holy Roman Church governed by the Pope and the bishops in communion with him.

The Church is apostolic. She must have the same powers, the same mission and the same fulfilment of that mission as the apostles. The power of bishops to teach and govern must derive from the apostles themselves. Again, Goodier contended, this is true only of the Church of Rome. To the extent that apostolic succession was claimed by others, it was only through the Church of Rome from which they had subsequently separated. The Catholic Church was accused of arrogance; similar accusations had been made against her Founder before her. 'She speaks as Jesus spoke, because He bids her; as the apostles spoke, because she is one with them, and can do no otherwise. She commands as they commanded, no more, no less.' The powers of the Church at the altar and in the confessional were exercised on the authority of Christ, transmitted through His apostles. The Anglicans insisted that they exercised the same sacramental ministry. The voice of Jarrett is behind the challenge issued by Goodier: 'By what sanction do those claim to use so sacred a power, who act only on their own authority?'

The Church is catholic, universal, open to all, never limited to one place or one people. But there was a false universality which the Church would never tolerate:

> She will not compromise, she will not surrender one tittle of the truth she holds, she will not modify her teaching to adapt herself to one people or another, she will not look for words that may contain two meanings for the sake of making a false friendship, she will not sacrifice unity for universality, for then she would not be universal.

If, for the sake of popularity, she chose to be guided by the spirit of the world, rather than by the Holy Spirit, then 'she would not be the Catholic Church of Jesus Christ. She would be but one of those organisations made by human hands which for ever spring up about her.'

Goodier pinned the full force of his argument to the fourth 'mark': the Church is holy. She offers her members the same ideal and means of sanctification as offered by Jesus Himself. Standards of holiness are not adaptable to time or place or whim of the world. The saints are one of the proudest boasts of the Church of Rome. That Church had been an overwhelming force for good in the world:

> Under her influence the social order has been lifted up; she has taught to a barbaric world humility, chastity and love; she has held up for man's veneration models of self-renunciation and sacrifice; never for the sake of a passing social problem has she yielded to the clamour of a self-indulgent world, sacrificed purity of life, lowered the standards of morals, public and private.

Goodier took a swipe at Anglican public school religion which, he felt, placed a greater emphasis on the values of the pagan, classical world than Christian revelation. Christ demanded more than 'a sound mind in a sound body'.

The Archbishop did not specifically mention the Lambeth Conference's sanction of artificial contraception. He did not have to. He reminded his audience that Christ would have us chastise our body, rather than yield 'to a self-indulgence which can only end, as it has always ended, in the suicide of the race'. Heresies could be moral, as well as doctrinal. The Papalists must have experienced severe discomfort. This had been their own criticism of the 1930 Resolution. Jones had simply urged that the Resolution be ignored. How could that be: a Church with no authority to teach? Goodier ruthlessly drove home the logic of his case: 'the faith or the morals of one generation cannot contradict the faith or the morals of another [...] the Church that teaches morals which have never been the morals of the Church of Jesus Christ, declares herself formally heretical.'

In summary, the Archbishop offered the Anglicans a (somewhat juridical) definition of *the* Church:

> The Church, the one and holy Church, is the union in one visible society of men upon this earth, professing the same faith, partaking of the same sacraments, under the authority or rule or jurisdiction of the same lawfully appointed pastors, and especially of the one chief pastor, the successor, the representative, the vice-regent of Him Who is the Head of all.

The Church of England failed to satisfy this definition as its members patently did not hold the same faith even between themselves. Papalists might argue that they were the true heirs of the pre-Reformation Church, but they were in communion with Protestants and Modernists. For Goodier, this constituted a contradiction. 'A union of opposites, or of those who believe opposites, can be no union.' Anglicanism lacked this capacity for unity of faith because it lacked a 'living authority to preserve it [...] [to] eject from itself false doctrine'.

In their Memorandum of the preceding October, the Papalists had made great play of their sacramental ministry exercised within the Anglican Communion. They could not deny the experience of grace they saw at work in their own lives and those of their people. Goodier responded. There should be a common definition and understanding of sacraments between members of the Church. Clearly this was not the case among Anglicans. Sacraments could only be administered and received as authorised by the Church. It was the Church of Rome which had 'always guarded, faithfully preserved, those visible signs and media of grace which were given to her by Jesus Christ Himself; in these above all things else she has kept the unity of the Spirit in the bond of peace'.

This, Goodier concluded, was the Ideal of the Church, but it was also the reality accomplished by Christ Himself. The Church did not depend upon 'the inner consciousness, or even the inner belief, of anyone'. The Archbishop built upon a much firmer, more Christological foundation than his earlier paper: 'I am a Catholic, not merely because I believe all that the Catholic Church teaches, but because, by His favour, I have been engrafted into Him, His living Body, and live by His life.' The action of Christ, and that alone, allowed him to recognise, accept and become a member of His one, holy, catholic and apostolic Church.[9] Goodier gave his audience much to consider. Jarrett noted that his 'paper created a great impression, because though written in a courteous manner it was yet uncompromising in doctrine'.[10]

Not a word of D'Arcy's paper has survived. And we have only a single quote from Butler's contribution:

> Reconciliation and reunion must come; I am confident, and today has made me more confident, that they will come. We cannot yet see how that will be; perhaps some devastating national calamity will sweep us into unity.[11]

We know from their correspondence that, doctrinally, there was nothing to distinguish the two, but it is easy to appreciate the Anglican preference for the Benedictine Abbot over the Jesuit Archbishop. There was a generosity, openness and imagination in Butler that was lacking in Goodier.

'The union of heart'

There is uncertainty as to the identity of the first two Anglican speakers. Comments by Pierce suggest that it may have been Monahan and Scott. The American ponders why Monahan did not rebut 'the Roman papers'. Pierce also makes reference to a response to Goodier's assertion that the Anglican position lacked authority: 'Dr Scott pointed to the Prayer Book etc. as the voice of Anglicana.' Struggling to justify his own continued presence in the Anglican Communion, Pierce found Scott's reply unconvincing. The Prayer Book was not a living voice. If Anglicanism still had a voice, it was that of the 1930 Lambeth Conference which had sanctioned birth control and communion with those lacking apostolic succession.[12]

Corbould spoke last in response to the Archbishop's paper on 'the Ideal of the Church'. Strictly speaking, it was not a response to that paper at all, but an impassioned plea for sympathy and progress towards Reunion similar to that which he had made in Chelsea four months earlier. The force of the Catholic papers seem to have hit home. While asserting that a perfectly good theological case could be made for the Anglican position, Corbould meekly stated that he and his colleagues were simply ordinary, hardworking parish priests who did 'not lay claim to great scholarship'.

For men such as these, Corbould claimed, 'the ending of the schism is essentially a practical matter'. They were not primarily concerned with producing a theological defence deemed adequate by their Catholic friends nor with matters 'of academic and historic interest' separating the two Communions. (This represented a considerable reversal of strategy from the papers delivered by Jones and Scott at the Thackeray Hotel.) Their overriding interest rather was to prevent the English people lapsing 'into entire godlessness'. They believed their objective could only be achieved through Christian unity and the return of the English Church to the Holy See.

Corbould asked again, as the Papalists had in their Memorandum, that Catholics be prepared to see 'the best and not the worst of the Church of England'. Could Catholics not admit that there were at least elements of Catholic truth in Anglican formularies when properly interpreted? Would Catholics not cooperate with Papalists to achieve their common goal of Reunion? Could Catholics not recognise those elements of 'Catholic life and practice' which appeared and flourished within the Church of England as soon as the hand of State persecution was stayed? Corbould did not deny tendencies to the contrary, but the revival of sacramental and religious life in the Church of England was a fact; 'Catholicism is natural to her'.

Corbould wished the Catholics to know that the policy towards Anglicans pursued by Rome was counterproductive. It served only to alienate the large Anglo-Catholic party and encourage them to seek to create 'a non-Papal Catholicism'. As a friend, he urged the Catholics to approach the Church of England with a new attitude 'of understanding, sympathy and conciliation, and the avoidance of harsh terms'. He was not asking Rome to compromise any dogmatic position, but the Catholic Church had to realise that anathematising those who lay beyond her visible boundaries was not a method of proceeding 'that commends itself to the English mentality'. Goodier would not have agreed with the proposition that 'union of heart must precede dogmatic agreement', but in conclusion Corbould begged his Catholic friends to cooperate with them in helping to create this 'union of heart'.[13]

'On the whole good'

How did the participants and others respond to the conference? Goodier remained impervious to Corbould's pleading. He was exasperated by the proceedings, failing to 'believe in the good faith of those Anglicans who had been eager to have conferences with him'. This, however, is more indicative of the Archbishop's lack of imagination than the Anglicans' sincerity.[14]

Other Catholics were less negative. Abbot Butler declared that in consequence of the St Ermin's conference he was now far more confident of the prospect of Reunion. Jarrett too spoke optimistically about the progress made. In his view the Papalist group 'is growing, in seriousness as well as in numbers. It is losing its undergraduate flippancy. It is maturing.'[15]

The Anglican reaction was also mixed. Whitton felt that little had been gained from the conference: 'We were told, very nicely, what we knew before.'[16] Monahan was unhappy, finding the Catholic papers 'weak, unfair and easily answerable'. As a Thomist scholar of some accomplishment, he would have bridled at Goodier's allegation that he dealt only in subjective truth and personal judgment. Monahan and others were critical of the Roman 'insistence that only individuals can be dealt with'. Pierce conceded that, in a sense, this was true. Ultimately, the issue was one of personal conscience. He felt Rome was eminently practical and would be more than willing to receive a group, while prudently reserving the right to treat each case on its merits. Pierce mused whether the Papalists had any real justification to blame the Catholics 'for harping on the chaos of Anglicanism', when this was one of their own favourite pastimes.

With time on his hands in Rome, Pierce corresponded with many who had attended the conference. Most were 'less gloomy' and less critical than Monahan. The consensus was 'that home truths were spoken, but in a charitable manner; that they needed to be stated; and that the result was on the whole good'.[17]

The End of the Road?

Many Papalists subscribed to the *Tablet*. They were aware of its polemical tone in speaking of all matters Anglican. Nevertheless, the issue of 12 November 1932 made particularly uncomfortable reading. It dealt ostensibly with the Papalist Manifesto dated 1 October 1932, but its criticism had equal application to the conference held in the same month. The *Tablet* accepted that the Papalists acted in all sincerity.

> None the less, we will tell them plainly that they are in an indefensible and presumptuous position. Holding such beliefs as theirs concerning the Catholic Faith and Catholic Unity, they have no right to remain another week or another hour in the Established Church [...] They say that they are a Catholic leaven, or salt, in the Establishment, keeping the bulk of Anglicanism from going utterly Protestant [...] In all kindness, we say that such a plea is presumptuous [...] To remain in communion with a majority of definite anti-Catholics is to 'do evil that good may come'.[18]

It was well known that the *Tablet* at the time was the house magazine of the Cardinal Archbishop of Westminster. The editor, Ernest Oldmeadow, had a standing appointment at Archbishop's House to discuss the weekly issue with the Cardinal. Was this Bourne telling the Papalists very publicly that his patience was finally exhausted, that there were to be no more conversations, no more conferences?

It would be an easy conclusion to draw, but probably incorrect. Despite his forbidding demeanour and stern reputation, Bourne operated a surprisingly *laissez-faire* attitude when it came to the initiatives of others. He would have seen no inconsistency between allowing Oldmeadow to run a harshly exclusivist line in the *Tablet* while himself sanctioning further contact with the Anglicans. Such an approach made the Cardinal difficult to read and had led to the general misunderstanding of his attitude towards the Malines Conversations.

It is true that there was no further contact between these Catholics and these Anglicans after 25 October 1932. The reason for that, however, may not lie in a Roman prohibition on future proceedings. Bourne was accustomed to visit Rome in December each year. (The preceding year he had taken the Memorandum with him to the Vatican.) The Cardinal is likely to have held his counsel as to his future policy regarding the Papalists until after he had had the opportunity to discuss the matter in audience with the Pope — and, as we shall see, Pius XI was increasingly favourably disposed to the possibility of a rapprochement with sympathetic Anglicans.

Bourne left London for Rome on 24 November. He arrived four days later suffering from a bronchial cold and gastric flu. His condition deteriorating, he was admitted to hospital and at one point his life was despaired of. The Cardinal staged a recovery of sorts. He was able to return to Westminster, but the final two years of his life were marked by prolonged periods of ill health. Cautious by nature, he had nevertheless consistently encouraged these London Conversations between Catholics and Anglicans. During his incapacity no other English Catholic felt authorised or inclined to do so.

Sickness and mortality dealt heavily with the Catholic participants too. Abbot Butler was troubled by occasional heart problems in the final years of his life. He suffered an attack and lost consciousness on a London bus in March 1933. The end came on 1 April 1934.[19] The loss of Bede Jarrett was a far greater shock to his many acquaintance when he died on 17 March 1934 aged just 52. Despite his uncompromising defence of Catholic truth, the Papalists appreciated that they had lost another friend, recalling their 'happiest memories' of Jarrett's 'charity and kindliness'.[20] Archbishop Goodier lingered on, increasingly isolated at his convent home in Devon, where he died on 13 March 1939.

Yet there is evidence of a continuing openness to further contact on the part of the Catholic hierarchy. When Corbould and

Fynes-Clinton wrote to Archbishop Lang in July 1932, they made clear their intention of holding 'a series of conferences' between Anglicans and Catholics. The invitation to Papalist clergy to St Ermin's Hotel that autumn was equally explicit that this was to be 'the first of a series of conferences'.[21] After one false start, Cardinal Bourne returned to his duties in Westminster in late March 1933. Is it coincidence that Corbould could write to Lord Halifax the very next month: 'The Roman authorities are willing to continue the conversations and conferences which we have held during the past 2½ years'?[22] There is no suggestion here of Catholic opposition to continued participation in talks on Reunion. What could not be relied upon was Bourne's health. He suffered a serious relapse in early June 1933. Thereafter he, and the prospect of dialogue, lived a twilight existence. The Cardinal died on 1 January 1935.

Notes

[1] Corbould and Fynes-Clinton to Lang, 27 July 1932, LPL, Lambeth Conference 1930, 153/386.

[2] *Ibid*.

[3] A. Sargent to Corbould, 28 July 1932(copy), LPL, Lambeth Conference 1930, 153/385.

[4] Goodier to Butler, 31 July 1932, DAA, Butler Papers, P/7.

[5] Goodier to Butler, 9 August 1932, DAA, Butler Papers, P/7; Circular letter, Jones, Fynes-Clinton and Corbould, Carshalton, October 1932, LPL, Young Papers, 4284/48; Goodier to Butler, 6 October 1932, DAA, Butler Papers, P/7; Goodier to Butler, 14 October 1932, DAA, Butler Papers, P/7.

[6] Circular letter, Jones, Fynes-Clinton and Corbould, Carshalton, October 1932, LPL, Young Papers, 4284/48; Circular letter, Baverstock, Corbould, Fynes-Clinton, Jones, Scott and Simmonds, Annotated 'Invitation to Conference held at St Ermin's Oct 25th 32', Fynes-Clinton Papers, LPL, 4297/26.

[7] Whitton to Pierce, 11 March 1933, cited Pierce to Bishop M. d'Herbigny, SJ, 17 March 1933 (copy), BCA, Pierce Bequest, Correspondence 1930–3/165.

[8] Editorial, *Blackfriars*, 14/155 (Feb. 1933), p. 85.

[9] A. Goodier, 'The Ideal of the Church'. The publication of the paper four months later in *Blackfriars*, 14/155 (Feb. 1933), pp. 90–100, is explained by the fact that Jarrett was the editor of that journal. Jarrett disclosed only that the paper had been 'read by request to a gathering of Anglican clergymen, assembled to discuss Reunion with the Church of Rome'.

[10] Editorial, *Blackfriars*, 14/155 (Feb. 1933), p. 85.

[11] *Reunion*, 1/2 (July 1934), p. 35.

[12] Pierce to D. Rea, 12 January 1933 (copy), PHA/Rea/CU3.

[13] 'Additional Notes on Archbishop Goodier's Paper by the Reverend W. Robert Corbould, Rector of Carshalton, Annotated 'Oct 1932?' LPL, Fynes-Clinton Papers, 4297/27–8.

[14] Whitton to G. P. Crookendon, 15 March 1933, Harris Papers, PHA.

[15] Editorial, *Blackfriars*, 14/155 (Feb. 1933), p. 85.

[16] Whitton to Pierce, 11 March 1933, cited Pierce to d'Herbigny, 17 March 1933 (copy), BCA, Pierce Bequest, Correspondence 1930–3/165.

[17] Pierce to Rea, 12 January 1933 (copy), PHA/Rea/CU3.

[18] *Tablet* (12 Nov. 1932), pp. 626–7.

[19] Knowles, 'Abbot Butler: A Memoir', pp. 417–18.

[20] *The Pilot*, 10 (June 1934), p. 2.

[21] Corbould and Fynes-Clinton to Lang, 27 July 1932, LPL, Lambeth Conference 1930, 153/386; Circular letter, Jones, Fynes-Clinton and Corbould, October 1932, LPL, Young Papers, 4284/48.

[22] Corbould to Halifax, 6 April 1933, BIY, Halifax, Ecclesiastical Papers.

✥ 8 ✥

'The Next Step'

The Centenary Manifesto[1]

If Corporate Reunion with Rome were ever to be achieved, the Papalists knew they faced a herculean task to inform and persuade the wider Anglican Communion. Most immediately, they had to formulate a response to the impending anniversary. Newman dated the beginning of the Oxford Movement to John Keble's Assize Sermon preached in the University Church of St Mary on 14 July 1833, when he deplored State encroachments on the liberties of the Church. For much of the following century, the Catholic Revival movement had endured persecution and suspicion in the Church of England. Most Anglicans retained significant misgivings. Nevertheless, Anglo-Catholicism emerged from the First World War with a newfound confidence and respectability. Nowhere was this more manifest than in the triumphalist Anglo-Catholic Congresses of the 1920s. The Centenary Congress of 1933 was to represent the high watermark. 70,000 attended the Congress itself, 50,000 were present at the Pontifical High Mass at White City on the Sunday. There were bishops in abundance, although tending to be colonial rather than home. Even if they wished him to be less timid, Anglo-Catholics felt that they enjoyed the sympathy of Archbishop Lang.

All this should have produced unqualified rejoicing on the part of the Papalists. It did not. In fact, numerical success served only to confirm their fears. They were concerned that the broader appeal of Anglo-Catholicism was being purchased at the cost of a lack of depth, of compromise in principle. Scott had been railing for a decade against the damage wreaked by Modernism among the Catholic Party in the Church of England. Anglo-Catholicism's failure to issue a firm denunciation of the 1930 Lambeth Conference's sanctioning of contraception seemed to vindicate Scott.

The 'Centenary Manifesto' originated, however, with a letter written on 21 March 1932 by Pierce, the American co-founder of the CU, to his fellow Papalist clergy Jones, Silas Harris[2] and Andrew Acheson.[3] His objective was a critique of the current state of Anglo-Catholicism and a call to return to the values of the early Tractarians. It was to be a 'Manifesto' broadcast widely in the press, its style 'very terse and plain spoken'. There was more than a hint of fatalism reflecting Pierce's personal anguish: the Church of England was 'changing in a way that will soon make it impossible for Catholics'.

Pierce was scathing in his assessment of contemporary Anglo-Catholicism, infected, as he claimed, by a spirit of Modernism and compromise: 'Some of its apparent triumph is really a defeat. Anglo-Catholicism has grown greatly in numbers; it has become respectable [...] We were in a more wholesome state when we were in the wilderness.' (While arguing for the 'corporate' conversion of the Church of England to Catholic belief and practice, there is always the sense that the Papalists felt more comfortable 'in the wilderness'.) The Catholic Faith, he claimed, was more than 'a revival of ceremonies and costume'. Pierce catalogued his misgivings concerning the stance of its 'self-elected leaders' on morals, Scripture and in other fields. They had traded 'a religion of authority' for acceptance as 'a tolerated school of thought' — something inimical to Catholic ecclesiology.[4]

Pierce was not directly involved in the subsequent drafting process. He deprecated the delay and the length of the final version.[5] Nevertheless, his original outline is still largely discernible in the Centenary Manifesto dated 1 October 1932. There was the same 'remonstrance and repudiation' over the direction taken by the Catholic movement within the Church of England, the same call to a return to the beliefs of the founding Oxford Fathers, 'to intellectual consistency and orthodoxy'.

The published Manifesto differed most substantially from Pierce's initial sketch in its emphasis on Reunion. Fynes-Clinton explained that the protest was against two tendencies in contemporary

'The Next Step'

Anglo-Catholicism: the theological surrender to Modernism and 'its acquiescence in, and even conscious aim of, consolidating a non-papal Catholicism'.[6] The Manifesto deplored Anglo-Catholic efforts 'to create and to justify an insular and particularistic interpretation of the Universal Faith which in practice results in the virtual denial of the "Catholic" and the undue stressing of the "Anglo" in their illogical use of the name'.[7] If faithful to its original principles, the Oxford Movement led logically and naturally to the 'Reunion of the English Church with the rest of Catholic Christendom'.

The Papalists reaffirmed their desire for the restoration of communion with the Eastern Orthodox, but the priority had to be Reunion with the successor of St Peter, upon whom Christ had founded His one Church. In the face of the Modernist dangers they had identified, the very survival of the Catholic movement in the Church of England depended on recognition of papal authority which alone could preserve unity and doctrinal integrity. The Manifesto concluded with an appeal for renewed prayer and labour for 'outward unity with the Catholic world and with the Holy See'.[8]

The list of the fifty-one signatories was headed by Corbould, Fynes-Clinton and Scott, suggesting their primary role in the drafting and coordination of the Manifesto. Jones and Monahan also signed. The absence of Simmonds's name is most probably explained by the fact that the first signatories were mainly, but not exclusively, parish priests. (Pierce had urged publication with a relatively small number of names initially to avoid delay.) In terms of geographical distribution, London led the way, but followed closely by the East Midlands, while a number of clergy from Yorkshire and East Anglia subscribed to the Manifesto. Critics made great play of the subsequent retraction of two of the signatories. They failed to mention that by February 1933 a further 350 Anglican clergy had subscribed to the Manifesto. Manifestly absent, however, are the names of any bishop, leading academic or layman.[9] The document decisively separated Papalist from Anglo-Catholic.

Without the insistence on Reunion with Rome, the Manifesto would probably have been ignored by the Anglican Establishment, or even welcomed as internecine squabbling weakening a subversive tendency in the Church of England. As it was, the Manifesto received significant coverage nationally and internationally from both the secular and Church press. Writing to the *Times*, Bishop Headlam, charged by Lambeth with responsibility for Reunion, dismissed the Manifesto as 'unintelligent'.[10] Fynes-Clinton and Corbould were called upon to make a personal sacrifice as a result of their identification with the Manifesto. Both had been long and intimately involved with the Anglican and Eastern Churches Association, promoting Reunion with Orthodoxy. Both were told that they were no longer welcome in light of their Papalist views, and asked why they did not simply 'go over to Rome'. Ultimately, both men resigned from the Association, but not without Fynes-Clinton censuring the 'prejudice' encountered there:

> The effect of this must be to cause division amongst those working for reunion on Catholic lines, to divert into separate camps those who have hitherto worked together with Rome and Constantinople, and so to exacerbate the antipathy between these two centres of Christendom. Once more the 'Bridge Church' proved a delusive conductor to divergent paths.[11]

The *Tablet* purported to offer 'friendly' advice to the signatories of the Manifesto, but the tone was entirely polemical. They were dismissed as Protestants, told to look to the salvation of their individual souls and 'to swallow bitter-tasting mortifications, including the sacrifice of local importance and material comfort'.[12] Apparently justifying earlier cautions, the Papalists had to look overseas for a sympathetic Catholic response. Pierce was able to write from Rome: 'The Manifesto is doing incalculable good. It is talked of with appreciation. The *Osservatore Romano* had two columns on 18 November—a portent for that highly conservative and cautious organ.'[13] Cardinal LaFontaine, Patriarch of Venice, came close to replacing Mercier in the affections of Anglican Reunionists, accepting their Catholic inclinations and writing to his clergy: 'Let us pray and pray anew, dearly beloved brethren and children, that the sacred union after which they aspire may be attained.'[14]

'The Next Step'

The Centenary Tractates

The Manifesto was not the only writing project in which the Papalists engaged in the months from the spring of 1932. Inspired by Jones's *Catholic Reunion*, the decision was taken to publish a series of tracts providing 'a comprehensive survey of the history of English relations with the Holy See'.[15] Surprise was expressed at the speed at which these Centenary Tractates emerged. They reflected Jones's life work, but also, of course, the response to Goodier's request the preceding year for evidence of a pro-Roman school within Anglicanism pre-dating the Oxford Movement.

The Council for Promoting Catholic Unity published eight Tractates in the first series. For the most part the authors and the subject matter are very familiar:

1. *What do the Celtic Churches Say?* by Silas Harris
2. *What does the Anglo-Saxon Church Say?* by Morton Howard
3. *What do the General Councils Say?* by Scott
4. *What did the Church of England Say?* by Morton Howard
5. *What does the XVI Century Say?* by Jones
6. *What do English Divines Say?* by Simmonds
7. *What do the Tractarians Say?* by Jones
8. *What are We to Say?* by Fynes-Clinton and Corbould

A second series was projected, but the only title which saw the light of day was by Scott as he returned to his favourite bugbear, *Modernism in Anglo-Catholicism*.

The Tractates constitute an interesting historical footnote, the result of considerable research and scholarship. They cite some fascinating examples and quotations, but it is difficult to make this tendentious revisionism of Reformation history stick with respect to Anglicanism as a whole. In his review, the Jesuit, Joseph Keating, notes that the authors failed to distinguish schism under Henry VIII from actual heresy under Elizabeth I. The Tractates were a partial presentation. Jones had nothing to say about the English recusant community. To ensure a balanced presentation, two more titles were required: *What did the Elizabethan Bishops say?* And *What did the English Martyrs say?*[16]

The tracts were primarily historical in character, as with so much produced by the Papalists, reflecting their expertise as historians rather than theologians. We need only concern ourselves with the final tract written by Fynes-Clinton and Corbould which surveyed the contemporary scene. At least here Keating was willing to concede that they provided a 'shrewd criticism of existing Anglicanism'. Pierce too was fulsome in his praise: 'I consider this to be one of the very strongest of the whole series. Fynes-Clinton writes very well and convincingly.'[17]

Fynes-Clinton rehearsed again the severe disadvantages under which the Church of England laboured: Modernism, indiscipline and disunity, and the 'shocking' instance of the Lambeth Conference sanctioning 'the vice of artificial contraception'. Heeding Goodier's words, he acknowledged the injury suffered in Catholic eyes by the recent decision to permit intercommunion with the Old Catholics. This was the first time Anglicanism had 'established such relations with a body schismatic from the historic hierarchy of a European country'. Nevertheless, his Church enjoyed openings simply not available to the Catholic: 'The Church of England has unrivalled opportunities of reaching every village and household, of influencing the greatest interests and powers of the kingdom.' He proceeded to challenge both Communions. Given Anglicanism's inherent difficulties, it was necessary to 'accustom our people therefore to look to the teaching of the Roman See as their guide in disputed doctrine'. Yet, simultaneously, Fynes-Clinton clung to the policy of Corporate Reunion, arguing that individual conversions served only to delay the day of Reunion.[18]

Corbould too summarised the current situation. 'Reunion' was being used in very different senses. For the Papalists it could never mean 'mere friendly relations and cooperation', but only 'true dogmatic agreement upon defined truth'. At least in principle, Papalist and Roman Catholic shared a common vocabulary and a common goal. Corbould's next thesis ought to have made him equally popular with Catholics and suspect in the eyes of his fellow Anglicans:

> As long as the Papacy lasts—and that will be until the world's end—so long must the Pope maintain his defined dogmas, and that acceptance of them is essential to communion with him. The Anglican habit of mind is always to believe that a compromise can be effected: in this matter no compromise is possible.

He cited verbatim the proposed terms of union between Rome and Canterbury contained in the 1931 Memorandum.

Corbould reaffirmed his optimism in Rome's willingness to treat with Anglicans on this, or a similar, basis:

> It is commonly said that Rome will do nothing to meet us. We have good reasons for believing that Rome will do so if in good faith we go to meet her [...] we have to pray and study, explain and understand. We have already seen with what alacrity our Roman brethren will respond to any true approaches made to them.

The Anglican made reference to the friendly overtures of the Patriarch of Venice, but he must surely also have had in mind the recent London Conversations. He continued in similar vein:

> If, hitherto, [Catholics] have made but little advance, it is because the wrong approach has been made on our side by demanding the impossible of them. When they know that we have no will to involve them in what they must regard as a denial of essential truth, but are their brethren in the faith, then joyfully will they come to meet us and the healing of the schism will be in sight.

Corbould is being wildly idealistic, but here at least, if he could persuade his fellow Anglicans, was the basis for rapprochement.[19]

Roman Holiday

Fynes-Clinton had led one Anglican pilgrimage to Rome in 1926. He proposed a second to mark both the Oxford Movement Centenary and the Holy Year declared by Pius XI for the 1,900th anniversary of the Redemption. Pierce was vehemently opposed to the enterprise. In the first instance he believed that, unless Cardinal Bourne could be persuaded to sponsor it, it would meet with a 'very cold and unsatisfactory' reception in Rome. He also feared that Fynes-Clinton himself would be the cause of the pilgrimage's failure: 'I dread it. I hope that I am not uncharitable, but to me his doings have always seemed of the stunt order.'[20] (There was a deep-seated antipathy between the two men. Pierce claimed ignorance of its source.[21] It was wholly personal: the effortless social superiority of the Englishman and the American who perhaps tried too hard. And, although he was too polite to say, Fynes-Clinton probably viewed the Americans and their CU as interlopers encroaching on the entirely English territory of his CL.)

The pilgrimage left London on 22 September 1933. It comprised eight clergy and a handful of the laity. Their intentions included 'the Conversion of England and its Reunion with the Holy See'. Stopping two nights at Turin, they were present among the huge crowd in the Cathedral for the Solemn Exposition of the Shroud. Fynes-Clinton, Scott and Baverstock were received by Pius XI in a private audience *as* Anglican clergymen. (The notion that in the pre-Conciliar Church there existed barriers in St Peter's Square at which non-Catholics were turned away is frankly absurd.) The Papalists presented the Pope with a copy of the Centenary Tractates bound by the Oxford University Press in tooled morocco.[22] Even Pierce had to concede that the pilgrimage had passed without incident. Simply seeing 'this wonderful Pope' and the vast crowds of devout pilgrims could only have done good. Nevertheless, he regretted that Fynes-Clinton and his companions had not 'presented any sort of proposals or asked any vital questions'. A practical opportunity to advance the cause of Reunion had been wasted.[23]

'The Pope's intimate friend'

The attraction of the 1931–2 Conversations to Bourne and his fellow English Catholics was the fact that they were held in London, thus keeping well-meaning, but clueless, foreigners off what they perceived as their turf. Yet it proved impossible to limit either the Catholic Church or the Anglican Communion to England.

Scott, Corbould and Fynes-Clinton already had their Belgian contacts at Malines and Amay. It was not long before others were

'The Next Step'

also taking an interest in these exotic Papalists. The care Pierce took over the presentation and content of the CU *Bulletin* paid dividends in attracting the attention of various European Catholics prominent in the field of Church unity.

Jacques de Bivort de la Saudée was a French Jesuit who interested himself in the phenomenon of Anglo-Catholicism and the problem of Reunion. He wrote articles, and his doctoral thesis on the subject was eventually published after the Second World War. Pierce found his involvement providential: 'He is another with the Mercier spirit.'[24] Visiting England in three successive summers from 1931, de la Saudée met extensively with the Papalists, who shared with him their papers from the London Conversations. Captivated by their charm and enthusiasm, he accepted their programme and imbibed their prejudices, which coloured his own writings. While allowing always for the possibility of individual conversions, de la Saudée agreed that unity would only come through Corporate Reunion, itself fostered by personal contact, conversations and conferences.[25] He was responsible for placing Scott's book, *The Eastern Churches and the Papacy*, into the hands of the Holy Father.[26]

Another important contact was the German Jesuit, Max Pribilla, who 'made a special study of the Reunion Movement', particularly the Conferences at Stockholm in 1925 and Lausanne in 1927. The CU *Bulletin* of January 1932 carried a review of Pribilla's published works, citing approvingly his advice to Catholics:

> As against an impatient Protestantism, which attacks our rights and our honour, we shall defend ourselves with the sword of the Spirit [...] But, with Protestants, who are concerned for the peace of the confessions and the unity of the Church, we shall go hand in hand in practical enterprises, but in religious questions keep our eyes open for ways and means to remove the mutual misunderstandings and prejudices and at least come nearer to the fulfilment of the words of our Lord, that in the whole Christendom there may be only *one* fold and *one* Shepherd.[27]

Pierce and his sister were migrants for a number of years. They travelled extensively between fashionable European resorts, ostensibly for the sake of health, principally because they could afford to. In the summer of 1931, they were several weeks at Zermatt in Switzerland, where Pribilla was a chaplain. Pierce declared him to be 'one of the most important people on the Roman side in the business of Reunion'. The German, in turn, furnished him with introductions to fellow Jesuits in Rome, including one of the most enigmatic Catholic prelates of the early twentieth century.[28]

Frustrated by Goodier's attitude towards the London Conversations, and judging Abbot Butler more sympathetic, a number of the English Papalists pressed for the Catholic conduct of any future talks to be transferred from the Jesuits to the Benedictines. Pierce was having none of it: 'I cannot agree with you as to Jesuits vs. Benedictines, in the work for reunion. Everything points to the Jesuits now being in charge of this work [...] The Jesuits now have the lead. They are the sort who *get things done*.'[29] Pierce's preference was partly due to his contact with de la Saudée and Pribilla, but owed much more to his meeting with the Jesuit to whom Pribilla had introduced him, Michel d'Herbigny.

Born in Lille in 1880, d'Herbigny was ordained a Jesuit priest in 1910. Influenced by a Russian Jesuit, he learned the language and wrote his thesis on the philosopher, Vladimir Solovyov, 'the Russian Newman', who converted to Catholicism. D'Herbigny taught Scripture in the Jesuit house of studies in Belgium before being appointed professor of ecclesiology at the Gregorian University in Rome in 1921. There he came to the notice of Pius XI and received rapid preferment. Secretary, then President, of the Pontifical Oriental Institute, d'Herbigny was made President of the Pontifical Commission for Russia in 1926. Opinions differ massively. Some thought d'Herbigny unprincipled or unbalanced, but there was an obvious ability and persuasiveness. For a decade and more he exercised an extraordinary influence at the highest level of the Catholic Church.

We have already met Lambert Beauduin, teaching at the Benedictine house of Sant' Anselmo in Rome. Beauduin became increasingly convinced that the West had much to learn liturgically from Orthodoxy. Through the agency of d'Herbigny, Beauduin brought his proposals before the Pope in a memorandum urging a monastic foundation to promote the work of unity. He argued that the Benedictines were ideally suited for this mission, sharing the Orthodox concern for liturgy and patristics. That memorandum was the genesis of the papal letter, *Equidem verba*, issued in 1924, but, influenced by d'Herbigny, there was a significant shift in emphasis to focus on Catholic relations with Russia. The same underlying tension was evident in Beauduin's foundation of the Benedictine community of Amay. Was the principal objective prayer, dialogue and mutual enrichment with the Orthodox, as Beauduin contemplated, or proselytism and individual conversions among the Orthodox, as d'Herbigny wanted? Our Papalists blamed Bourne for the ecclesiastical condemnation of Beauduin. They had more reason to censure the French Jesuit.

The Bolshevik Revolution unleashed prolonged and severe religious persecution in Russia. For d'Herbigny, Orthodoxy's misfortune was Catholicism's opportunity. He saw Amay as a potential training ground for Catholic missionaries who would enter Russia to win the country for Rome. The hierarchy of the tiny Catholic minority in Russia had also been decimated by Soviet persecution. D'Herbigny persuaded the Pope to sanction schemes indicative of either the utmost bravery or the utmost folly. In 1925, d'Herbigny made a clandestine visit to Russia under the auspices of the French diplomatic service. He returned the following year, having been secretly consecrated a bishop by the papal nuncio in Berlin (the future Pius XII), and proceeded himself to consecrate Catholic bishops within Russia. In a moment of madness, d'Herbigny celebrated a public Pontifical Mass in Moscow, blowing his cover to the ubiquitous Soviet agents. His imprudence caused the French authorities to disown him and compromised those Catholics whom he sought to succour. Within a decade all those he had consecrated in Russia were exiled or executed.

The Catholic Church finds it difficult to accommodate such colourful and unconventional characters, at least when they are not successful. When it came, the fall from grace was swift and complete. In October 1933, d'Herbigny visited Brussels for routine surgery. He was expected back in Rome within the month.[30] Instead, he was relieved of office. Four years later he was stripped of all marks of episcopal dignity, spending the remaining twenty years of his life in enforced seclusion. There were hints of personal scandal. Pierce, however, believed that d'Herbigny's initial downfall and the abolition of the Commission for Russia were the result of petty jealousy. D'Herbigny had antagonised and circumvented both the Vatican Secretariat of State and the Polish bishops, who resented his intrusion in Russian affairs, which they regarded as their sphere of competence. It did not help that the Jesuit General of the day was a Pole.[31]

D'Herbigny's focus was never exclusively on the East. His interest was aroused wherever there were converts to be gained or intrigue to be furthered. Cardinal Mercier first raised the possibility of ecumenical dialogue with d'Herbigny while he was teaching in Belgium. His move to Rome allowed him to pursue the question of Catholic-Anglican unity with the sympathetic Secretary of State, Cardinal Gasparri. D'Herbigny needed no encouragement. In no time at all he was corresponding with Leslie Walker in Oxford in an attempt to establish either Jesuit representation at Malines or their own parallel set of conversations. It required Mercier's firm intervention in May 1922 to quash this potential for confusion and ensure that his were the only officially-sanctioned talks.[32] D'Herbigny was no stranger to England and was familiar with the Papalist landscape of St Magnus-the-Martyr, Fynes-Clinton and Jones.

When Pierce first met him in October 1931, d'Herbigny was still a force to be reckoned, eager to seize any opportunity to advance the conversion of England. Also present at that meeting was the American Jesuit and Librarian at the Oriental Institute, Francis McGarrigle. He was eager to emphasize his superior's standing in the Vatican for the benefit of the Anglican: 'Mgr d'Herbigny is the Pope's intimate friend, and has an audience at least once a week with him, often spending two or three hours with him.' Pierce told d'Herbigny how much it would mean to the Papalists if they could know the Holy Father was aware and approved of their work. Imagine his excitement, therefore, when d'Herbigny assured him, 'He does, *he does*'. Pierce left in raptures, feeling that he received nothing but sympathy and understanding from

'The Next Step'

the Bishop.[33] In a series of interviews in the following weeks d'Herbigny encouraged the Papalists in their work, stressing the importance of prayer and mutual explanations.[34]

It would appear that the two French Jesuits, d'Herbigny and de la Saudée, colluded in the cause of Church unity. When the latter returned to Oxford in the summer of 1932, he assured the Papalists that 'For a group holding the Confraternity credenda the Holy Father is ready to do *anything*'.[35] De la Saudée is unlikely to have made so extravagant a claim without authorisation, and, indeed, he impressed upon Pierce the importance of keeping d'Herbigny abreast of developments.[36]

Back in Rome in October 1932, Pierce found doors opening at the very highest levels. The Bishop obtained a private audience for the American at which the Pope 'said that he blessed, and prayed for, me and mine, and all of us in this work; and the work itself'.[37] D'Herbigny arranged for Pierce to meet with Michael Browne, Irish Rector of the Angelicum University and future Master-General of the Dominicans, and Cardinal. Having quizzed Pierce on the state of Anglicanism and his friends' plans, Browne turned to practicalities:

> If a body of clergy like you should come over, those who are really stable and with sufficient preparation should be re-ordained the *next day*. Authority might choose one or more of you to vouch for the individuals; decide which were completely equipped; which needed further brief preparation; then take action accordingly, at once, quietly.

Pierce was careful not to commit himself, but his head was swimming with possibilities in the light of the new attitude he found in Rome.[38]

There was nothing d'Herbigny was not prepared to do to advance the cause of Reunion. He arranged favourable coverage of the Centenary Manifesto in the Vatican newspaper, the *Osservatore Romano*. When the Centenary Tractates emerged, Pierce forwarded copies to the Bishop who, in turn, passed them on to Pius XI. D'Herbigny assured Pierce that the Pope read them with the greatest interest and approved their content. It was d'Herbigny who arranged the special audience with the Pope for Fynes-Clinton, Scott and Baverstock on the Catholic League pilgrimage to Rome. Pierce was entirely won over by d'Herbigny's kindness. He accorded the Jesuit his highest accolade: 'I found in him the interest and spirit of Cardinal Mercier.'[39]

Why was d'Herbigny so helpful? He was certainly attentive to anything that might extend the visible confines of the Catholic Church. But it is not necessary to strip the Frenchman of all claim to charity and spirituality. D'Herbigny insisted on the primacy of prayer in the work of Reunion. Pierce was no fool. He was convinced that d'Herbigny was 'a holy and humble man'.[40] One has to wonder, however, as to the Jesuits' grasp of reality. De la Saudée wrote:

> I hope the number of A.C. clergymen adopting the position of the CU are growing more and more numerous. When you will be a few thousands, I am morally sure Rome will grant you the disciplinary concessions you are wishing to have.[41]

Like Mercier before them, the Frenchmen seemed inclined to see what they wanted to see, and what Catholically-minded Anglicans wished to show them.

'No one answers'

Since *Apostolicae Curae*, the line of Anglicanism generally and of most Anglo-Catholics was that Reunion was impossible through no fault of their own. Eric Milner-White, Dean of King's College, Cambridge, explained the difficulty to those attending the First Anglo-Catholic Congress in 1920: 'Rome has shown as yet no desire whatever to approach other communions [...] Face the facts: anything like reunion or intercommunion with the Church of Rome is at the moment not practical, because Rome will have none of it.'[42] Malines could be dismissed as the benign eccentricity of one Belgian prelate. For many Anglicans, *Mortalium Animos* was a comforting document which allowed them to rest undisturbed amid old prejudices. Suddenly, the attitude and action of Pius XI and d'Herbigny appeared to challenge prevailing assumptions.

'The Next Step'

With no pastoral work or intellectual apostolate in Rome to occupy him, Pierce wrote often and at length to his associates in England and the United States. D'Herbigny and Pierce convinced themselves that a seismic change in the ecclesiastical landscape was imminent. The American wished those in England to know 'what an immense impression the Manifesto has made here [...] For the moment we have the ear of the public, in England and in Rome. It seems a wonderful opportunity.' Conceding that they were well written, Pierce feared that the Tractates would reach only a small scholarly audience. 'We have in Rome an attitude that is without precedent, as far as I know, since the schism.'[43] What practical steps were being taken in England to take advantage of this newfound benevolence?

For the final six weeks of 1932, this was Pierce's constant refrain: what was the Next Step to be?[44] He argued that the 1930 Lambeth Conference had fatally compromised the Church of England with respect to both morals and ecclesiology. The Manifesto had attempted to 'recall Anglicanism from the suicide it is preparing, or Anglo-Catholicism from the betrayal it is so committed to'. But what if the call went unheeded or was rejected? Could the Papalists continue indefinitely in communion with those who advocated such 'evils'? '*I don't know what the next step is. But I believe that we should all be thinking of the matter* [...] Ought you not to be discussing and planning?'[45]

Desperately seeking a future strategy, Pierce was even prepared to bury the hatchet and seek reconciliation with Morton Howard (if not Scott). Morton Howard could only suggest that the Papalists 'keep on teaching'. He himself proceeded to write what was, in effect, simply another CPCU Tractate: *Epistola ad Romanos*. Yet it only rehearsed the arguments of the earlier Tractates and the London Conversations. Indeed, there is a certain hardening of defensive attitudes and, despite protestations to the contrary, a desire to be defined as against Rome.[46]

There were various replies to his letters, but 'no one answers' Pierce's questions. There came the dawning realisation that there was to be no Next Step. 'No one will admit there is any definite point in the Anglican Communion's disintegration beyond which we can't be associated with it.' Jones was the founder of Papalism and for thirty years its fearless proponent. He was normally as prolific in his correspondence as Pierce himself. So his silence at this point was the most difficult for Pierce to bear. In his search for truth and personal integrity, the American felt abandoned and utterly alone.[47]

A call to action to his fellow Papalists, Pierce's letters can also be read as his own spiritual journal. The climax is imminent. Earlier that year he had been rethinking what was meant by 'Corporate Reunion' and dissociating himself from those who urged against any split within the Anglican Communion:

> On the contrary, I think most of us look forward eagerly to the day which must be coming when the faithful in our communion shall separate themselves, or be separated, from the protestant and modernist wings. It is just such a split that will make possible some sort of corporate reunion of the faithful part.[48]

These thoughts returned to the fore of Pierce's mind in December 1932. He shared them with two of his closest friends: 'I said there would come some point when we could no longer stick. Then what? What stands in the way of a considerable group "submitting"?'[49]

For Pierce that 'point when we could no longer stick' was reached with the moral apostasy of the 1930 Lambeth Conference. Having failed to coordinate a collective Papalist response, he felt constrained to act personally. Papalists had always argued that they remained in the Church of England both to work for Corporate Reunion and because they could not deny the validity of their Anglican Orders. Pierce felt the first condition was now an impossibility. He continued to struggle with the second issue. The crisis and the resolution came early in 1933, eased by d'Herbigny's tact and sympathy. Pierce and his sister were received into the Catholic Church by the Irish Dominicans at San Clemente on 4 March and confirmed by Bishop d'Herbigny the following week.

'The Next Step'

'Now or never'[50]

Sir James Marchant had contacted the Archbishop of Canterbury and the Cardinal Archbishop of Westminster in the preceding decade with grandiose schemes for the Reunion of the Anglican and Catholic Communions. Was this the sole tangible result—the conversion of one itinerant Episcopalian minister and his spinster sister in an ancient Roman basilica in the presence of a couple of seminarians?

So many clerical converts to Catholicism, whether by accident or design, allow contact with their former co-religionists to lapse following their move to Rome. Pierce planned otherwise. He and his sister took a flat in the Palazzo Doria Pamphilij and sent for their furniture from New York. D'Herbigny arranged matters so that Pierce was accepted as a seminarian at the Beda College for convert clergy in Rome. In a rare display of creative imagination, he was ordained a priest for the Diocese of Westminster on 28 March 1936 on the understanding that he could retire immediately 'in order to devote his time and talents to helping Anglicans, and particularly Anglican clergymen and religious, towards a better understanding of the Catholic Church'.[51] He was to do so assiduously until his death in 1962.

Pierce was in contact with the Essex clergyman, Thomas Whitton, who had been similarly shaken by Lambeth's sanction of contraception and who had derived little comfort from the St Ermin's Conference. Pierce outlined his spiritual journey in his correspondence; Whitton used his book, *The Necessity for Catholic Reunion*, for the same purpose. It was an indictment of both Anglo-Catholics and Papalists. 'Unfortunately,' Whitton wrote, 'the ordinary Anglican Catholic estimates the "catholicity" of a priest not from his dogmatic and moral teaching but from the standard of his ceremonial.' Goodier's influence is apparent in Whitton's assessment of the Papalists: 'It is extraordinary that they do not see how serious is their defiance of Rome, whether right or wrong, and how their religion is not the Roman Catholic, but a very similar religion on a totally different foundation.' It is difficult to fault his rationale:

> If an Anglican is convinced that the Roman Catholic Church is the one true Church, he is bound to join her at once, on her terms, without waiting for concessions; and if he does not so believe, if he thinks the Church can be divided, he cannot be received by Rome into communion and no concessions are of any value.

Corporate Reunion, he felt, was a fantasy. Whitton waited to see how many Papalists would follow the logic of their own arguments.[52]

Whitton shared Pierce's pessimism, feeling that after the Centenary Manifesto 'things seem to be settling down into quiet again'. By letting the Papalists know that he was prepared to do all he possibly could for them, Pius XI had 'called their bluff'.[53] Nevertheless, Whitton continued to press for action:

> I have been writing to Fynes-Clinton urging a move of some sort and publicity; also a meeting of Anglicans to discuss and, if possible, agree on what they want from Rome. For my own part I think they would find that they do not know what they want, or that they cannot agree on it.[54]

Pierce took up the matter with Jones: 'Do you not, yourself, believe that Whitton's thesis is the right one, of an exodus of those who hold the old faith?'[55] Again, the response was silence.

The leading Papalists did meet in London in mid-May 1933, under the auspices of the CPCU, to consider the future. The meeting was neither pleasant nor productive 'with Scott and Morton Howard getting very angry and going on the war path [...] The London people are now saying that nothing less than the return to Rome of the entire Anglicana is the goal, with no exodus short of that.'[56] Pierce dismissed the CPCU as hopeless, and was scathing of its attitude and inaction: 'Is it that these people (or some of them) want the "kick" of talking about Rome, without really meaning to do anything about it but talk?'[57]

If Whitton failed to receive a hearing among Anglicans in England, it was different in Rome. The Pope himself read his book, supplied through the agency and d'Herbigny. Whitton knew that, as a matter of conscience, he could no longer remain in the Church of England. Could he, as a married clergyman, be ordained a Catholic priest? Bishop Doubleday of Brentwood raised the matter

'The Next Step'

with Pius XI. Doubleday relayed how the Pope was 'impressed' by the Papalists he had met 'and was wondering what could be done to meet them'. It was the English Catholic Bishops who put paid to the suggestion, urging 'that the *laity* would not stand a married priesthood in England'.[58] Converting to Catholicism, Whitton remained a layman. In his late fifties, he struggled to support his family and re-establish his role in life.

Society for Catholic Reunion

If Papalists in London and Oxford were proving themselves capable of accommodation with post-Lambeth Anglicanism, there was one part of the country where it appeared this might not be the case. Silas Harris, otherwise known as 'Father Dominic Mary' in the Third Order Anglican Dominicans, was an irascible Welshman with a scholarly interest in Welsh Church history and liturgy. English was merely to be tolerated as a liturgical language—his preference was for Latin or Welsh—banning the use of 'the State Book of Common Prayer' at his own funeral. Nevertheless, having graduated from Keble College, Oxford, Harris's priestly ministry was exercised principally in rural England. For almost thirty years he was Vicar of Egmanton in the Diocese of Southwell. There he endeavoured, with decidedly mixed results, to re-establish a pre-Reformation Marian shrine as a rival focus to Walsingham for Anglican pilgrimage.

It was at Egmanton in October 1929 that Harris founded the Society for Catholic Reunion, one of the most zealous and extreme of all Papalist groups. It began as a local branch of the CU, a handful of East Midlands clergy gathering monthly to share 'common discussion and action'. As clergy invited their friends, the numbers grew to around twenty and the Society was formally constituted in January 1931. Why the need for another reunionist society? With staggering inconsistency, the CPCU posed that very question, regretting the SCR's capacity to 'divide and weaken the forces of reunionists'. The SCR claimed its distinctiveness lay in the urgency with which it viewed the problem and its insistence on practical action.[59] It was the SCR which appeared most unsettled by developments within the Church of England and most determined to take further action. The SCR proposed that the Centenary Manifesto signatories contact the Anglican Bishops directly with their grievances. If the response was unsatisfactory, they would investigate the possibility of conversion as a group.[60] To the irritation of other Anglican clergy, the SCR later wrote to parishes offering to address their people on the reunionist vision.[61]

Pierce had attended a SCR meeting as he toured the country attempting to build up support for the CU, and it was to Pierce that the members of the Society now turned for help. Bishop d'Herbigny laid before the Pope their request for disciplinary concessions, particularly a possible temporary relaxation of the rule on clerical celibacy. Pierce reported back: 'The Holy Father is intensely interested and sympathetic, and realises the gravity of the problem for many.' The Pope promised nothing specific, but nor did he rule anything out. Rome wished to study the relevant facts and once more was most interested in 'the number of individuals involved'. It seemed that matters were about to move rapidly. D'Herbigny proposed visiting England in April 1933 to discuss the issue with Cardinal Bourne in his sick room. Harris's disclosure that he was probably talking of only a score or so of interested clergy somewhat dampened proceedings, but Pierce still spoke in terms of a delay rather than outright rejection, and indicated that d'Herbigny might visit England that summer.[62]

The SCR sought to advance matters again by writing directly to the Pope during the centenary year of the Oxford Movement. They felt it politic to inform Bishop McNulty of Nottingham. The Bishop himself responded positively, sending his Cathedral Administrator to meet the Anglican clergy at Markham Clinton in April 1934. Unfortunately, they found the man 'rigid and unsympathetic'.[63] Harris took the advice which Whitton had given the SCR the preceding year: '*if* and *when* you are *pledged to a move, go to Rome direct.*'[64] It was not just the presumption that Rome was more kindly disposed to Anglicans than English Catholics, but only Rome could grant the requested concessions.

The address submitted to Pius XI by Harris and 19 others was sincere and uncomplicated, expressing their 'profound

'The Next Step'

gratitude' for his restatement of traditional Christian moral teaching in the Encyclical Letter, *Casti connubii*. Having assured the Pope of their desire for Reunion with Rome, they asked whether he might feel able 'to take some action which will tend to advance this desire and yearning of ours, and make its fruition and realisation possible'.[65]

Nothing further was heard for four months when Harris may have been surprised and alarmed to receive a letter from the Jesuit, Francis Woodlock, whose opposition to the Malines Conversations was notorious. But Woodlock came in no hostile spirit. He was giving effect to the instructions of the Secretary of State, Cardinal Pacelli. The Anglican address had filled Pius XI with 'great joy and consolation', and he entrusted Woodlock with 'the task of, with loving charity, enquiring further into the mind of these clergymen'.[66] It was not to be a repeat of the London Conversations, but an attempt to ascertain the nature of the disciplinary concessions sought by the Anglicans.[67]

The SCR group met with Woodlock at Egmanton on 23 and 24 October 1934. It is difficult to know how much information Harris had shared with the wider group in advance. At least one Anglican was surprised to discover himself treated as a potential convert. Certainly, the agenda was eminently practical. What action were the Anglicans looking for from Rome? What disciplinary concessions did they hope for?[68] Harris expressed his satisfaction with the proceedings: 'We all appreciate very much the friendly and cordial attitude you brought to the conferences, and we are grateful to you for the kindly sympathy and charity you displayed throughout our discussions.' The concessions the Anglicans hoped for closely resembled those contained in the 1931 Papalist Memorandum: a vernacular liturgy; retention of the Authorised Version of the Bible; the option of communion under both kinds; a relaxation of the discipline of clerical celibacy. The SCR sought communion with the Apostolic See while maintaining their own distinct identity, governed by a Vicar-Apostolic and with their own separate constitution.[69]

Once more there was something of a hiatus. Pierce wrote at Christmas reassuring Harris that his Memorial was 'being treated with the utmost seriousness'. His sources informed him that 'no doors are to be closed against these memorialists', but, at the same time, there was a reluctance in Rome to do anything which might deter individual conversions. The Vatican's 'definitive' answer was finally delivered via Woodlock in February 1935. While not specifically rejecting such a possibility, it held out no 'encouragement of the hope of the scheme proposed of uniate status for groups who should "come over"'.[70] The numbers involved were just too small for Rome to contemplate such a significant step.

Country House Ecumenism

Before this disappointing news was communicated, Pierce was already suggesting to Harris new avenues to pursue in the cause of Reunion, urging him 'to become friends with Fr St John'. Henry St John was a convert clergyman whose entry into the Catholic Church and the Dominicans had been facilitated by discussions with Vincent McNabb. As a Catholic, he shared the Irishman's benign attitude towards Anglicanism.

After the First World War, England was awash with large country houses which families were obliged to sell or rent to meet the challenges of high taxation and social and economic change. Religious orders were in the market for such properties, filling them with novices or schoolboys, even when they struggled to heat and maintain them. Laxton Hall, in fine Northamptonshire hunting country, had once been the seat of Lord Carbery. There in 1924 the Dominicans opened a school, where St John was sent to teach, being appointed headmaster in 1932.

Harris visited Laxton in December 1934. The Welshman and the Dominican agreed to friendly meetings between Anglicans and Catholics, sharing the conviction 'as to the necessity of some sort of uniate scheme'.[71] St John met the SCR on 1 June 1935 to deliver a paper. Conscious of the difficulties into which McNabb's ecumenical forays had landed him, St John insisted on absolute confidentiality. To avoid the complication of having to seek permission from his superiors, he came 'as an ordinary private person paying a friendly visit and having a friendly discussion'.[72] The

'The Next Step'

Dominican seems to have been expecting a robust exchange of views. Instead, the Anglicans he met took full dogmatic agreement for granted and seemed intent on demonstrating that they were more Catholic than the Pope. It did not help that St John subsequently went into print, criticising the Papalists for their rejection of Anglican traditions. Obsession with Roman liturgy and devotions, St John felt, hindered rather than helped the cause of Reunion with the wider Anglican Communion.[73] Conversations continued, but the Anglicans were now represented by the Society of the Sacred Mission ('the Kelham Fathers').

Kelham Hall, designed in the High Victorian Gothic style by Sir George Gilbert Scott, is St Pancras Station dropped into the Nottinghamshire countryside. For seventy years this was the home of the Society of the Sacred Mission, founded by Herbert Kelly in 1890 to train men for missionary work in Korea. It rapidly developed as a general Anglican theological college, the largest in the country in the 1930s, recruiting non-graduates and working class men not normally considered for Anglican Orders. Run along the lines of a religious order, its Anglo-Catholicism, like that of its founder, was decidedly *sui generis*. Papalist in neither doctrine nor devotions, Kelham's initial ecumenical endeavours turned in an altogether different direction.

Although critical of its liberal propensities and the practice of intercommunion, Kelly was, surprisingly, an enthusiast of the annual Student Christian Movement conference held at Swanwick in Derbyshire. (He was also a member of the drafting committee of the 1910 Edinburgh Missionary Conference.) Kelly went partly in a mischievous spirit of good humour to challenge Evangelical prejudice, but there was a common zeal for the missions and relish in being outside the Anglican Establishment.[74] The SCM also provided a link to Henry St John. As a prickly, young High Anglican, he too found himself, against his better judgment, attending the SCM summer conference in 1910. Arriving with a disdain for Presbyterians and Dissenters, St John was humbled to discover a shared 'deep personal love of our Lord Jesus Christ'. It required a readjustment of his attitude towards other Christians. He left the SCM conference 'profoundly convinced that the divisions of

Christendom were a world tragedy and the healing of them a primary necessity'.[75] A generation later, his conviction reinforced by his experience of ministering to soldiers of different denominations in the trenches, St John as a Dominican friar was in a position to make his personal contribution to this healing.

Interrupted by the Second World War, the Laxton conferences were held approximately every three years. By the mid-1950s there had been eight conferences, and more were planned. With the approval of the Bishop of Northampton and the religious superiors on both sides, Dominican and other Catholic theologians met with their Anglican counterparts, normally four on each side. Prominent among the Anglicans was Gabriel Hebert. A product of Harrow and New College, Oxford, he was not the average Kelham Father, although, like their founder, he too was an enthusiast of the SCM summer conferences.[76] Hebert's liturgical scholarship had given him an introduction to both Lutheran and Catholic ecumenical circles in Europe; his work on Aquinas brought him to the attention of St John.[77] It is typical, however, that his biographer, having detailed Hebert's involvement with the Free Churches, the Nordic Churches and the continental Liturgical Movement at some length, passes over his participation in the Laxton conferences in a single sentence.[78]

Over two or three days, papers were read and discussed at those conferences on subjects such as dogma, Scripture, the meaning of revelation and Church unity. St John recalled their approach:

> The method has been that of slow and sympathetic discussion, concerned less to argue than to interpret each other's minds, and to realise the angle from which those who differ from us see the truth as it is in Jesus Christ. No immediate results are looked for save a growing together in understanding, an appreciation of each other's point of view. We soon came to realise that this growing together is promoted as much by social intercourse and by meeting alternately as hosts and guests around a common table as by the more formal times of discussion.

The lack of direct involvement from either hierarchy may have made for a more relaxed ambience. It may have helped to remove

'The Next Step'

the pressure of expectations of 'immediate results' but, eighty years on, one is entitled to ask what practical results have been attained.

St John was viewed as an innovative progressive in his day, but he too came to understand that 'at the very heart of the problem of our divisions is the fact that there are beliefs which for us are truths revealed by God, but for them human inventions'. His conclusion might have been penned by Archbishop Goodier: 'Even where, as in the case of some Anglo-Catholics, doctrinal divergence is reduced almost to vanishing point, the foundations upon which these doctrines are held to rest, the presuppositions which lie behind them and the atmosphere in which they are lived, belong to a world different from that of Catholics.'[79]

These meetings of Laxton and Kelham were not the only instance of country house ecumenism. In its day the community of Nashdom held a special place in Papalist affections. Aelred Carlyle's colourful attempt to re-establish Benedictine life in the Anglican Communion on Caldey Island off the Welsh coast had ended in tears in 1913 when the majority of the community converted to Catholicism rather than comply with Bishop Gore's demand that they abandon Catholic liturgical practice and devotions. The Anglican remnant settled at Pershore in Worcestershire until new vocations after the First World War necessitated larger premises. Nashdom — the name means 'our home' in Russian — was a suitably flamboyant location. The house was built by Sir Edwin Lutyens to enable the Russian diplomat, Prince Alexis Dolgorouki, and his English wife to entertain in style in suburban Buckinghamshire. The 1913 defections did not lead the community to reject all things Roman. On the contrary, in the ballroom-turned-chapel Anglicans monks celebrated the Roman liturgy with the greatest precision. In these whimsical surroundings, the *orarium*, the daily round, was that of a traditional European monastery.

While still resident at Pershore, 'a most welcome addition to the community' arrived: 'an enchanting person, gay, good looking, witty and brilliant [...] he brought to our rather stuffy recreations something of the flavour of an Oxford common room'.[80] Dom Gregory Dix was Nashdom's most famous monk, possibly the most celebrated Papalist of them all. He ought to have been an irrelevance: an Anglican religious from a suspect community whose views placed him on the extreme fringe of his Communion. Yet he was a force to be reckoned with in the Church of England during his own lifetime, his work still read sixty years after his death. An Archbishop of Canterbury (Michael Ramsey) and one of Anglicanism's most eminent historians (Henry Chadwick) both expressed the desire to write Dix's biography. Neither work materialised.

Alston Dix was born in 1901, the son of an Anglo-Catholic teacher who took Anglican Orders later in life. After scholarships to Westminster School and Oxford, he followed his father into the Church, being appointed tutor and lecturer in Modern History at Keble College. His teaching career at Oxford was brief. Taking the name 'Gregory', he entered the Anglican Benedictines shortly before their move to Nashdom. Although later elected their Prior, for more than a decade Dix's relationship with his community was ambiguous. Due to take final vows in 1929, he became a priest oblate instead, only re-entering the novitiate in 1936 and being solemnly professed in 1940. The delay is the cause of some speculation. Health was an issue following a posting to West Africa. It probably reflected more his doubts as to his ability to remain in the Church of England.

With great candour, Dix tells of his spiritual anguish as to whether to submit to Rome around the time of the 1930 Lambeth Conference.[81] He resolved against such a step, but only later became reconciled to his own Communion, representing the Diocese of Oxford on Convocation, holding the hierarchy to account on matters of importance to the Catholic movement within Anglicanism. Nevertheless, years later, a mutual friend mused that while Gabriel Hebert believed in 'Anglicanism as a specific form of Christian thinking and living [with its own] unique and peculiar excellence', he was not certain that Dix did. For Dix, Anglicanism was no more than a temporary expedient to bring the English people back to the wider Catholic Church.[82]

That Dix enjoyed considerable influence way beyond his own limited constituency was due in large measure to his affability and wit. 'Mischievous' was the adjective most frequently applied

'The Next Step'

to him, invariably and immediately qualified—'not malevolent'. He hated the Anglican Establishment and Modernism with a passion because he believed them destructive of true religion and the search for personal sanctity. Yet logic, history and humour were the only weapons he employed against their proponents. (The effects were still devastating.) Dix's capacity to teach and communicate was employed to greatest effect when his message was most controversial or unpopular. And all this was founded upon impressive scholarship. Today Dix is remembered principally for his seminal tome which emerged in 1945, *The Shape of the Liturgy*. However, it was his work on the Church Fathers that brought him into contact with the English Jesuits.

Heythrop in north Oxfordshire was on an altogether grander scale than Nashdom, originally built in the Baroque style for an eighteenth-century Duke of Shrewsbury returning from the Grand Tour. Heythrop was purchased by the Jesuits in the 1920s to gather together Philosophers from Stonyhurst and Theologians from St Beuno's in North Wales. That amalgamation was not judged a success by members of the Society as a whole.

Maurice Bévenot arrived at Heythrop in 1936, and taught at the College until his death in 1980. Born in 1897, he was the son a French papal zouave who came to England to lecture in modern languages. Joining the Jesuit novitiate, Bévenot was ordained in 1930 and sent to Rome for further studies. He rapidly established a reputation for patristic scholarship.[83] In this capacity Dix wrote to him in June 1937. Writing himself on the question of jurisdiction in the early Church, the Anglican wanted Bévenot's opinion on St Cyprian's ecclesiology, the subject of the Jesuit's doctoral thesis. Dix had an ulterior motive. His Abbot, Martin Collett, had recently been in Rome. There he had encountered the English Jesuit, Bernard Leeming, professor of sacramental theology at the Gregorian University, who had been 'very anxious' that Nashdom should make contact with Bévenot.[84] Two years earlier Pierce had reported that Leeming had been won over to a more sympathetic stance towards Anglicans in general and Papalists in particular.[85]

Dix followed up Bévenot's response to his initial enquiry by issuing an invitation to Nashdom. The Jesuit accepted, but only arrived after he had attended the Faith and Order Conference in Edinburgh as a Catholic observer. Initially, there were definite limits to his ecumenical openness, criticising the 'comprehensiveness' and 'compromise' he had encountered in Edinburgh.[86] The same reservation is apparent in Bévenot's reply to a CU request to write an article for *Reunion*. While he agreed to do so, he disassociated himself entirely from the journal's recent publication of Beauduin's Malines paper, which he thought detrimental to the cause of Reunion.[87]

During Bévenot's visit to Nashdom in November 1937, Dix suggested the possibility of conferences between Catholic and Anglican theologians. 'The idea was to keep it quite informal and make the primary aim to understand one another better.'[88] Leeming suggested possible Catholic participants, but was not involved himself, fearing lest the Jesuit General in Rome refuse permission. In the event, four other Jesuits from Heythrop were to accompany Bévenot, including Edward Helsham, until recently Rector of Heythrop, and George Hayward Joyce.

The Anglicans, although all firmly at the Catholic end of the spectrum of their Communion, were a much more disparate group. Indeed, Dix feared that the Jesuits would ruthlessly exploit divisions between the Anglicans. Dix invited Gabriel Hebert from Kelham; the two men were already collaborators in liturgical scholarship and dialogue with Orthodox theologians. Two more of the Anglican participants had also been involved in those talks with the Russian Orthodox held at Mirfield in 1936: Lionel Thornton, a Scripture scholar and a member of the Community of the Resurrection, and Eric Mascall, Sub-warden of Lincoln Theological College. The fifth Anglican was Vigo Demant, a sociologist, theologian and vicar of St John the Divine in Richmond, Surrey, later Regius Professor of Moral and Pastoral Theology at Oxford.

The effort required to assemble the Anglican team necessitated delay. That time allowed the participants on both sides to read and review the most recent contribution to the debate, the work of the French Dominican, Yves Congar, *Chrétiens désunis*. Hebert argued that this represented Catholicism's definitive commitment to the ecumenical endeavour. Bévenot summarised Congar's contention:

'The Next Step'

'That it is a mistake to try to envisage by what process the Holy Spirit will eventually bring all Christians to unity, and that we must rather study the actual situation as it is in concrete, and ask ourselves what the situation calls on us to do here and now.'[89] Immediately, we notice the dramatic shift from the position of the Papalists and their Catholic counterparts for whom full dogmatic agreement and the acceptance of papal claims had been the very basis of all their thought.

Catholics and Anglicans met at Nashdom over two days in June 1938. It is inconceivable that Dix was unaware of the London Conversations six years earlier. The St Ermin's Conference had hardly been a secret within Papalist circles, Dix knew Fynes-Clinton well and Simmonds was curate at All Saints, Margaret Street, where the parish priest was another Nashdom monk and Dix a frequent visitor. While the Anglicans were now represented by a younger generation, Dix did not dismiss out of hand the methodology of the earlier Conversations. For him too, it was of paramount importance that the talks were being conducted in England by Englishmen. Reunion meant dealing with English Roman Catholics rather than Frenchmen and Belgians.[90]

Seeking to avoid unnecessary controversy at the outset, Bévenot had suggested that the conference consider 'The nature of Tradition, and its function in the Church'.[91] No records were kept, but forty years later Bévenot recalled the experience:

> We plunged into very unknown waters, feeling our way at first, and experiencing the wanderings of discussions as they kept getting off the point. That did not matter much and often corrected itself. We were not negotiating, nor even preparing for negotiation; but we were getting to know one another and understanding something of our respective outlooks.[92]

Writing later still, Eric Mascall's memories of this 'extremely secret' conference were even more vague. Accepting the proceedings as a whole ran relatively smoothly, the only fact that remained impressed upon his mind was Gabriel Hebert insisting repeatedly that Luther was 'terribly sincere', while 'that inflexible old moral theologian Fr Joyce' retorted on each occasion that Luther was 'a bad man'.[93]

Were the Laxton and Nashdom conferences successful? Yes, on their own criteria of 'getting to know one another and understanding our respective outlooks'. Bévenot and Dix entered in a fruitful correspondence (which never lost the capacity for critical analysis) which lasted until Dix's death in 1952. Others were encouraged by the experience. There were further talks at Mirfield between Catholics, including Christopher Butler of Downside, and, on the Anglican side, Hebert, Mascall and members of the Community of the Resurrection.[94] Suddenly, it seemed that everyone wished to talk to each other. Only the outbreak of the Second World War brought a temporary halt to this epidemic of fraternisation. But it appeared that the groundwork had been laid for something more significant in the new world which was to emerge from that War.

Invariably, the fleeting references to these conferences describe them, and particularly the willingness of the Catholic Church to engage, as unique and unprecedented.[95] A wider perspective is lacking,[96] especially a knowledge of the London Conversations which gives the context to this ecumenical contact on English soil. Would it be too much to suggest that it was those London Conversations which gave the English Dominicans and Jesuits the confidence and tools to enter into such dialogue and the Anglicans the knowledge that English Catholics were prepared to engage with them seriously and with official recognition?

Whatever the answer, we have travelled quite a distance from those ground-breaking Conversations of the early 1930s and we should return to those pioneers.

Notes

[1] The full text of the Centenary Manifesto is given in the Appendix.

[2] Silas Harris, Welsh scholar and Vicar of the shrine church of Egmanton, Nottinghamshire.

[3] Andrew Acheson, Vicar of Down Ampney, Gloucestershire.

[4] Pierce to Harris, Jones and Acheson, 21 March 1932 (copy), BCA, Pierce Bequest, Correspondence 1930–3/20–1.

[5] Pierce to Harris, 2 May 1932 (copy), BCA, Pierce Bequest, Correspondence 1930–3/22–3.

6 Fynes-Clinton, in H. J. Fynes-Clinton and W. R. Corbould, *What are We to Say?* (London: Council for Promoting Catholic Unity, 1933), p. 4.

7 See Mascall, 'The Ultra-Catholic', p. xix.

8 'The Oxford Movement: A Centenary Manifesto', 1 October 1932.

9 De la Saudée, *Anglicans et catholiques*, p. 198.

10 Pierce to Acheson, 11 December 1932 (copy), BCA, Pierce Bequest, Correspondence 1930–3/43.

11 Fynes-Clinton and Corbould, *What are We to Say?*, p. 12.

12 *Tablet* (12 Nov. 1932), pp. 626–7.

13 Pierce to Howard, 6 December 1932 (copy), BCA, Pierce Bequest, Correspondence 1930–3/37.

14 Cited *Bulletin*, 17 (Chair of Peter, 1933), p. 4.

15 *Bulletin*, 15 (Sacred Heart, 1932), p. 4.

16 J. Keating, SJ, 'Anglicanism Merely a Schism?', *The Month*, 162 (1933), pp. 430–1.

17 *Ibid.*, p. 431; Pierce to d'Herbigny, 16 July 1933 (copy), BCA, Pierce Bequest, Correspondence 1930–3/244.

18 Fynes-Clinton, *What are We to Say?*, pp. 5–15.

19 Corbould, in Fynes-Clinton and Corbould, *What are We to Say?*, pp. 21–7.

20 Pierce to Harris, 2 May 1932 (copy), BCA, Pierce Bequest, Correspondence 1930–3/23; Pierce to Gillam, 9 July 1933 (copy), BCA, Pierce Bequest, Correspondence 1930–3/237.

21 Pierce to Hussey and Gillam, 4 January 1933 (copy), PHA/Rea/CU3.

22 'Pilgrimage to Rome' in *The Pilot*, December 1933, no. 4.

23 Pierce to Gillam, 30 October 1933, PHA, Rea/CU3/229.

24 Pierce to Howard, 6 December 1932 (copy), BCA, Pierce Bequest, Correspondence 1930–3/37.

25 De la Saudée, *Essai sur le Mouvement Anglo-Catholique* (Paris: Louis de Soye, 1932).

26 De la Saudée to Pierce, 25 September 1932, PHA/Rea/CU3/718.

27 M. Pribilla, SJ, *Um kirchliche Einheit* (Freiburg: Herder & Co., 1929) cited *Bulletin*, 14 (Epiphany 1932), p. 18.

28 Pierce to Joblin, 31 July 1931, PHA/Rea/CU3/204c; Pierce to Joblin, 6 August 1931, PHA/Rea/CU3/204d.

29 Pierce to Rev. G. Nuttall-Smith, 13 January 1933 (copy), BCA, Pierce Bequest, Correspondence 1930–3/81.

30 Pierce to Gillam, 30 October 1933, PHA, Rea/CU3/229.

31 Pierce to Harris, 16 January 1934, PHA, Harris Papers; T. Barnas, OSB,

'Paul Couturier and the Monastery of Amay-Chevetogne', *Messenger* (Oct. 2003), accessed online at www.paulcouturier.com/pcbook12barnas.pdf; Salter, *The Anglican Papalist*, pp. 155–65.

32 Barlow, *The Malines Conversations*, pp. 74–81.

33 Pierce to Jones, 31 October 31 (copy), PHA/Rea/CU3.

34 Pierce to Jones, 14 November 1931 (copy), BCA, Pierce Bequest, Correspondence 1930–3/12.

35 Pierce to Jones, 15 December 1932 (copy), BCA, Pierce Bequest, Correspondence 1930–3/49.

36 Pierce to C. R. Hussey, 8 August 1932 (copy), PHA/Rea/CU3.

37 Pierce to Hussey and Gillam, 8 November 1932 (copy), PHA/Rea/CU3.

38 Pierce to Harris and Acheson, 1 December 1932 (copy), BCA, Pierce Bequest, Correspondence 1930–3/35.

39 Pierce to d'Herbigny, 11 December 1932 (copy), BCA, Pierce Bequest, Correspondence 1930–3/42; Pierce to Howard, 6 December 1932 (copy), BCA, Pierce Bequest, Correspondence 1930–3/37; Pierce to Gillam, 18 December 1932 (copy), BCA, Pierce Bequest, Correspondence 1930–3/53; 'Pilgrimage to Rome' in *The Pilot*, December 1933, no. 4.

40 Pierce to Jones, 31 October 1931 (copy), PHA/Rea/CU3.

41 De la Saudée to Pierce, 10 September 1932, PHA/Rea/CU3.

42 E. M. Milner-White, 'The Church of Rome', in *Report of the First Anglo-Catholic Congress, London, 1920* (London: SPCK, 1920), pp. 86–7.

43 Pierce to Jones, 15 December 1932 (copy), BCA, Pierce Bequest, Correspondence 1930–3/49.

44 *Ibid.*

45 Pierce to Gillam, 28 November 1932 (copy), BCA, Pierce Bequest, Correspondence 1930–3/34.

46 Pierce to Morton Howard, 6 December 1932 (copy), BCA, Pierce Bequest, Correspondence 1930–3/37–8; Pierce to Acheson, 3 January 1933 (copy), BCA, Pierce Bequest, Correspondence 1930–3/73; Morton Howard, *Epistola ad Romanos: An Open Letter to our Brethren of the Roman Catholic Church* (London: Talbot & Co., 1933).

47 Pierce to Acheson, 3 January 1933 (copy), BCA, Pierce Bequest, Correspondence 1930–3/73; Pierce to Jones, 15 December 1932 (copy), BCA, Pierce Bequest, Correspondence 1930–3/49.

48 Pierce to Hussey, 17 June 1932 (copy), PHA/Rea/CU3.

49 Pierce to Harris and Acheson, 1 December 1932 (copy), BCA, Pierce Bequest, Correspondence 1930–3/35.

50 Whitton to Pierce, 15 May 1933, cited Pierce to d'Herbigny, 18 May 1933 (copy), BCA, Pierce Bequest, Correspondence 1930–3/203–4.

'The Next Step'

51 C.A.C.H., 'Monsignor Henry Pierce', p. 8.

52 Whitton, *The Necessity for Catholic Reunion*, pp. 110, 125, 152–3, 42.

53 Pierce to D. Fenwick, 30 April 1933 (copy), BCA, Pierce Bequest, Correspondence 1930–3/193.

54 Whitton to Pierce, 15 May 1933, cited Pierce to d'Herbigny, 18 May 1933 (copy), BCA, Pierce Bequest, Correspondence 1930–3/203–4.

55 Pierce to Jones, 2 June 1933 (copy), BCA, Pierce Bequest, Correspondence 1930–3/214.

56 *Ibid.*

57 Pierce to Gillam, 7 February1934, PHA, Harris Papers.

58 Whitton to Crookendon, 15 March 1933, PHA, Harris Papers.

59 Harris to Campbell, 3 March 1931, PHA/CU/Rea/CU3; Harris to Jack, 4 December 1951, PHA/Rea/CU4/1052; *Reunion*, September 1935, vol. I, no. 6, p. 192.

60 Harris to Pierce, 4 March 1933 mentioned Pierce to Harris, 22 March 1933 (copy), BCA, Pierce Bequest, Correspondence 1930–3/169.

61 SCR Memorandum signed by Harris and others, undated [1935], PHA, Harris Papers.

62 Pierce to Harris, 22 March 1933 (copy), BCA, Pierce Bequest, Correspondence 1930–3/169; Pierce to Harris, 5 April 1933 (copy), BCA, Pierce Bequest, Correspondence 1930–3/172; Pierce to Harris, 16 April 1933 (copy), BCA, Pierce Bequest, Correspondence 1930–3/181.

63 Harris to Woodlock, 21 December 1934 (copy), PHA, Harris Papers.

64 Whitton to Crookendon, 15 March 1933, PHA, Harris Papers.

65 SCR Address to Pius XI, 7 March 1934 (copy), PHA, Harris Papers.

66 Eugenio, Cardinal Pacelli to Woodlock, 8 July 1934 (copy), PHA, Harris Papers.

67 Woodlock to Harris, 13 and 24 July 1934, PHA, Harris Papers.

68 Notes of SCR Committee Meeting, 2 October 1934, PHA, Harris Papers.

69 E. Wass to Harris, 4 December 1934; Harris to Woodlock, 31 October 1934; Memorandum, 'Conference with Fr Woodlock, Oct 23 and 24: Note of Agreed Points', PHA, Harris Papers.

70 Pierce to Harris, 28 December 1934; Woodlock to Harris, 24 February 1935, PHA, Harris Papers.

71 St John to Harris, 1 December 1935; Pierce to Harris, 28 October 1934 and 30 January 1935, PHA, Harris Papers.

72 St John to Harris, 10 May 1935, PHA, Harris Papers.

73 *Blackfriars* (March 1937); *Reunion*, 2/13 (June 1937), pp. 385–6; 2/14 (Sept. 1937), pp. 417–22.

74 A. Morton, *History of the Society of the Sacred Mission* (Norwich: Canterbury Press, 1993), pp. 62, 95.

75 St John, *Essays in Christian Unity*, pp. xii–xv.

76 C. Irvine, *Worship, Church and Society: An Exposition of the Work of Arthur Gabriel Hebert* (Norwich: Canterbury Press), p. 56.

77 Morton, *History of the Society of the Sacred Mission*, pp. 162, 167, 176.

78 Irvine, *Worship, Church and Society*, p. 67.

79 St John, *Essays in Christian Unity*, pp. xvi–xviii.

80 B. S. James, *Asking for Trouble* (London: The Catholic Book Club, 1962), p. 41.

81 G. Dix, OSB, to M. Bévenot, SJ, 28 March 1941, cited J. G. Leachman, OSB, 'Across the Fence: The Conversation between Maurice Bévenot, SJ, and Gregory Dix, OSB', *Sewanee Theological Review*, 53/1 (2009), p. 30.

82 E. L. Mascall, *Saraband: The Memoirs of E. L. Mascall* (Leominster: Gracewing, 1992), p. 169.

83 R. Murray, SJ, 'Maurice Bévenot, Scholar and Ecumenist (1897–1980)', *Heythrop Journal*, 23/1 (1982), pp. 1–17.

84 Leachman, 'Across the Fence', p. 16.

85 Pierce to Harris, 28 February 1934, PHA, Harris Papers.

86 Leachman, 'Across the Fence', pp. 18–19.

87 Bévenot to Gillam, 1 September 1937, PHA, Rea/CU3/907.

88 Bévenot to Dix, 23 January 1938, cited Leachman, 'Across the Fence', p. 21.

89 Bévenot, *Month* (May 1938), p. 431, cited Leachman, 'Across the Fence', p. 21.

90 Dix to Bévenot, 28 March 1941, cited Leachman, 'Across the Fence', p. 37.

91 Leachman, 'Across the Fence', p. 22.

92 Bévenot, 'Dix Redivivus: *Jurisdiction in the Early Church* by Dom Gregory Dix', *Heythrop Journal*, 17 (1976), p. 183.

93 Mascall, *Saraband*, pp. 163, 168.

94 Pawley, *Rome and Canterbury through Four Centuries*, pp. 301–2.

95 P. Dunstan, *The Labour of Obedience: The Benedictines of Pershore, Nashdom and Elmore* (Norwich: Canterbury Press, 2009), p. 204n.; Morton, *History of the Society of the Sacred Mission*, p. 176.

96 Bernard and Margaret Pawley were almost alone in discerning this pattern of growing contact between Anglican and Catholic religious communities in England, but even they were unaware of the London Conversations which preceded them.

✣ 9 ✣

A Different Direction

The Abbé Couturier

The decisive blow to Papalist ambitions of Reunion came from the least expected of quarters. It was the result of neither condemnation by Canterbury nor rebuff by Rome. Instead, it was delivered by an unassuming French priest, the Abbé Paul Couturier. For someone who spent only a matter of weeks in England, Couturier is given significant coverage in most accounts of the search for unity between Rome and Canterbury—because, unlike the Papalists, he fits the narrative of the ecumenical establishment.[1] This holy and humble man took the outdated and exclusive Church Unity Octave and single-handedly transformed it into the more meaningful Week of Prayer for Christian Unity in one seamless development and to common acclaim. Unfortunately, such an interpretation does not quite match the facts.

Couturier was born into conventionally bourgeois circumstances, conservative and Catholic, in Lyon in 1881. He followed other family members into the Church, being ordained in 1906 for the Society of Priests of St Irenaeus. Then he settled down to teach maths and natural sciences in the Society's school for the next four decades, struggling to maintain discipline and interest among his younger charges. And in this obscurity he might have remained, a conscientious priest and an indifferent schoolmaster, had a Jesuit not encouraged him in 1923 to engage in the pastoral care of the large Russian émigré community settled in Lyon. So Couturier was introduced to the clergy and liturgy of the Russian Orthodox Church.

These contacts among the Orthodox in Lyon led him to make his retreat at the Benedictine Priory of Amay in the summer of

1932. The community's founder had already begun his long period of exile, but Couturier picked up a copy of *A Monastic Work for Church Unity* in which Beauduin set out Amay's objectives and methods in working for Reunion, involving study, respectful dialogue and the shared experience of the different liturgical traditions of East and West. Completely won over, Couturier became an oblate of Amay. He saw in the vision of Beauduin and Mercier the means of achieving not just full communion with the Russian diaspora among whom he ministered in France, but Christian unity generally.

Corresponding with Wattson in the United States, Couturier introduced prayer for unity to Lyon. It began very tentatively in January 1933 with just three days of prayer among Catholics and Orthodox 'for the return of Unity'. However, with the support of Cardinal Maurin, Couturier felt emboldened the following year to keep the full Octave, culminating in a service in Lyon Cathedral.[2]

'A rather wider view of things'[3]

Initially, the Octave Couturier introduced to Lyon was that founded by Wattson and Jones.[4] But already by 1935 the Lyon Octave was developing a different emphasis to that practised in England and America, and endorsed by Rome. Couturier's vision was not limited to Catholicism and Orthodoxy. Anglicans, Protestants and Jews—indeed all mankind—had an indispensable place in his understanding of unity in Christ.[5]

Couturier himself acknowledged that he came to Anglicanism through Russia. He learnt about the Church Unity Octave through Amay. Hearing of the French priest's interest, Fynes-Clinton sent him and Cardinal Maurin the Council's material concerning the Octave. Jones too was soon corresponding with Couturier, who persuaded him to write regular articles on Reunion for the *Revue apologétique* which eventually appeared as the book, *L'Église d'Angleterre et la Sainte-Siege*. In 1934, Couturier's Orthodox friend and assistant, Serge Bolshakoff, told him of the Anglican religious communities of the Society of St John the Evangelist in Oxford (the Cowley Fathers) and Nashdom. In its work for Christian unity,

A Different Direction

Nashdom prided itself as fulfilling the role of Amay in England, helping to popularise the person and writings of the Abbé.

Through prayer and reflection, Couturier's ideas on unity had developed sufficiently by 1935 for him to present these to an English audience in Nashdom's journal *Laudate* and the CU's *Reunion*. There was much that was right and attractive in the Frenchman's vision. There was the recognition of human inability to mend the scandal of division and the necessity for supernatural intervention, for prayer. And not only prayer, but also for penance. Couturier had no difficulty in owning a shared culpability for division and denouncing 'a kind of spiritual pride' which prevented some Catholics from admitting this. He urged on his co-religionists the duty 'to be the first to restore mutual sympathy and the cordial welcome of hands outstretched. His heart must be open and sincere in its fraternal love, and charity in the fullest sense of the word.'

But then Couturier strayed into more controversial territory, characterising the methods of the existing Octave as 'proselytism' and 'spiritual conquest'. Based on papal claims and having as its predetermined end union with Rome, Couturier maintained that the Church Unity Octave was doomed to failure unless given a significant change of direction. 'For an Orthodox, a Protestant or an Anglican to participate means falling into a spiritual ambush, a net spread for the good faith of men by the spiritual imperialism of Rome', whereas for the Catholic 'the Octave can have only one meaning, and that is to lead other Christian sects into a humble submission to the Pope of Rome'. Couturier dismissed the value of historical study, preferring to 'leave the past unspoken (for all know it)'—anathema to our Papalist scholars!

The Abbé was never anything other than a good and loyal Catholic. Yet he felt it a serious mistake to urge his beliefs and practices upon others. For Couturier, unity would happen only in God's time and in the manner of His choosing. Consequently, his proposals were somewhat vague. The Octave 'should be spread and made universal in each denomination, each working on the lines of its own way of thought'. No one would be called upon to abandon their practice or theology. Unity would be sought and prayed for by different means, with different Christians meaning different things by it. Convergence would be left in God's hands.[6]

All this constituted a radical departure from the concept of Catholic Reunion promoted by the Anglican Papalists since the beginning of the century. Spencer Jones's response was surprisingly mild. It is difficult to lambast genuine holiness. Jones praised not so much Couturier's thought as his attitude to non-Catholic Christians: 'his general way of looking at us; and his manner of approach; in other words the *line of sympathy* that runs through all he has to say'. Jones had no difficulty with 'spiritual unity', if by that was meant the principle of sympathy which arose from personal contact and joint conferences. (As he wrote, was he remembering the London Conversations?) The Englishman distinguished this, however, from 'United Services in the Church', which he rejected as the 'vain attempt at the compulsory resolution of contradictory factors'. (In a later clarification Couturier stated that he too viewed such shared services as 'most harmful and disastrous', tending to 'religious indifference'.[7]) Jones insisted that he had no intention of accusing Couturier of abandoning Catholic principles but one has to wonder why he felt it necessary to mention this: 'There is no fear, then, of our misunderstanding the attitude of the Abbé, or of our regarding him as having given away his own case; nor would it be of any service to ours if he had.'[8]

Couturier implemented his proposals fully for the first time in Lyon in January 1936. The *Octave* was replaced by the *Week of Universal Prayer of Christians for the Unity of Christians*, generally referred to as the Week of Universal Prayer. Couturier himself was clear that this represented more than just a mere change of name: 'We do not imply that the older way has been absorbed into the new one.' Rather,

> retaining only the intention of Christian Unity to be recovered according to God's will, by means which are according to His will and in His own time, those octave prayers progressed along a glorious road. They were accepted and observed in Orthodoxy and Protestantism.[9]

A Different Direction

Couturier also retained the dates, 18–25 January, despite Papalist protests. Not unreasonably, they argued that having two octaves on different bases running simultaneously was bound to confuse.[10] The co-founder of the older Octave pointed out forcefully 'those 8 days signify the double dedication of the Church of Rome, and are intended to lay the stress on that aspect; and it seems to me out of all reason to destroy its very character, and yet to go on using the condition of 8 days, which is intended to express it'.[11]

Fynes-Clinton was often perceived, even by his friends, as a well-intentioned old buffer, but not endowed with the greatest intellect. Yet immediately he grasped the issue at stake here. The Anglican Establishment was rattled by the fact that the Church Unity Octave, with its explicit acceptance of papal claims, was becoming accepted overseas as mainstream Anglicanism's response to the widespread desire for unity. To counter this, Douglas (Fynes-Clinton's former sparring partner in the Anglican and Eastern Churches Association) and Lambeth Palace wished to establish 'some "oecumenic" form of the Octave' on a very different basis to that which Jones, Fynes-Clinton and the Papalists had toiled for so long and which finally appeared to be bearing fruit in terms of the number of supporters and overseas interest. Were Couturier and the French Church to sanction this alternative octave, then the Papalists risked being 'smothered' and their work destroyed. Fynes-Clinton urged his fellow Papalists to press ahead with their original vision 'all the harder'.

So there already existed an underlying tension when, at Couturier's invitation, Fynes-Clinton and Dix travelled to Lyon in September 1936 to see at first hand this 'remarkable movement in France'. This tension was aggravated by the Anglican Establishment which, in the person of Douglas, had 'rather nobbled Couturier' with a view to gaining his support for a non-papal octave in England.[12] Fynes-Clinton sought to remind Couturier of the Octave's origins and bring him back onside. Any discord was immediately dispelled by the warmth of Couturier's welcome and the busy schedule he had arranged for his guests. Fynes-Clinton delivered a paper in French setting out the standard Papalist line on the ecclesiastical position in England and the work for Church

Unity.[13] Dix spoke more spontaneously on the Papalist interpretation of the Reformation and subsequent English Church history. Dix thought that they had gained their objective in ensuring the French stuck to the traditional Octave, but this may have been a misreading of general reunionist enthusiasm for actual agreement on a specific proposal.[14]

Fynes-Clinton attempted to secure Couturier for the Papalist position by issuing him a return invitation to visit England. Initially hesitant, he pleaded poverty, health concerns and ignorance of the language. All these objections were swept aside. So, in September 1937, Couturier arrived in the wonderful world of Anglican Papalism, hosted by Fynes-Clinton at St Ermin's. There he met Jones, Corbould and Harris, who took Couturier to the shrine church at Egmanton. The Frenchman's itinerary also included Nashdom and, briefly, Cowley. Fynes-Clinton could not be faulted for charm and effort, but, ultimately, he failed. The Abbé may have been self-effacing, but he was sufficiently astute to recognise that the version of Anglicanism presented to him was wildly unrepresentative. William O'Brien, Superior of the Cowley Fathers, impressed on Couturier that there was more even to Anglo-Catholicism than this.

Couturier pressed ahead in developing contacts of his own in the Church of England. Having received visitors from Cowley and Mirfield in the spring of 1938, he himself returned to England that July. Freed from Fynes-Clinton's tutelage, his second tour was more wide-ranging. Seeking to build an 'invisible monastery' of anonymous souls united in prayer for Christian unity, Couturier particularly welcomed meeting the religious communities of Nashdom, Mirfield, Kelham, Cowley and various Anglican female houses. In Oxford he saw Bishop Kirk and Dr Kidd, sole survivor of the Anglican participants of Malines. Most importantly, this diminutive French schoolmaster struck up friendships with the two Archbishops, Temple of York and Lang of Canterbury. Flouting convention, Couturier felt no qualms about praying with his non-Catholic hosts. He asked the Archbishops to invite Anglicans everywhere to join in his Week of Universal Prayer. So manifestly 'a man of God', there was a general disposition to grant what he asked. He radiated Rome's love for all those who bore the name of Christian and explained patiently why prudential considerations meant that sometimes Rome had to move more slowly than others might wish.[15]

'Sold to the enemy'

Always courteous, Couturier was utterly convinced of the rightness of his approach and impervious, therefore, to Papalist persuasion. Back in Lyon, he wasted no time in following up his English contacts, inviting the Anglican religious communities to join his inclusive version of the Octave. He made plain his wish 'to draw in the Evangelicals and ultimately the Nonconformists'.[16] Clearly, the Anglicans were captivated by Courturier's simplicity and goodness. Victor Shearburn indicated Mirfield's intention to throw in its lot with his 'wider vision'. He shared Couturier's concern that many 'will not touch the Octave on the plea that it is entirely in the hands of folk, whose line they disapprove'. A less exclusive, less papal octave opened up new opportunities: 'official Anglicanism is ready to mutter a guarded blessing, and the Bishop of Oxford is especially keen'. Shearburn reasoned that Couturier's 'call to prayer skips nimbly over innumerable ecclesiastical prejudices'. He hoped that the Week of Universal Prayer would prove acceptable to everyone, including Fynes-Clinton and the CPCU.[17]

Shearburn hoped in vain. Fynes-Clinton had no intention of abandoning the Church Unity Octave. The Papalists rejected out of hand the reasons advanced to justify change. Couturier sought maximum participation by allowing everyone to pray in a way in which they felt comfortable for 'the unity which Christ wishes for His Church by the means which He wishes'.[18] Couturier insisted that in no manner was doctrine being compromised, he was simply issuing an invitation to prayer freed from any preconditions, taking an imperative of Christ and leaving the mode of its realisation in God's hands. But, for the Papalists, God had revealed the means of Christian unity. Its realisation and maintenance were inseparable from St Peter, upon whom Christ had founded His

Church, and his successors, the Popes. Ignoring this could only impede, rather than advance, the cause of unity. If papal claims proved unpalatable to many, then it was a case of teaching the truth, as Jones and his disciples had done for well nigh forty years, and to pray, but always on a correct doctrinal basis.

Shearburn's other reason for change—its appeal to the Anglican Establishment—was even more abhorrent to the Papalists. The Abbot of Nashdom wrote somewhat intemperately: 'I too am deeply distressed about the Octave. Fr Couturier, although unknown to himself and with the best of motives, has sold us to the enemy.'[19] 'The enemy' was what Dix scathingly referred to as 'the National Religious Establishment'. It was typified by the Anglican Bishops and the BBC, and its creed was: 'God is nice and in Him is no nastiness at all.' Lacking doctrinal and moral substance, the power to communicate holiness and to prophesy, it was, in Dix's humble opinion, the complete antithesis of the Catholic Church.[20] The Church Unity Octave thus found itself on the front line of this battle for the soul of the Church of England.

To the uncharitable, Papalist hostility could appear to be motivated by jealousy. In four decades of tracts, societies and conversations they had signally failed to achieve official Anglican commitment to the cause of Catholic Reunion. This obscure French priest seemed to have obtained it in the course of two brief visits by dint of his evident sanctity and sincerity. But there was more substance to Papalist opposition than this.

The Papalists thought Couturier naïve. For the first time in his life Dix admitted approval of the views of the late Cardinal Bourne concerning 'the interlopings of foreign ecclesiastics in matters Anglican which they could hardly understand *au fond*'.[21] Pierce in Rome was similarly critical of 'the harm [Couturier] may do to the pro-Roman movement'. He complained: 'The good Abbé's wonderful sympathy and charity rather blind him to many facts.'

Pierce did not doubt the Frenchman's good faith, but his downplaying of doctrine, his 'soft pedalling' of 'papal connections and implications' was storing up confusion and trouble for the future. It allowed the Anglican Bishops to 'find in the approaches of the good Abbé simply the cheerful sign that "Rome is at last coming

A Different Direction

to her senses!"'' There was a failure to ascertain whether everyone was proceeding from the same premise: Courturier

> has no notion that these cordial Anglican prelates speak a different language. Undoubtedly bitter experience is bringing them to see the necessity for Christian unity. But by 'unity' they mean something radically different from what you and I mean. They have not the slightest notion in their woolly minds of accepting the full Catholic faith, and in its full and traditional meaning.

Pierce feared by 'unity', the Anglican Establishment meant no more than friendly cooperation, whereas, for any Catholic, it had to mean full communion in belief and practice. Pierce was also anxious lest some indiscretion on Couturier's part might invite Rome's intervention and censure, 'a catastrophe' for the cause of Reunion.[22]

It seemed an uneven contest in England. Lining up in favour of change were the Anglican Establishment and virtually all the Anglo-Catholic religious communities. Defending the old Octave were Fynes-Clinton and his Catholic League, Corbould and the CPCU and Nashdom. At least in Dom Gregory Dix the Papalists possessed one of the finest minds and sharpest tongues in the Anglican Communion. Or they thought they did.

There were other factors at play. Dix was a fully-committed Papalist. Yet, like others of his generation, he was critical of the old guard and disparaging of them: 'The present *personnel* are standing in the way of their own object. Papalism as such is growing fast. Public support of the Papalist Movement is at a standstill.' While he mentioned no names, it is not difficult to guess whom Dix had in mind when he wrote later to Bévenot that the 'Papalist party' at that time had comprised 'only a handful of eccentrics, some of whom have been our biggest handicaps'. Dix held Fynes-Clinton in genuine affection, but did not rate him intellectually and thought him 'constitutionally incapable of working *with* other people'. Logically, Dix's analysis was flawless:

> You *cannot* have *two* Octave Councils issuing rival appeals on a different basis [. . .] The main purpose of the manoeuvre

> *is* to get *two* Councils. So the Papalists will be isolated. That is the *terminus ad quem,* so to speak. And a Council presided over by Kirk and backed up by Cowley, Mirfield and CU will inevitably *swamp* a Council presided over by FC (who is not always wise) and backed only by Nashdom, with all the suspicion still attaching to it. That is inevitable — and *designed.* Ergo: there must *not* be two Councils. And since we cannot prevent the formation of the second, we must abolish the first and *muck in.* Only so we prevent the profound isolation of the Papalists, with all that involves.

It was a nonsense to run simultaneously two separate octaves for nominally the same purpose yet on different bases. Dix accepted that Couturier's approach was 'fraught with mischief of very serious kinds'. Although a monk, his political antennae were highly attuned. He conceded that Courtier's idea of the Week of Universal Prayer was irresistible. Rather than fight it, Dix sought to control it.

It was clear to Dix that the good of the wider Catholic movement within the Church of England demanded a united front. He hoped to persuade Fynes-Clinton of this: 'one man's *amour propre* and personal feelings must not be allowed to stand in the way'. The Church Unity Octave should be celebrated on the old basis for one last time in January 1939, and then the CUOC would be wound up and Fynes-Clinton gracefully retire. Failing persuasion, Dix was willing to act as 'assassin'.[23]

Dix prevailed upon Abbot Collett and the Nashdom community to endorse the new Week of Universal Prayer. Fynes-Clinton felt the defection keenly, but Dix had under-estimated the older man's tenacity and, within Papalist circles, his popularity.[24] The final denouement was scheduled for the CUOC meeting in March 1939. Perhaps Dix was distrusted as being too clever and subtle by half. But Fynes-Clinton also had a trump card to play, the backing of the Papalist founder, Spencer Jones. Too unwell to travel up to London himself, Jones nevertheless supplied the required assistance. Accounts of ecumenical history like to present the development from the Church Unity Octave to the Week of Prayer for Christian Unity as a seamless transition. Couturier's biographer

A Different Direction

claims that, of the two pioneers, at least Jones lived long enough to appreciate the changes wrought by the Frenchman, 'to recognise that, at the hands of another apostle of unity [...] the Octave had been baptised into a larger and more evangelical life'.[25] The reality is otherwise. Jones lived long enough to spit blood at what he saw as the destruction of his life's work.

He categorically denied that the Week of Universal Prayer was the equivalent of what he and Wattson had initiated thirty years earlier: 'You cannot go on saying "We still mean CUO" when you have deprived it of the very meaning which constitutes its soul and substance.'[26] Jones repeated his point days later:

> The Octave he had founded was 'concerned with reunion with Rome as the primary and substantive conditions not as conditions kindly and considerately *allowed*; and to reverse this order is to convert *CUO* into a misnomer, and into a term which cannot be used—or abused—without betraying our brethren at home or abroad.[27]

His response emboldened Fynes-Clinton to continue the fight: 'I am and you are equally determined to continue a committee on the Roman basis! In so far as the Lyons basis differs consciously from the Roman it differs from what the Pope has sanctioned.'[28] With Jones's support, Fynes-Clinton carried the Council with him, and Dix resigned from the CUOC.[29]

Matters then proceeded to fall out very much as Dix had predicted. Having shown such signs of growth and promise in the early 1930s, observance of the old Church Unity Octave dwindled away as the original Papalists died out in the post-War world. By contrast, sponsored by Cowley, Mirfield, Kelham and Nashdom, the Week of Prayer rapidly became the official expression of prayer for Christian unity in England, accepted by the Faith and Order Conference, the Church Union and the Anglican hierarchy. By 1958 the involvement of the World Council of Churches ensured its international status. In 1968 the support of the Catholic Church for the Week of Prayer for Christian Unity was secured with the participation of the Pontifical Council for Promoting Christian Unity. The irony would not have been lost upon Fynes-Clinton and his colleagues. The ecclesiastical certainties of the early twentieth century had been turned upside down.

Notes

[1] Pawley, *Rome and Canterbury through Four Centuries*, pp. 304–6.

[2] T. Burke, CP, 'The Abbé Paul Couturier, Pioneer of Spiritual Ecumenism', in M. Woodruff, *The Unity of Christians: The Vision of Paul Couturier* (London: The Catholic League, 2003), p. 4.

[3] Dix to Young, 29 October 1936, LPL, Young Papers, 4290/13.

[4] P. Couturier, 'Towards the Unity of Christendom: The Psychology of the Church Unity Octave', *Reunion*, 1/7 (Dec. 1935), p. 198.

[5] Curtiss, *Paul Couturier and Unity in Christ*, pp. 65–7.

[6] Couturier, 'Towards the Unity of Christendom', pp. 194–209; 'The Universal Prayer of Christians for Christian Unity—II', *Reunion*, 3/16 (March 1938), p. 9.

[7] Couturier, 'The Universal Prayer of Christians for Christian Unity—I', *Reunion*, 2/15 (Dec. 1937), p. 464.

[8] S. J. Jones, 'Lambeth and Loyalty', *Reunion*, 2/9 (June 1936), pp. 259–66.

[9] P. Couturier, 'Rapprochement between Christians in the XXth Century', *Reunion*, 5/36 (Dec. 1946), pp. 187 and 186.

[10] Fynes-Clinton to F. E. Biggart, CR, 23 April 1945, cited *Reunion*, 5/45 (Dec. 1945), p. 124.

[11] Jones to Fynes-Clinton, 20 January 1939, LPL, Fynes-Clinton, 4297/66.

[12] Fynes-Clinton to Young, 2 September 1936, LPL, Young Papers, 4284/70.

[13] Fynes-Clinton, 'The Current Position of Anglicanism', pp. 61–76.

[14] Dix to M. J. Dix, 4 October 1936 cited S. Jones, ed., *The Sacramental Life: Gregory Dix and his Writings* (Norwich: Canterbury Press, 2007), p. 146.

[15] Curtiss, *Paul Couturier and Unity in Christ*, pp. 197–224.

[16] W. B. O'Brien, SSJE, to Fynes-Clinton, 27 September 1938, LPL, Fynes-Clinton Papers, 4297/44.

[17] V. Shearburn, CR, to Dix, 5 October 1938, LPL, Fynes-Clinton Papers, 4297/46.

[18] P. Couturier cited M. Villain, *Unity: A History and Some Reflections* (London: Harvill Press, 1963), pp. 198–9.

[19] Abbot M. Collett, OSB, to Young, 15 October 1938, LPL, Young Papers, 4285/8.

[20] S. Bailey, *A Tactful God: Gregory Dix, Priest, Monk and Scholar* (Leominster: Gracewing, 1995), p. 105.

A Different Direction

[21] Dix to Young, 26 October 1938, LPL, Young Papers, 4290/38.

[22] Pierce to Young, 25 October 1938, LPL, Young Papers, 4285/19; Pierce to Gillam, 28 October 1938, PHA/Rea/CU3.

[23] Dix to Young, 26 October 1938, LPL, Young Papers, 4290/38–40; Dix to Young, 29 October [1938?], LPL, Young Papers, 4290/13; Dix to Bévenot, 27 January 1940, cited Leachman, 'Across the Fence', p. 30.

[24] Fynes-Clinton to [Jones?], 12 January 1939, PHA/Rea/CU3.

[25] Curtiss, *Paul Couturier and Unity in Christ*, p. 61.

[26] Jones to Fynes-Clinton, 20 January 1939, LPL, Fynes-Clinton, 4297/67.

[27] Jones to Fynes-Clinton, 24 January 1939, LPL, Fynes-Clinton, 4297/69.

[28] Fynes-Clinton to [Jones?], 3 February 1939, PHA/Rea/CU3.

[29] Dix to Fynes-Clinton, 9 May 1939, LPL, Fynes-Clinton Papers, 4297/90.

✝ 10 ✝

Ut unum sint

The Passing Generation

What became of the participants in the London Conversations? Death came swiftly to the Catholics. In addition to Cardinal Bourne, three of the four Catholic Conversationalists were dead by the end of the decade. D'Arcy alone survived. Boasting an impressive catch of illustrious converts, he is unlikely to have given a second thought to the London Conversations. On his criteria, they had not yielded a result. For another generation D'Arcy sparkled and shone in the academic and social milieu of Oxford, London and the United States. Yet his time as Provincial of the English Jesuits was not a success. He alone of the Catholics lived through the Second Vatican Council. He died in 1976, disillusioned by the direction taken by the Church and the Society of Jesus in the post-Conciliar world.

The Anglicans fared rather better in terms of longevity, although only Jones enjoyed a lengthy retirement. He left Moreton-in-Marsh in 1932 after 45 years as Vicar there. Despite protestations of extreme age and ill health, he survived another decade in the West Country, cared for by a spinster daughter. He continued a copious correspondence with past collaborators. There were articles for various reunionist journals, but all with a retrospective tone, reminiscing on the origins of Papalism. An exception was his fulsome tribute in praise of General Franco as the saviour of Spanish Catholicism.[1] Having completed one final Church Unity Octave, Jones died on 28 January 1943 at the age of 85. McNabb lamented the passing of a friend, 'a deep thinker, a humble soul [. . .] [and] a prophet'.[2]

The remaining Papalists died in harness, Simmonds presiding at Evensong, teaching maths and tending roses in Gloucester, the others still in parish ministry. Monahan was the first to go, aged 80, in 1948. His sight no longer permitting him to indulge his passion for watercolour painting, he retreated into memories of his earliest years, penning sporadic entries in his highly personal and melancholy memoirs. Scott died the following year. Ill health and the death of friends had dissipated much of his former vehemence. To those who remained, he mused wistfully: 'We have not left the Anglican Church; the Anglican Church has left us.'[3]

Corbould and Fynes-Clinton soldiered on through the 1950s. Both gave the impression of being Edwardian gentlemen of substantial means. The reality was rather different. High taxation and the rising cost of domestic staff took their toll. Corbould never really adapted to the massive changes his parish underwent during his long incumbency, continuing to run it as an overgrown Surrey village, rather than the sprawling London conurbation Carshalton had become. Even he had to dispense with the services of his valet, although dying in the Hotel Berchielli in Perugia in 1957 demonstrated a certain style and a refusal to capitulate to more functionalist expectations of clerical life.

Fynes-Clinton's friends were shocked when they discovered how meagre were the remaining investments on which he sought to live out his final years. Like many of his class, he felt the chill winds of post-War austerity Britain, moving out of St Ermin's and into a cheaper flat in St James's Court, where he died on 4 December 1959. A statue of St John the Evangelist was placed in his memory in the Fynes-Clinton Chantry Chapel he had funded in the Anglican Shrine in Walsingham. Naturally enough, the inscription was in Latin. It can be translated: 'Of your charity, pray for the soul of Henry Joy Fynes-Clinton, priest, whose life was given in the defence of Catholic truth and working for Christian unity.' Not a bad epitaph for a Papalist.

Fynes-Clinton, Corbould and their ilk made no concessions to modernity in terms of liturgy nor the reunionist message. Papalist churches could still attract sizeable congregations, but there was not the same sense of being at the cutting-edge of Anglicanism as there had been between the Wars. No new leaders or theologians emerged to replace the passing generation. Perhaps Pierce had been right all along: the early 1930s had constituted the decisive moment for action to be taken. At least our Papalists were spared the indignity of having to make sense of the post-Conciliar Catholic Church, many of whose members seemed intent on embracing similar errors to those the Papalists had spent a lifetime denouncing in the Church of England.

And what of Sir James Marchant, the man responsible for initiating the Conversations in the first place? A leopard does not change its spots. The Second World War found Marchant with a minor role at the Ministry of Information. The Establishment still received the benefit of his views. Following the Fall of France, he wrote to Archbishop Lang requesting the King summon a council of the great and the good to seek a negotiated peace with Nazi Germany.[4] Having made the wrong call, Marchant had no compunction subsequently in editing an anthology in praise of Winston Churchill as the wartime Premier. Marchant died in Sherborne in Dorset in 1956. Despite his best endeavours to ingratiate himself with the leaders of Church and State, today he is remembered by no one.

'Why don't they go over?'[5]

Goodier concluded his résumé of the Thackeray Hotel Conversations by expressing his disappointment 'that the idea of "conversion" to the Catholic Church never so much as entered once into the discussions'.[6] Many on both sides of the confessional divide simply expected the Papalists to go over to Rome, accusing them of bad faith when they failed to do so. That, however, is to misunderstand Papalism. Yet the question remains legitimate. The Papalists had claimed that the 1930 Lambeth Conference represented a decisive watershed in terms of moral teaching and ecclesiology. Why then did only Pierce, Whitton and a handful of others—none of our Conversationalists—make the crossing to Rome?

The *Tablet* was predictably rude in the aftermath of the Centenary Manifesto, insinuating that undue attachment to status and money held back the signatories from doing the right thing. Fr

Albert Gille was an erratic Belgian Jesuit working in India and Britain whose Anglican sympathies in his book, *A Catholic Plea for Reunion*, landed him in very hot water with the Society. Many of the views expressed there were impractical and highly questionable, yet he displayed a shrewd insight into the psychological pressures operating upon the Papalists: 'More than one Anglican will give away a good deal of his dogmatic belief, if he can keep his church, his ceremonial, his Authorised Version, his hymns and his friends.'[7]

The Americans might have been Anglophiles romantically attached to Oxford's dreaming spires, yet they were less encumbered by historical and cultural baggage, explaining perhaps why three of the CU founders converted to Rome when none of the leading English Papalists did so. As if to emphasize the point, the only Conversationalist who seems seriously to have entertained the possibility following the 1930 Lambeth Conference was the Irishman, Monahan. At the very end of his life he mused on the option of conversion and returning to Ireland. The fear of publicity and the improbability of being ordained a Catholic priest at his advanced age deterred him.[8]

The reality was complex. The Papalists were sincere in decrying the disaster of a division which was not of their making and wanting to ensure the corporate return of the English Church to full unity with the successor of St Peter. They were, however, caught on the horns of a dilemma. Should conscience dictate, could they possibly fail to act personally? Yet was not each individual conversion another blow to the attempt to persuade the Church of England of its Catholic identity and ultimate destiny? As a matter of conscience, many Papalists felt unable to disown the tangible signs of holiness they saw associated with their ministry and their people. And, while this remained the case, many Catholics would not have wanted them to have converted.

Few describe the anguished difficulties better than Dix. Writing to the Catholic Bévenot, gone is the bravado and savage humour employed to such effect against his fellow Anglicans. Instead, Dix bares his soul: '*we* take the Anglican Church seriously—not merely as a going concern in which we are personally involved

Ut unum sint

but as a living part of the Body of Christ grievously sick but living and curable, to which we have a desperate sort of duty'. Dix fully acknowledges the nigh-impossibility of the task.[9] Yet such transparency clears the Papalists of the accusations of being either knaves or traitors.

'What useful purpose'?[10]

Even at the time some of the participants, most noticeably Goodier, queried the usefulness and significance of the London Conversations. Today, the same question will be asked. Now that these Conversations have been exposed to the light of day, do they really contribute anything to our understanding of the history of ecumenism? There are those who will dismiss them as no more than an interesting footnote, a dialogue with a completely unrepresentative group of Anglicans which was never going anywhere.

At the very least, the London Conversations contradict the 'Whig historiography' of the ecumenical Establishment written by the likes of Bernard and Margaret Pawley who unquestioningly presented the Church of England as on the side of progress and enlightenment, with the pre-Conciliar Catholic Church committed to a policy of reaction and obscurantism. It has suited both the Anglican Establishment and more ultramontane Catholics to portray Rome as a latecomer to the ecumenical endeavour. English Catholics in particular are meant to carry a collective sense of shame at their obtuse insularity. Donald Allchin was typical of a generation when, in an offhand manner, he discounted Catholic engagement in the search for Reunion: 'The Roman Catholic Church, as opposed to occasional Roman Catholic theologians, stood massively apart from the movement towards Christian unity.'[11] The London Conversations call for historical reassessment and a little humility on the part of some writers.

It was the head of the Roman Catholic Church in England and Wales, Cardinal Bourne, who sanctioned these Conversations and authorised the Catholic participants. It was successive Archbishops of Canterbury, Davidson and Lang, who refused such official approval. If the participating Anglicans were unrepresentative of their Communion, then the blame for that cannot be laid at the door of the Catholics.

The Malines Conversations are rightly held to be of significance as the first direct contact between Catholic and Anglican theologians. (Contact preceding *Apostolicae Curae* a generation earlier can hardly be said to have been a bilateral attempt at Reunion.) The London Conversations demand equivalent recognition as the first direct contact on English soil between English Catholic and Anglican conversationalists. The team assembled by the Catholics was hugely impressive by any standards. And the Catholic authorities continued to support engagement at this level over a period of almost two years. Indeed, the evidence suggests a continued willingness to participate subsequently.[12] One should not always judge Rome at the level of her official pronouncements. It is instructive to look at what is happening on the ground.

What was actually achieved by the London Conversations? In 1978 the *Catholic Herald* ran a short piece on Spencer Jones entitled, 'Cotswold Vicar who inspired ecumenism'.[13] That article got it spectacularly wrong, claiming that it was Jones who encouraged Couturier to broaden the scope of the Week of Universal Prayer. Jones would be horrified to be considered the precursor of a movement whose proponents today can appear an ageing and diminishing constituency sitting in church halls sipping tea and coffee, telling one another that they are 'all the same really'. The London Conversations teach us the need to face up to real differences honestly. Those involved in the 1930s talks sought Reunion. They meant by this more than friendly recognition of and collaboration between competing and contradictory denominations. Reunion for them meant no less than full unity in faith and life. It should mean no less for us.

The London Conversations achieved precious little in terms of the visible unity of the two Communions or even the reception of significant numbers of individuals into full communion with Rome. Nevertheless, a huge debt is owed to the Papalists. They proposed a way forward, unpopular to many, from Rome's condemnation of Anglican Orders. Courageously, Jones and his disciples told their fellow Anglicans that there were fundamental issues upon which they could not ask Rome to adapt her teaching. Indeed, it was the successor of Peter's refusal to compromise with the spirit of the age in matters of faith and morals which makes unity with him attractive and essential. Even if they were not to cross the threshold themselves, the Papalists pointed the way to a full and proper understanding of Reunion.

To the Present Day

As the subtitle makes clear, this work is concerned with the search for Christian unity in the 1930s. Yet, just as a little history of the preceding period is necessary to appreciate the endeavours of that decade, so it is appropriate to reflect briefly on what happened subsequently.

Our Papalists would have rejoiced at the increased commitment to Christian unity shown by the Catholic Church at the highest levels. They knew that that desire for unity had always existed, but there has been a change of tone and vocabulary, for which our Conversationalists pleaded and prayed. Initially, that development was slow and hesitant. Rome officially took note of the Ecumenical Movement in the years immediately following the Second World War. Care was taken at the outset to put down cautions and boundaries. Although the Catholic Church followed all efforts to attain unity 'with the most intense interest' and earnestly prayed for them, she herself did not participate in ecumenical congresses and conventions. She might exhibit 'maternal affection', but her objective was always to reconcile 'dissident Christians to the Catholic Church'. What was shared with other Christians should not be excessively emphasized if it would encourage 'a dangerous indifferentism'. Yet couched in decidedly cool terms was approval of involvement in conferences with non-Catholics to promote the work of Reunion—for those 'well instructed and strong in their faith' who were specifically authorised by their bishop. They might even pray the Lord's Prayer with non-Catholics at the beginning and end of such meetings—provided they avoided any form of shared worship.[14]

The Second Vatican Council fifteen years later did, therefore, represent a significant official change of emphasis when it declared 'the restoration of unity among all Christians' one of the Council's 'principal concerns'. The division existing between Christians 'openly contradicts the will of God, scandalises the world and damages that most holy cause, the preaching of the Gospel to every creature'. The primacy of the Holy Spirit as 'the principle of the Church's unity' was acknowledged. At the level of its highest teaching, the Catholic Church now urges 'all the Catholic faithful to recognise the signs of the times and to take an active and intelligent part in the work of ecumenism'.[15]

Our Conversationalists struggled to define the relationship of the Anglican Papalists to the Church. The Papalists themselves maintained that they were full members of the Catholic Church, willing to concede, at most, that they were only in a state of internal schism within the Church. The Catholics participants were having none of it. All Anglicans were heretics or, possibly in the case of the Papalists, schismatics—but definitely outside the Church. Vatican II provided a vocabulary and concepts which were both more accurate and more charitable, an ecclesiology of *degrees* of communion. All validly-baptised Christians are members of the Church. By virtue of baptism they are already in communion, albeit imperfect, with the Catholic Church, already joined to Catholics 'in the Holy Spirit'. They are called to full communion with the successor of Peter. In order that Eucharistic communion might be restored, the issue of the validity of Orders has to be addressed. Nevertheless, as the Papalists had maintained three decades earlier, the Church accepts that 'many elements of sanctification and of truth are found outside its visible confines'.[16]

The special status Vatican II accorded to the Anglican Communion, distinguishing her from other ecclesial communities of the Western Reformation, would have delighted the Papalists.[17] They would not have been surprised, however, to learn that Rome is not thereby reducing herself to the status of one equal among many. For some others it comes as an unpleasant shock that, while they welcome her softer terminology, Rome does not and cannot abandon her exclusive claims. The Second Vatican Council

Ut unum sint

affirmed: the Church of Christ 'constituted and organised as a society in the present world, subsists in the Catholic Church, which is governed by the successor of Peter and by the bishops in communion with him'. Moreover, 'they could not be saved who, knowing that the Catholic Church was founded as necessary by God through Christ, would refuse to enter it, or to remain in it'.[18]

The Papalists knew that Rome cannot change in her fundamentals. But they argued that she might learn from Canterbury: in respecting a legitimate academic freedom, in the courtesy extended to her own members and to others who approached her in a spirit of goodwill. Eric Mascall was not uncritical of his own Communion: 'The Roman See and its occupant are only too often ignored by Anglicans or else are dismissed with a few airy and superficial generalisations.'[19] Yet, he held, the Catholically-minded Anglican is uniquely placed to help heal divisions. Too conscious of the havoc wrought in his own Communion by a hermeneutic of rupture, he readily accepts Tradition and Rome as the principle of unity. But his sense of independence and history made him less susceptible to the errors of ultramontanism still present in the pre-Conciliar Church. He appreciates how even the Pope is a member of the Church and not above her, how even he is subject to Scripture and Tradition.

Progress made between the two Communions in the second half of the twentieth century seemed to justify the Papalists in their decision to remain in the Church of England and to work as a catalyst for Corporate Reunion from within. In 1960 Geoffrey Fisher travelled to Rome, becoming the first Archbishop of Canterbury since the Reformation to meet with the Pope. A rather warmer encounter took place in 1966 concluding with Paul VI taking his episcopal ring from his finger and presenting it to Archbishop Michael Ramsey. The following year the Anglican-Roman Catholic International Commission (ARCIC) was established. Between 1970 and 2005 meetings of Anglican and Catholic theologians produced nine agreed statements on a wide range of issues including the Eucharist, authority and Mary. All this culminated in the historic visit of John Paul II to Britain in 1982 when Pope and Archbishop of Canterbury prayed together in Canterbury Cathedral. It seemed legitimate to hope that the convergence of the two Communions, the realisation of full communion, was imminent.

Yet there were already dark storm clouds on the horizon. The Papalists had always feared the forces of liberalism, that the Church of England might take some action or commit itself to some position which made Catholic Reunion impossible. Both Communions suffered high levels of dissent at the local and personal level in the post-Conciliar period. Two events in particular, in the autumn of 1992, crystallised Papalist fears at the institutional and official level. Both were the result of lengthy processes, but seemed for those of Catholic sensibilities to represent points of no return. On 13 October 1992, the Poorvo Common Statement agreed in Finland set the basis for full communion between the Church of England and the Lutheran churches of Scandinavia and the Baltic, some of which made no claim to apostolic succession, understood in a Catholic sense. On 11 November 1992, the General Synod of the Church of England voted for the ordination of women to the Anglican priesthood. Those who took these decisions did so in good faith, believing them to be the will of the Holy Spirit. But they constituted a unilateral departure from the belief and practice of the Catholic Church of which the Papalists claimed to be part. Beyond these debates, issues of human sexuality have torn apart the Anglican Communion.

How would our Anglican Conversationalists, and those they represented, have reacted to these new dilemmas? Faith and the decision to move between Communions are intensely personal matters. It is impossible to know, therefore, with any degree of certainty. It is possible that there would have been some surprising reactions. Some who had never identified as Papalist or even Anglo-Catholic might have recognised the gravity of the situation immediately and decided, in conscience, that they had to be reconciled with Rome. Others, more prominent and outspoken, might simply have raised the drawbridge and determined that the one, true Faith would be maintained in their parish come hell or high water. No doubt, as in the 1930s, others would have reacted instinctively by wishing to form more societies and committees with which to continue the fight against the enemy.

Ut unum sint

Whatever the response of individuals, Anglican Papalism generally, defined by its desire for Corporate Reunion, seemed to be between a rock and a hard place. Into this predicament, Pope Benedict XVI cast an unexpected lifeline, reminiscent of some of the proposals of the 1930s. The 2009 Apostolic Constitution, *Anglicanorum Coetibus*, allowed for 'Personal Ordinariates' for Anglicans wishing to be received into full communion with Rome, while retaining elements of their Anglican heritage. For the first time, the Catholic Church provided structures for the reception of groups coming from the communities of the Reformation.

It seemed to be the answer to our Papalists' prayers. Provision was made for Anglicans to be received corporately, clergy and people continuing together after reception into the Catholic Church. Of the concessions sought in the 1931 Memorandum, use of the vernacular and Communion under both kinds were already the norm in the Catholic Church. Ordinariates were permitted to celebrate the liturgy 'according to liturgical books proper to the Anglican tradition', as approved by the Holy See. Former Anglicans were to be subject to the jurisdiction of their own ordinaries, rather than the local bishop. They might erect their own religious communities. The arrangements also allowed for the ordination of married clergy.[20] Rather than feeling a requirement to repudiate their past in its entirety, members of the Ordinariate were positively encouraged to enrich the Catholic Church by those aspects of Anglican patrimony consistent with Catholic truth. Fynes-Clinton could have continued to enjoy the cadences of the Prayer Book and the King James Bible.

The provisions were generous and prophetic. It offered an imaginative solution to reconciling the imperative of unity with the desire for legitimate diversity. Personal Ordinariates were established for England and Wales, North America and Australia. To date the response, in England at least, has been limited. As of the summer of 2015, 89 priests have been ordained for the Personal Ordinariate of Our Lady of Walsingham. There has been no widespread influx from the Anglican laity. *Anglicanorum Coetibus* constitutes both an invitation and a challenge to those Anglicans who sought Catholic Reunion. Not only in the 1930s voices were raised: if only Rome would do something, then they would act. Rome has done something. Whitton posed the question in 1933 in the light of Pius XI's benign attitude. Perhaps it should be asked again, even more insistently: has the Papalists' bluff been called?

At the beginning of the twenty-first century Reunion can seem more, not less, distant than in the 1930s. The Church of England appears to have chosen another path. The imperative of Christian unity remains—because it is Our Lord's prayer: *ut unum sint*, that all might be one.

Notes

1. S. J. Jones, 'General Franco and what brought him to the Front', *Reunion*, 3/24 (Dec. 1940), pp. 268–79.
2. V. McNabb, 'Tribute to Father Spencer Jones', *The Pilot*, 117 (May 1943), p. 37.
3. Morton Howard, 'Sidney Herbert Drane-Scott', p. 19.
4. Beaken, *Cosmo Lang*, p. 188.
5. 'Paulinus', 'Why don't they go over?', *The Pilot*, 59 (July 1938), pp. 1–8.
6. Goodier to Bourne, 28 October 1931, AAW, Bo. I/107.
7. A. J. A. Gille, SJ ('Fr Jerome'), *A Catholic Plea for Reunion* (London: Williams & Norgate, 1934), pp. 29–30.
8. Monahan, Memoirs, vol. II, early 1948, PHA/Monahan Papers.
9. Dix to Bévenot, 27 January 1940, cited Leachman, 'Across the Fence', pp. 28–34.
10. Goodier to Butler, 27 October 1931, DAA, Butler Papers, P/7.
11. A. M. Allchin, Foreword in Irvine, *Worship, Church and Society*, p. xii.
12. Corbould to Halifax, 6 April 1933, BIY, Halifax, Ecclesiastical Papers.
13. *Catholic Herald* (13 Jan. 1978).
14. Holy Office Instruction, *On the 'Ecumenical Movement'*, 20 December 1949.
15. Vatican II, *Unitatis Redintegratio* (1964), n. 1, 2, 4.
16. *Lumen Gentium*, nn. 8, 11, 15; *Unitatis Redintegratio*, n. 22.
17. *Unitatis Redintegratio*, n. 13.
18. *Lumen Gentium*, nn. 8, 14.
19. E. L. Mascall, *Recovery of Unity* (London: Longman, Green & Co., 1958), p. 194.
20. Pope Benedict XVI, *Anglicanorum Coetibus* (2009).

Appendix

The Oxford Movement: A Centenary Manifesto

The purpose of this Manifesto is to draw attention to certain grave questions which arise in connection with the Anglo-Catholic observance of the Centenary of the Oxford Movement. These questions are concerned especially with the inconsistency of many who are looked on as Anglo-Catholic leaders, and the injuries that the Catholic cause is suffering by their utterances.

The original Oxford Movement from its beginnings in 1833 set on foot a steady and progressive return to the faith and practice of historic Christendom. The leaders, whose attitude from the outset was of a constitutional and not of a revolutionary character, made their appeal to the consent of the Universal Church as evidenced by the decrees of the Oecumenical Councils, the writings of the Fathers, and the standards and formulated teachings of the historic Christian Body; on these they based their teaching and founded their efforts. Deriving their inspiration from such sanctions, they stood pre-eminently for **Catholic Orthodoxy** — for the Catholic faith in its true and historic sense, as defined and professed by the whole Church. Opposing and rejecting the usurped power of the State over the Church in England in spiritual matters, they strove to restore to that Church its former liberty and true heritage. Hence the Movement, as it gathered force, necessarily brought the goal of **Reunion of the English Church with the rest of Catholic Christendom** before the eyes of its followers as an ideal to be accepted and pursued with zeal and devotion.

In the modern Anglo-Catholic Movement much of the enthusiasm over the observance of the Centenary cloaks a marked departure from the original Oxford principles and ideals as progressively unfolded during the first sixty years of the Revival. There is manifest today a drift and tendency leading the main body of Anglo-Catholics to depart fundamentally from the religion of the great leaders who began the Movement. It is now infected with a spirit of compromise and Modernism which is gradually leavening the whole and threatens to divert it from its true course. Representative leaders are continually endeavouring in speech and writing to commit the Revival—the rank and file of the followers of which is largely innocent and unsuspecting of such tendencies—to these departures from its origins. So marked a character have these efforts assumed that Liberal theologians, antagonistic to the Catholic Revival and its ideals, have expressed their satisfaction with the extent to which the Movement has become permeated with modernistic teaching. In current Anglo-Catholic expositions of the Faith, novel theories, marked by evasions and accommodations of a modernistic character and contradictory of the historic Catholic position, are frequently set forth. On such supreme and vital matters as:

the Person of our Lord, and the union of the Two Natures in Him;
the Interpretation of Holy Scripture;
the Authority and Infallibility of the Church;
the moral standards of historic Christianity;
much of the teaching openly propagated within the modern Movement is in sad contrast with the orthodoxy of the original Oxford Fathers, and with the Catholic standards to which *ex professo* the Anglo-Catholic Movement itself makes its appeal. Hence a large section of modern Anglo-Catholics are rapidly becoming false to their own past and to the standards of that original Movement from which they profess to draw their inspiration and ideals.

Uneasily conscious of the radical departure from normal Catholic tradition which is involved in much of their current teaching, many of the leaders today attempt to create and to justify an insular and particularistic interpretation of the Universal Faith which in practice results in the virtual denial of the 'Catholic' and the undue stressing of the 'Anglo' in their illogical use of the name. Abandoning the necessarily exclusive claim of Catholic Truth, they now begin to advocate and justify a novel comprehensiveness and

The Oxford Movement: A Centenary Manifesto

mutual tolerance of opposed teaching on fundamental matters within the English Church, in which they express themselves as willing henceforth to occupy the position of one among many mutually contradictory 'schools of thought'.

The abandonment of the original Oxford Movement involved in all this has resulted in a certain amount of official patronage and recognition from those who are at their heart indifferent or opposed to Catholic ideals; while the recent readiness to compromise on unpopular doctrines and moral standards has earned for the later Anglo-Catholic Movement a dubious popularity and a certain numerical increase. But it is clear that much of the success over which rejoicing is made has been bought at the expense of its original *raison d'être* and primary message. It has produced an atmosphere of unreality which prejudices and hinders the progress of the Catholic Revival—and among those who take seriously the claim involved in the Catholic name it has resulted in considerable uneasiness and disquiet.

In the face of these sinister developments it becomes a necessary duty for us, on the occasion of this Centenary, to voice our remonstrance and repudiation. We urge upon all who value consistency and are jealous for the Catholic claim of the English Church, the need of awaking to the dangers involved in recent developments and the duty of taking strong action against such a distortion of Catholicism as now threatens the Movement. We desire to disassociate ourselves as publicly and as comprehensively as possible from all such tendencies and to sound a recall, long overdue, to the ideals, standards and goal of the Oxford Fathers—a recall to intellectual consistency and orthodoxy and to the rational and historic use of the word 'Catholic'. We reaffirm our unwavering acceptance of the whole Catholic Faith as defined by the Oecumenical Councils and set forth and interpreted in the official teaching of the historic Catholic Church. We utterly reject Modernism and reprobate all theories and accommodation of a modernistic character which impugn or innovate upon that Faith so formulated.

In particular in view of modern hesitations and denials in the Anglo-Catholic party, we deem it necessary at this time to set forth explicitly the following statement:

1. We confess **the Catholic doctrine of the Incarnation** of the Divine Word, our Lord and Saviour Jesus Christ, one Divine Person in the two Natures, Perfect God and Perfect Man, in the sense in which the Councils and Fathers of the Church have defined that saving truth. In particular, we repudiate the Kenotic teaching, so prevalent within the Anglo-Catholic Movement, conflicting with and minimising, as it does, the truth of the immutability and omniscience of the Divine Person of Christ in His Incarnate Life.

2. We reject all theories concerning **Holy Scripture** which detract from its inspiration and authority, and we declare that the Catholic Church alone has the right and power authoritatively to interpret it.

3. We proclaim that the Catholic Religion is divinely revealed and essentially **a religion of authority**, and that therefore the Faith is not at the mercy of the speculation or imagination of any individual teacher. The ultimate and absolute authority to explain and define that Faith belongs to the visible, historic, Catholic Church, founded by our Lord. As a necessary consequence we repudiate any local and lesser authority as final: the utterances of Anglican bishops and their interpretations of Anglican formularies are only worthy of consideration just so far as they are faithful to the Catholic Faith and practice—when they depart from these they must be disowned. Hence we wholly reject the idea or claims of a specific Anglican religion, and *a fortiori* of an Anglo-Catholicism which departs from Catholic standards in faith, practice or morals. As a grave instance of the last-named, it is incumbent upon us to reprobate the toleration and even positive support of certain Anglo-Catholics of the immoral sanction of artificial contraception given by many Bishops at Lambeth.

4. We emphasise that the Catholic Religion cannot take a place as one of many contending 'schools of thought' or versions of Christianity. We hold it as **the one authentic Christian Religion**, and we acknowledge its exclusive and absolute claim upon us and upon all men. To this Universal Faith, and this alone, the Church of England is wholly committed by her origin, by her history and by her representative teachers in every age.

The Oxford Movement: A Centenary Manifesto

5. We affirm that **the claim of the Church of England to continuity** with the Church of St Augustine and St Theodore, consistently maintained by the Oxford Fathers, involves oneness of Faith and Practice with the historic Church of the past, which was in unquestioned communion with the whole Catholic Church and which held the common Faith of Christendom. That essential continuity is not satisfied by mere succession in property, nor by revival of ceremony, nor by use of words, but only by complete identity of Faith, the possession of which is the sole justification of her existence.

6. With the original Oxford Fathers, we reject **State control of the Church in spiritual matters** and the Erastian philosophy which attempts to justify it. We see in that control the efficient cause of most of the evils from which we suffer, and in particular of our *de facto* separation from Catholic Communion. We denounce the culpable silence and acquiescence of the main Anglo-Catholic body in the face of **appointments of Modernists** to important and influential positions in the Church, at the Universities and in Theological Colleges, and we protest against the insidious attempt to change the character of the witness of the Church of England by according favour and advancement to Modernist teachers.

7. We share **the hope and ideal of reunion** with the rest of the Catholic Church which was cherished by the Oxford leaders and which it was early perceived was included in their appeal. The logic of the principles which animated the original Movement necessarily brought the goal of Reunion to the forefront. Our Lord set up but One Church, the members of which were to be in communion one with another. This one Catholic Church was constituted with St Peter as its Foundation and Head, and for ever has as its Centre and Guide on earth the successor of St Peter. This truth we confess, and hence, while striving also for Reunion with the Orthodox Churches of the East, we declare that **the real and essential goal** is Reunion with the Apostolic See of Rome. This was recognised by some even of the earliest Oxford leaders and the lapse of time has made it more apparent. The Movement throughout its course has been marked with this instinctive desire for the restoration of the English Church to her normal position in

relation to the Centre and the whole. The existence of the Church of England as a body separate *de facto* from the rest of the Catholic Church is only tolerable when it is regarded as a temporary evil, destined to disappear when God shall please to restore us to our normal place among our brethren.

It is well to bear in mind that the Catholic revival in the Church of England will only be safeguarded and made permanent by the recognition of that Authority whose divinely-appointed office it is to 'strengthen the brethren' and who always and everywhere preserves the one Faith in its integrity. We assert that Reunion with Rome is the logical and highest goal and the natural consummation of the movement celebrated by the present Centenary. For that consummation it is a supreme duty to work and pray.

We commend what we have set forth to all who look with sympathy to the Oxford Movement as the origin and source of the modern Catholic Revival. We call them to a realisation of the present dangers to that revival in the conditions which obtain in the Anglo-Catholic body. We urge upon all a renewed adhesion to normal Catholic teaching and a wholehearted acceptance of the *de fide* standards of the Church. We sound once more the call to repudiate prevailing errors: to advance the spiritual freedom of the Church of England: and to labour and pray for that outward unity with the Catholic world and with the Holy See which alone will justify and crown the efforts and sacrifices of our forerunners, and by the grace of God bring the seed sown by the Oxford Fathers to full fruition, and the Oxford Movement to its perfect term.

1 October 1932

Sources and Bibliography

Primary Sources

Archives of the Archdiocese of Malines
    Mercier Papers
Archives of the Archbishop of Westminster
    Bourne Papers
Beda College Archives, Rome
    Pierce Bequest
Bodleian Library, Oxford
    Marchant Papers
Dominican Archives, Douai Abbey
    Jarrett Papers
    McNabb Papers
Downside Abbey Archives
    Abbot Cuthbert Butler Papers
Lambeth Palace Library
    Bishop Bell Papers
    Archbishop Davidson Papers
    Rev. Henry Fynes-Clinton Papers
    Archbishop Lang Papers
    Lambeth Conference Papers
    Rev. Ivan Young Papers
Pusey House, Oxford
    Harris Papers
    Monahan Papers
    Rea Papers—Confraternity of Unity

Magazines, Newspapers and Periodicals

Beda Review
Bulletin of the Confraternity of
 Unity (subsequently renamed
 Reunion)
The Messenger

The Pilot
Reunion
Revue apologétique
The Tablet
The Times

Primary Printed Sources

Bévenot, M., SJ, 'Dix Redivivus: *Jurisdiction in the Early Church* by Dom Gregory Dix', *Heythrop Journal*, 17 (1976), pp. 183–7.

Bourne, F. A., Cardinal, 'The Catholic Apostolic Roman Church', in J. Marchant, ed., *The Reunion of Christendom: A Survey of the Present Position* (London: Cassell & Company, 1929), pp. 15–21.

Butler, C., OSB, *The Life and Times of Bishop Ullathorne*, 2 vols (London: Burns Oates and Washbourne, 1926).

── *Religions of Authority and the Religion of the Spirit with Other Essays Apologetical and Critical* (London: Sheed & Ward, 1930).

── *The Vatican Council: The Story Told from Inside in Bishop Ullathorne's Letters*, 2 vols (London: Longman, Green & Co., 1930).

Clayton, J., *The Historic Basis of Anglicanism* (London: Sands & Co., 1925).

The Conversations at Malines 1921–1925 (Oxford: Oxford University Press, 1927).

Corbould, W. R., et al., *The Oxford Movement: A Centenary Manifesto* (1932).

Couturier, P., 'Towards the Unity of Christendom: The Psychology of the Church Unity Octave', *Reunion*, 1/7 (Dec. 1935), pp. 194–209.

── 'The Universal Prayer of Christians for Christian Unity—I', *Reunion*, 2/15 (Dec. 1937), pp. 455–69.

── 'The Universal Prayer of Christians for Christian Unity—II', *Reunion*, 3/16 (March 1938), pp. 3–16.

── 'Rapprochement between Christians in the Twentieth Century', *Reunion*, 5/36 (Dec. 1946), pp. 169–89.

D'Arcy, M. C., SJ, ed., *The Life of the Church* (London: Sheed & Ward, 1934).

Sources and Bibliography

de la Saudée, J. de Bivort, *Anglicans et catholiques: Le Problème de l'union anglo-romaine (1833–1933)* (Paris: Libraire Plon, 1948).

—— *Essai sur le mouvement anglo-catholique* (Paris: Louis de Soye, 1932).

Frere, W., CR, *Recollections of Malines* (London: Centenary Press, 1935).

Fynes-Clinton, H. J., 'The Current Position of Anglicanism', *Revue apologétique*, 64/616 (Jan. 1937), pp. 61–76.

—— and W. R. Corbould, *What are We to Say?* (London: Council for Promoting Catholic Unity, 1933).

Garvie, E., 'The Free Churches in England', in J. Marchant, ed., *The Reunion of Christendom* (London: Cassell & Co., 1929), pp. 129–48.

Goodier, A., SJ, *The Passion and Death of Our Lord Jesus Christ* (London: Burns, Oates & Washbourne, 1933).

—— *The Public Life of Our Lord Jesus Christ*, 2 vols (London: Burns, Oates & Washbourne, 1930).

—— et al., *Why I am and why I am not a Catholic* (London: Cassell & Co., 1931).

Halifax, C. L., Viscount, ed., *The Conversations at Malines 1921–1925: Original Documents* (London: Philip Allan & Co., 1930).

Harris, S., *What do the Celtic Churches Say?* (London: Council for Promoting Catholic Unity, 1932).

Hole, D., *Anglican Papalists* (London: Society for Promoting Catholic Unity, 1942).

Jones, S. J., *Catholic Reunion* (Oxford: Blackwell, 1930).

—— *The Clergy and the Catechism* (London: Skeffington & Son, 1895).

—— *The Counter-Reformation in the Church of England* (London: Skeffington & Son, n.d.).

—— *England and the Holy See: An Essay towards Reunion*, 2nd edn (London: Longman, Green & Co., 1902).

—— 'England and the Holy See in the Middle Ages', in A. H. Mathew, ed., *Ecclesia: The Church of Christ* (London: Burns & Oates, 1906), pp. 159–82.

—— 'Lambeth and Loyalty', *Reunion*, 2/9 (June 1936), pp. 259–66.

—— *L'Église d'Angleterre et le Saint-Siège: Propos pour la réunion* (Grenoble: B. Artaud, 1940).

—— *Rome and Reunion: The Inaugural Lecture to the Members of the Society of St Thomas of Canterbury* (London: Longman, Green & Co., 1904).

—— *What does the XVI Century Say?* (London: Council for Promoting

Catholic Unity, 1932).

Lambeth Conference 1930: Encyclical Letter from the Bishops with the Resolutions and Reports (London: SPCK, 1930).

Marchant, Sir James, ed., *The Claims of the Coming Generation* (London: Kegan Paul, Trench, Trubner & Co., 1923).

——, ed., *The Reunion of Christendom: A Survey of the Present Position* (London: Cassell & Co., 1929).

McNabb, V., OP, Tribute to Spencer Jones, *The Pilot*, 11/117 (May 1943), p. 36.

Milner-White, E. M., 'The Church of Rome', in *Report of the First Anglo-Catholic Congress, London, 1920* (London: SPCK, 1920).

Morton Howard, J. G., *Epistola ad Romanos: An Open Letter to our Brethren of the Roman Catholic Church* (London: Council for Promoting Catholic Unity, 1933).

—— *What does the Anglo-Saxon Church Say?* (London: Council for Promoting Catholic Unity, 1932).

Orchard, W. E., *From Faith to Faith* (London: Putnams, 1933).

—— 'A Vision of the Reunited Church', in J. Marchant, ed., *The Reunion of Christendom* (London: Cassell & Co., 1929), pp. 269–91.

Oxford Dictionary of National Biography (Oxford: Oxford University Press)

Pierce, H. K., *The Message of Modernism* (New York: League for Catholic Action, 1926).

Pius XI, *Selected Papal Encyclical and Letters* (London: Catholic Truth Society, 1933).

Scott, S. H., *Anglo-Catholicism and Re-union* (London: Robert Scott, 1923).

—— Article on Reunion, *The Pilot*, 11 (May 1943), p. 117.

—— *The Eastern Churches and the Papacy* (London: Sheed & Ward, 1928).

—— *Modernism in Anglo-Catholicism* (London: Council for Promoting Catholic Unity, 1933).

—— *What do the General Councils Say?* (London: Council for Promoting Catholic Unity, 1932).

Simmonds, L. F., *The Framework of Faith* (London: Longman, Green & Co., 1939).

—— *What do English Divines Say?* (London: Council for Promoting Catholic Unity, 1932).

Simmonds, L. F., *What Think ye of Christ?* (London: The Centenary Press, 1938).
St John, H., *Essays in Christian Unity, 1928–1954* (London: Blackfriars Publications, 1955).
Tugwell, S., OP, and A. Bellenger, OSB, *Letters of Bede Jarrett, Letters and Other Papers of the English Dominican Archives selected by Bede Bailey, OP* (Bath: Downside Abbey, and Oxford: Blackfriars Publications, 1989).
Walker, L. J., SJ, *The Problem of Reunion: Discussed Historically in Seven Essays* (London: Longman, Green & Co., 1920).
Whitton, T., *The Necessity for Catholic Reunion* (London: Williams & Norgate, 1933).

Secondary Printed Sources

Angell, C., SA, and C. LaFontaine, SA, *Prophet of Reunion: The Life of Paul of Graymoor* (New York: Seabury Press, 1975).
Anson, H., *T. B. Strong: Bishop, Musician, Dean, Vice-chancellor* (London: SPCK, 1949).
Aubert, R., 'The History of the Malines Conversations', *One in Christ*, 1 (1967), pp. 56–66.
—— 'Cardinal Mercier, Cardinal Bourne and the Malines Conversations', *One in Christ*, 4 (1968), pp. 372–9.
Bailey, S., *A Tactful God: Gregory Dix, Priest, Monk and Scholar* (Leominster: Gracewing, 1995).
Barlow, B., OSM, *'A Brother Knocking at the Door': The Malines Conversations 1921–1925* (Norwich: Canterbury Press, 1996).
Barnas, T., OSB, 'Paul Courturier and the Monastery of Amay-Chevetogne', *The Messenger* (Oct. 2003), accessed online at www.paulcouturier.com/pcbook12barnas.pdf.
Barnes, J., *Ahead of his Age: Bishop Barnes of Birmingham* (London, Collins: 1979).
Beaken, R., *Cosmo Lang: Archbishop in War and Crisis* (London: I. B. Tauris & Co., 2012).
Bell, G. K. A., *Randall Davidson*, 3rd edn (London: Oxford University Press, 1952).

Bouyer, L., *The Memoirs of Louis Bouyer: From Youth and Conversion to Vatican II, the Liturgical Reform, and After* (Kettering, OH: Angelico Press, 2015).

Caraman, P., SJ, *C. C. Martindale: A Biography* (London: Longman, 1967).

Curtiss, G., *Paul Couturier and Unity in Christ* (London: SCM Press, 1964).

Davie, P., *Raising up a Faithful People: High Church Priests and Parochial Education, 1850-1910* (Hereford: Gracewing, 1997).

Dick, J. A., *The Malines Conversations Revisited* (Leuven: Leuven University Press, 1989).

Dunstan, P., *The Labour of Obedience: The Benedictines of Pershore, Nashdom and Elmore* (Norwich: Canterbury Press, 2009).

Gordon-Taylor, B., and N. Stebbing, ed., *Walter Frere: Scholar, Monk, Bishop* (Norwich: Canterbury Press, 2011).

Farmer, R. J., *The Catholic League 1913–1988* (London: The Catholic League, 1988).

— *Father Alban Baverstock SSC: An Exploration of his Life* (London: The Catholic League, 1997).

Hastings, A., ed., *Bishops and Writers: Aspects of the Evolution of Modern English Catholicism* (Wheathampstead: Clarke, 1977).

— *A History of English Christianity 1920–1990* (London: SCM Press, 1991).

Hemmer, H., *Fernand Portal (1855–1926): Apostle of Unity* (London: Macmillan & Co., 1961).

Hughes, A., *The Rivers of the Flood: A Personal Account of the Catholic Revival in England in the Twentieth Century* (London: Faith Press, 1961).

Iremonger, F. A., *William Temple, Archbishop of Canterbury: His Life and Letters* (London: Oxford University Press, 1948).

Irvine, C., *Worship, Church and Society: An Exposition of the Work of Arthur Gabriel Hebert* (Norwich: Canterbury Press, 1993).

Jack, L., 'The Church Unity Octave Golden Jubilee', *Reunion*, 6/51 (Dec. 1958), pp. 57–62; 6/52 (June 1959), pp. 90–6.

James, B. S., *Asking for Trouble* (London: The Catholic Book Club, 1962).

Jasper, R., *Arthur Cayley Headlam: Life and Letters of a Bishop* (London: Faith Press, 1960).

Sources and Bibliography

Jones, S., ed., *The Sacramental Life: Gregory Dix and his Writings* (Norwich: Canterbury Press, 2007).

Kaye, E., *The History of the King's Weigh House Church: A Chapter in the History of London* (London: George Allen & Unwin, 1968).

—— and R. Mackenzie, *W. E. Orchard: A Study in Christian Exploration* (Oxford: Education Services, 1990).

Keane, H., SJ, 'Archbishop Goodier: A Memoir', in A. Goodier, SJ, *St Ignatius Loyola and Prayer: As Seen in the Book of Spiritual Exercises* (London: Burns, Oates & Washbourne, 1940), pp. 1–49.

Keldany, H., 'Father Vincent McNabb: Pioneer Ecumenist', *New Blackfriars*, 60 (1979), p. 367.

Kreeft, P., *Ecumenical Jihad: Ecumenism and the Culture War* (San Francisco: Ignatius Press, 1996).

Leachman, J. G., OSB, 'Across the Fence: The Conversation between Maurice Bévenot, SJ, and Gregory Dix, OSB', *Sewanee Theological Review*, 53/1 (2009), pp. 9–64.

Leslie, S., *Cardinal Gasquet: A Memoir* (London: Burns & Oates, 1953).

Lockhart, J. G., *Charles Lindley, Viscount Halifax*, 2 vols (London: Geoffrey Bles, Centenary Press, 1935–6).

Lunn, B., and J. Haselock, *Henry Joy Fynes-Clinton* (London: The Church Literature Association, 1983).

Macaulay, R., *Letters to a Friend, 1950–1952* (London: Collins, 1961).

Mason, A., *History of the Society of the Sacred Mission* (Norwich: Canterbury Press, 1993).

Mascall, E. L., *Pi in the High* (London: The Faith Press, 1959).

—— *Recovery of Unity* (London: Longman, Green & Co., 1958).

—— *Saraband: The Memoirs of E. L. Mascall* (Leominster: Gracewing, 1992).

Morton, A., *History of the Society of the Sacred Mission* (Norwich: Canterbury Press, 1993).

Murray, R., SJ, 'Maurice Bévenot, Scholar and Ecumenist (1897–1980)', *Heythrop Journal*, 23/1 (1982), pp. 1–17.

Oldmeadow, E., *Francis Cardinal Bourne*, 2 vols. (London: Burns, Oates & Washbourne, 1940 and 1944).

Pawley, B. and M., *Rome and Canterbury through Four Centuries: A Study of the Relations between the Church of Rome and the Anglican Churches 1530–1981* (London: Mowbrays, 1981).

Poulter, G. C. B., *The Corbould Genealogy* (Ipswich: Suffolk Institute of Archaeology, 1935).

Radano, J. A., ed., *Celebrating a Century of Ecumenism: Exploring the Achievements of International Dialogue* (Geneva: World Council of Churches, 2012).

Salter, A. T. J., *The Anglican Papalist: A Personal Portrait of Henry Joy Fynes-Clinton* (London: The Anglo-Catholic History Society, 2012).

Sire, H. J. A., *Father Martin D'Arcy: Philosopher of Christian Love* (Leominster: Gracewing, 1997).

Stephenson, C., *Walsingham Way*, 2nd edn (Norwich: Canterbury Press, 2008).

Symondson, A., SJ, and S. A. Bucknall, *Sir Ninian Comper: An Introduction to his Life and Work with Complete Gazeteer* (Reading: Spire Books, 2006).

Taylor, T. F., *J. Armitage Robinson: Eccentric, Scholar and Churchman, 1858–1933* (Cambridge: James Clarke & Co., 1991).

Valentine, F., OP, *Father Vincent McNabb: The Portrait of a Great Dominican* (London: Burns & Oates, 1955).

Vickers, M., *By the Thames Divided: Cardinal Bourne in Southwark and Westminster* (Leominster: Gracewing, 2013).

Villain, M., *Unity: A History and Some Reflections* (London: Harvill Press, 1963).

Woodruff, M., ed., *The Unity of Christians: The Vision of Paul Couturier* (London: The Catholic League, 2003).

Woods, E. S., and F. B. MacNutt, *Theodore, Bishop of Winchester: Pastor, Prophet, Pilgrim* (London: SPCK, 1933).

Wykeham-George, K., OP, and G. Mathew, OP, *Bede Jarrett* (London: Blackfriars Publications, 1952).

Yelton, M., *Alfred Hope Patten and the Shrine of Our Lady of Walsingham* (Norwich: Canterbury Press, 2006).

—— *Anglican Papalism: A History, 1900–1960* (Norwich: Canterbury Press, 2008).

Index

Members of the Church are indexed under the latest title used in the text.

Ad Anglos (1895) 26
Allchin, Rev. Donald 257
All Saints, Carshalton 111
Amay 44, 51, 94, 133, 215, 239–40
Anglican and Eastern Churches
    Association 29–30, 105, 208
Anglicanorum Coetibus (2009) 263
Anglican-Roman Catholic International
    Commission (ARCIC) 261
Anglo-Catholicism 2, 5, 20, 33, 39, 40,
    52, 54–5, 56, 62, 118, 205–7, 218,
    221, 265–70
Anglo-Papalism 87–90, 103, 138, 140,
    142, 143, 148, 150–1, 155–6, 158–9,
    165, 181, 184, 191, 196, 198, 199,
    200, 207, 210, 221, 227, 245–6, 247,
    255–7, 258–9, 260–4
Apostolicae Curae (1896) 27, 38, 88, 183
Association for Promoting the Unity of
    Christendom (APUC) 23–4, 28
Athenaeum 16

Barnes, Bishop Ernest 54–5
Battifol, Mgr Pierre 43
Baverstock, Rev. Alban 133, 189, 212, 218
Beauduin, Dom Lambert, OSB 43–4, 45,
    94, 159, 161–2, 214–15, 240
Bell, Bishop George 174, 176
Benedict XV, Pope 32, 41
Benedict XVI, Pope 21, 263
Bévenot, Rev. Maurice, SJ 231–4
Bidwell, Bishop Manuel 10, 14, 66
Blackfriars 79–80, 202n.
Bourne, Francis, Cardinal 4, 6–16, 38,
    39, 40, 44, 48, 56, 61–3, 65, 66, 67,
    74–5, 80, 94, 108, 113, 131, 134, 136,
    153–6, 164–5, 166, 167–8, 173, 174,
    175–6, 177, 188, 189, 190, 200–1,
    202, 224, 246, 257
Brent, Bishop Charles 19–20
Browne, Rev. Michael, OP 217
Bulletin (of the Confraternity of Unity)
    50, 52, 213
Butler, Dom Christopher, OSB 234
Butler, Abbot Cuthbert, OSB 24, 67–71,
    85, 130, 131, 135, 137, 138, 139–40,
    141, 143, 152, 156, 164, 167, 177–8,
    180–1, 182, 183, 189, 191, 197, 199,
    201

Campbell, Rev. Bowyer 51, 56, 77, 95,
    102, 103, 115, 130, 135, 136
Casti Connubii (1930) 134–5, 225
Catholic League (CL) 33–4, 39, 51, 56,
    106, 114, 115, 133, 189, 212, 218, 247
Centenary Manifesto (1932) 200, 206–8,
    217, 219, 255, 265–70
Centenary Tractates 209–11, 212, 217, 219
Church Unity Octave (CUO) 32–4, 88,
    97, 102, 106, 132, 239, 240, 241,
    243, 244, 245–6, 247, 248–9, 253
Church Unity Octave Council
    (CUOC) 34, 114–15, 116, 240,
    247–8, 249
Collett, Abbot Martin, OSB 231, 246,
    248
Confraternity of Unity (CU) 50–2, 54,
    56, 94, 95, 96, 102, 106, 114, 115,

122, 129, 130, 134, 189, 212, 217, 218, 223, 224, 232, 248, 256
Congar, Rev. Yves, OP 232
Corbould, Rev. Robert 109–16, 133, 135, 156, 157, 159, 160, 163, 168, 173, 176–7, 178, 179–80, 182–5, 187–9, 197–9, 201–2, 207, 208, 209, 210–11, 244, 247, 254
Council for Promoting Catholic Unity (CPCU) 114–115, 189, 209, 222, 223, 245, 247
Couturier, Abbé Paul 239–48, 258
Cowley Fathers 240, 244, 248, 249

D'Arcy, Rev. Martin, SJ 76–8, 118, 130–131, 132, 135, 137, 142, 145–6, 152, 157, 167, 177, 178, 180, 188, 191, 197, 253
Davidson, Archbishop Randall 1–2, 6, 12–16, 35, 40, 41, 42–3, 44, 45–7, 48, 49, 54, 61, 62, 63, 101, 105, 112–13, 257
de la Saudée, Rev. Jacques, SJ 213, 217, 218
de Lisle, Ambrose Philipps 22–3, 24
Demant, Rev. Vigo 232
Dix, Dom Gregory, OSB 229–34, 243–4, 246, 247–9, 256–7
d'Herbigny, Bishop Michel, SJ 214–19, 220, 221, 222, 224
Dominicans 29, 78–80, 234
Doubleday, Bishop Arthur 222–3
Douglas, Canon John 113, 243
Drane-Scott – see Scott, Dr S. H.

Edinburgh Missionary Conference 1910 19, 21, 227
Egmanton 223, 225, 244

Faith and Order Movement 20–1, 213, 232, 249
Fisher, Archbishop Geoffrey 261
Frere, Dr Walter 41, 43, 113, 161
Fynes-Clinton, Rev. Henry 33, 34, 51, 55, 56, 104–9, 115, 133, 134, 135, 157, 160, 162, 178, 179–80, 187–8, 189, 190, 202, 206–7, 208, 209, 210, 211–12, 216, 218, 222, 233, 240, 243–4, 245, 247, 248, 254

Gasparri, Pietro, Cardinal 46, 183, 216
Gille, Rev. Albert, SJ 255–6
Goodier, Archbishop Alban 72–6, 78, 129–130, 131, 132, 135, 136–7, 138–9, 141–53, 155, 156–7, 163–4, 165–9, 174, 175, 176–82, 183, 185, 188, 189, 191–7, 199, 201
Gore, Bishop Charles 42–3, 46, 48, 54, 93, 113, 119, 120–1, 132, 229
Goudge, Professor Henry Leighton 86
Halifax, Charles Wood, Viscount 6, 7–8, 10, 11, 24–7, 28, 40–2, 44–9, 51, 54, 80–1, 99, 110, 112, 160–1, 202
Harris, Rev. Silas 101, 207, 209, 223–6, 244
Headlam, Bishop Arthur 37, 133, 208
Hebert, Rev. Gabriel, SSM 228, 230, 232, 233, 234
Helsham, Rev. Edward SJ 232
Hemmer, Rev. Hippolyte 43
Heythrop 146, 231, 232
Hough, Bishop William 132–3

Jarrett, Rev. Bede, OP 78–81, 130, 133, 135, 137, 142, 145–6, 152, 167, 177, 178, 180, 188, 191–2, 194, 197, 199, 201, 202n.
Jesuits 14, 29, 56, 66–7, 214, 231, 232, 234, 253
John Paul II, Pope 261
Jones, Rev. Spencer 28–32, 34, 51, 54, 55, 77, 87, 92, 95–6, 97–104, 107, 108, 111, 129, 130–1, 132, 133–4, 135, 136, 137–9, 142, 157, 158, 187, 188, 189, 207, 209, 216, 220, 222, 240, 242, 244, 248–9, 253, 258
Joyce, Rev. George, SJ 232, 233

Index

Keating, Rev. Joseph, SJ 67, 209–10
Kelham Fathers 227, 244, 249
Kelly, Rev. Herbert, SSM 227
Kidd, Dr Beresford 42, 46, 85–6, 244
Kirk, Bishop Kenneth 244, 245, 248

LaFontaine, Pietro, Cardinal 208, 211
Lambeth Conference 1908 36, 157–8, 189
Lambeth Conference 1920 4, 35–7, 55, 62, 72–3, 101, 157–8, 183
   Appeal to All Christian Peoples (1920) 37–9, 40, 41, 45, 46, 47, 162
Lambeth Conference 1930 52–6, 64, 96, 102, 114, 122, 219
   Anglican relations with Nonconformists 52–3, 197
   contraception 55–6, 86, 96, 102–3, 108, 129, 134, 195, 197, 206, 210, 268
Lambeth Palace 6, 12
Lang, Archbishop Cosmo 5, 7, 36, 40, 45, 55, 62–4, 65–6, 86, 87, 131, 136, 153–4, 173, 176, 177, 187–8, 202, 205, 244, 255, 257
Laxton Hall 226, 228, 234
Leeming, Rev. Bernard, SJ 231, 232
Leo XIII, Pope 26–7
Life and Work Conferences 20–1, 213

Major, Rev. Henry 95–6, 133
Malines Conversations 6, 7–10, 15, 16, 21, 40–9, 63, 67, 70–1, 80, 161, 164, 216, 258
Manning, Henry, Cardinal 23, 182
Marchant, Eleanor, Lady 176
Marchant, Sir James 1, 2–6, 10–15, 48, 61–7, 71, 72, 75–6, 78, 85–7, 129–38, 152, 153–4, 155, 157, 164–8, 173–9, 180, 187, 255
Mascall, Rev. Eric 232, 233, 234, 261
Maurin, Louis-Joseph, Cardinal 240
McGarrigle, Rev. Francis SJ 216
McNabb, Rev. Vincent, OP 31, 38, 80–1, 89, 102, 103, 104, 130, 226, 253
McNulty, Bishop John 224
Mercier, Désiré-Joseph, Cardinal 6, 7, 8, 9, 40–8, 71, 80, 94, 112–14, 162, 183, 216
Merry del Val, Rafael, Cardinal 67, 82n., 102
Messenger 33
Mirfield 232, 234, 244, 245, 248, 249
Modernism 42, 50, 54–5, 74, 93, 96, 133, 148, 205, 207, 266–70
Monahan, Rev. William 119–22, 133, 135, 197, 199, 207, 254, 256
Month 66–7
Mortalium Animos (1928) 16, 21, 46, 63–4, 131, 218
Morton Howard, Rev. James 92, 94, 96, 97, 209, 219, 222
Moyes, Canon James 39
Myers, Canon Edward 10, 66

Nashdom 229, 230, 231, 232, 233, 234, 240–1, 244, 247, 248, 249
Newman, John Henry, Cardinal 22, 99, 182, 205

Old Catholics 36, 53, 169, 180, 210
Orchard, Dr William 64–5, 173–5, 176
Ordinariate 263
Orthodox Church 20, 21, 23, 26, 30, 36, 41, 53, 86, 105–6, 113, 140–1, 146–7, 160, 208, 214–15, 232, 239
Oxford Movement 22–4, 25, 54, 100–1, 121–2, 138, 205, 207, 265–70
Oxford University Society for Reunion (OURS) 77, 95, 107, 113–14, 116, 130–1, 162

Pacelli, Eugenio, Cardinal 215, 225
Paul VI, Pope 261
Pawley, Canon Bernard & Margaret 90, 238n., 257
Pierce, Mgr Henry 49–51, 56, 86–7, 95–6, 102, 109, 129, 130, 135, 142,

152–3, 155, 197, 199–200, 206, 207, 208, 210, 211–12, 213–14, 216–18, 219–222, 224, 225–6, 231, 246–7, 254–5
Pius IX, Pope 23
Pius X, Pope 32, 54, 74, 111, 116
Pius XI, Pope 9, 16, 21, 44, 46, 62, 106, 134–5, 166, 168, 201, 212, 213, 214, 215, 216–18, 222–3, 224–5
Portal, Rev. Fernand 25–7, 40, 44, 46, 162, 215
Porvoo Common Statement (1992) 262
Prayer Book Revision 2, 6, 14, 16, 43
Pribilla, Rev. Max, SJ 213–14

Rampolla, Mariano, Cardinal 26
Ramsey, Archbishop Michael 230, 261
Robinson, Dr Armitage 41, 47, 70–1, 85–6, 161

Sargent, Rev. Alec 188
Scott, Dr S. H. 90–7, 130, 131, 132, 133, 134, 135, 136, 137, 140–1, 144, 146–53, 156–7, 158, 160, 162, 177, 189, 197, 205–6, 207, 209, 212, 213, 218, 222, 254
Shearburn, Rev. Victor, CR 245
Simmonds, Rev. Leslie 116–19, 133, 135, 142, 156, 173, 175, 177, 178, 189, 207, 209, 233, 253
Society for Catholic Reunion (SCR) 223–7
Society of St Thomas of Canterbury 30–1, 97, 114, 130, 134
St Andrew's, Oddington 91–2, 96
St David's, Moreton-in-Marsh 97–8
St Ermin's Hotel 106, 190, 202, 244, 254

St John, Rev. Henry, OP 89, 226–9
St Magnus-the-Martyr, London 34, 55, 104, 106, 216
St Mary's, Chelsea 75, 179–80, 185n.
St Swithun's, Worcester 119–21
Student Christian Movement (SCM) 19, 227–8
Strong, Bishop Thomas 86

Tablet 5, 8, 93, 200, 208, 255
Temple, Archbishop Frederick 25–6, 55, 131, 154, 244
Thackeray Hotel 131, 132, 133, 135, 144, 174, 177
Thornton, Rev. Lionel, CR 232
Thurston, Rev. Herbert, SJ 67

Van Roey, Mgr Joseph-Ernst 41
Vatican II 21, 145, 151, 167, 253, 260–1
Vaughan, Herbert, Cardinal 26

Walker, Rev. Leslie, SJ 39, 216
Walker, Rev. Sheafe 51
Walsingham 104, 254
Wattson, Rev. Paul 31–2, 95, 102, 240
Week of Prayer for Christian Unity 239, 248, 249
Week of Universal Prayer (for the Unity of Christians) 242–3, 244–5, 248–9, 258
Whitton, Rev. Thomas 89, 199, 221–3, 224, 255, 264
Wiseman, Cardinal Nicholas 23
Woodlock, Francis, SJ 9, 67, 108, 167, 225–6
Woods, Bishop Theodore 4, 12, 55, 86
World Council of Churches 20, 249